Building a City: C.S. Daley an

Also by Jennifer Horsfield and published by Ginninderra Press
Mary Cunningham: an Australian life
Rainbow: the story of Rania McPhillamy

Jennifer Horsfield

Building a City

C.S. Daley and the story of Canberra

Building a City: C.S. Daley and the story of Canberra
ISBN 978 1 76041 038 4
Copyright © text Jennifer Horsfield 2015
Cover and chapter heading design: Rosanna Horn
Cover images: background – the Federal Capital Site, Canberra, Australia, 1913,
W. Lister Lister, by permission National Library of Australia;
foreground – Capital Hill, showing W.M. Hughes, C.S. Daley and P.G. Stewart,
reproduced with permission of Canberra & District Historical Society

First published 2015 by
GINNINDERRA PRESS
PO Box 3461 Port Adelaide 5015
www.ginninderrapress.com.au

Contents

Acknowledgements 7

Prologue 9

1 Victorian Years 17

2 Towards Canberra 33

3 The Most Beautiful City in History 49

4 Greening the Capital 71

5 Transition 87

6 Commission Rule 107

7 Town and Country 127

8 The Long Slump 139

9 A People's City 157

10 Another War 179

11 A New Beginning 197

12 A Private Citizen 217

References 227

Bibliography 233

Index 237

For Nancy, Joan and Billie

Acknowledgements

Members of C.S. Daley's extended family gave me invaluable help in the writing of this book. His two surviving daughters, Nancy Boyd and Joan Dahl, shared many memories of their beloved Papa. As well, Joan cast an expert editorial eye over the manuscript and provided useful advice on some historical and family details. Mirian ('Billie') Daley was always a most helpful and encouraging source of advice and information. Her late husband Geoff was custodian of his father's papers before depositing many of them at the National Library; however, Billie was able to share some letters and photographs that are still part of a treasured family archive. Billie's son, Nigel, also read the manuscript and offered some helpful corrections. C.S. Daley's granddaughter, Sally Williams, provided the original motive for the writing of this book, when she invited me to look at the public records about her grandparents and to tell their story, which she was convinced was an important part of Canberra's history. Sally was especially keen to discover more details about the life and work of her grandmother, who died many years before Sally was born. Jessie Daley's story does not, however, feature strongly in this book. Before her early and untimely death, Jessie played an active role in many community organisations in Canberra but for the biographer she remains a shadowy figure. There are no surviving letters or other personal papers, and no first-hand accounts of her friendships or her life in Canberra. However, I hope I have done justice to her story, as much as I was able to.

Canberra institutions gave me much appreciated support in writing this book. I would like to thank the knowledgeable and expert staff of the Petherick Room at the National Library and in the Reading Room of the National Archives. My thanks also to Antoinette Buchanan of the ACT Heritage Library, Mark Dawson of ACT Archives and Helen Digan at Canberra & District Historical Society for their expert advice and assistance.

Stan Goodhew, Margaret McAuslan, Ann Gugler and Dawn Waterhouse all provided me with useful background to C.S. Daley's life in Canberra and my thanks to them for their kindness. Lenore Coltheart's discussion groups at the Albert Hall in 2013 gave me much appreciated insights into this building and its special place in Canberra's history.

I am grateful to Stephen Matthews of Ginninderra Press for his continuing support, and for Rosanna Horn, who generously offered her expert design skills with images used in the book.

I hope *Building a City: C.S. Daley and the story of Canberra* will be a worthwhile addition to the growing literature about Canberra and the building of Australia's federal capital.

Prologue

On a day in late summer in 1932, a party of visitors drove out from Canberra to the little village of Tharwa on the Murrumbidgee River. The driver, a veteran on these bush tracks, then took the party up the steep and rocky pinch of Fitz's Hill and over a formidable granite range that led down eventually to the old sheep station of Gudgenby on the valley floor. After a picnic lunch at the station, the party was guided on foot across the valley floor to inspect two remarkable rock shelters. The first, a rounded granite monolith with a sloping shelter, contained depictions in red ochre and white clay of a number of native animals. The second shelter, half an hour's walk away, was a spacious cave whose high concave interior also contained representations of animals.[1]

One of the visitors was an amateur naturalist and historian from Victoria, an elderly gentleman by the name of Charles Daley. He had a long-standing interest in the country's prehistory and Australia's indigenous people and he wanted to preserve evidence of their culture. He considered that both collections of cave paintings were perhaps of a great age and he thought it likely that in that wild and lonely country to the south-west of Canberra there were probably other rock shelters of similar interest.

Daley shared with others of his generation the belief that no Aboriginal people survived in the federal territory. Subsequently, in a meeting he had with the Minister for the Interior, he urged the preservation of these easily defaced paintings. A keen advocate in Victoria for the creation of national parks and nature reserves, Daley saw how the pressures of growing populations, industrial development and land clearing threatened to destroy huge swaths of the Australian landscape, and with it, the evidence it contained of Aboriginal people and their vanishing way of life.

Daley's advocacy of government protection for these Aboriginal sites was not successful, and it was not till 1998 that the sites were formally registered, which led to their ongoing management and preservation.

Canberra residents have little reason to know Charles Daley's name or be aware of the details of his life in Victoria as a teacher, botanist, writer and historian. But they might be more familiar with the name of his eldest son, Charles Studdy (C.S.) Daley, whose close connection with the story of Canberra for over fifty years is the subject of this book. Father and son had much in common. Both took seriously the notion of public service as a high and honourable calling. Daley senior retired after forty-six years of zealous and effective teaching in Victorian schools, and thereafter devoted his energies to numerous voluntary cultural and educational projects.

His son was to be involved with a wide range of community groups in Canberra during his working life with the Commonwealth Government and in retirement. Both men shared a schoolmasterly desire to educate others, to help their fellow Australians appreciate their country's history and its unique but fragile environment. During his lifetime, Daley senior published a number of well-regarded books, including two that became standard references in their field. His last book, *The Story of Gippsland*, was published by his sons after his death.

C.S. Daley, for his part, always hoped that he would be given the chance to write the official history of Canberra, whose early years he had been so closely involved with. He was disappointed in this hope, but until the end of his life he saw himself as an authentic spokesman for early Canberra and a reliable witness to those first decades when the Commonwealth's new city was being planned and built on the Limestone Plains.

C.S. Daley attracted his own share of controversy during his working life. He was not a man who sought the limelight, but his role at the centre of Canberra bureaucracy for nearly fifty years made it inevitable that he would be criticised by those hostile to the government he served. He was secretary for four years to the Federal Capital Advisory Committee, which was appointed in 1921 to plan the transfer of the seat of government from Melbourne to Canberra and to advise on the first stage of construction of the new federal capital. Daley then became secretary to the Federal Capital Commission, an independent authority set up by the government and vested with important financial and legal powers. The Commission, under the decisive leadership of Chief Commissioner John Butters and with a large technical and administrative staff, constructed all the early buildings of note in Canberra, including the provisional Parliament House. From 1925, the Commission managed an enormous business with its construction of homes and hostels, early administrative buildings and other public buildings, all public utilities, construction sites and roads plus a hospital, schools and a bus system. For five years, it ran every aspect of life in the federal territory.

The Commission was bound by law to proceed with the development of Canberra in accordance with the gazetted plan of the city, a 1918 version of Walter Burley Griffin's prize-winning 1912 design. After a period of prolonged controversy and uncertainty, the government had decided that Griffin's plan would be the official city design, only to be altered by ministerial consultation with Parliament. In fact, over the years a number of important changes to the gazetted plan were endorsed by Parliament, a body of men with no particular knowledge of or interest in city design or town planning.

The scattered suburbs that were taking tentative shape on the Molonglo plain during the Commission years bore little resemblance to Griffin's grandly symbolic and spacious capital which he had hoped would become 'the most beautiful city in history'.[2] The Great War, followed by a period of changing political alliances and then by the Great Depression, gave the Commonwealth little chance to focus on the building of a great national capital. Many Australians were either indifferent to the idea of a new capital city or actively hostile, seeing it as an extravagant and unnecessary folly. The Melbourne press, especially, fought to scrap the project and maintain Melbourne as the seat of the federal government. Other critics, among them many architects and town planners, wanted to see the city built but deplored the fact that Griffin's plan was being compromised and its integrity destroyed by the government's need for economies and quick results. In our own time, a new generation has become familiar with the Griffin plans, and some writers have passed a severe judgement on the Advisory Committee and the Commission. Their officials – and C.S. Daley was included as one of them – are condemned as bureaucrats who either did not understand the Griffin plans or who betrayed Griffin's vision by the compromises they made with his plans in order to get the building of the city underway.

As a young man, C.S. Daley was very attracted to the idea of helping build the new federal capital. In 1905, as an eighteen-year-old, he joined the Department of Home Affairs in Melbourne. The department's key officials included Colonel Percy Owen, soon to be Director General of Works in Canberra, and John Smith Murdoch, who would become its chief architect. Under their tutelage, Daley gained an interest in architecture, engineering and the relatively new and exciting field of town planning. He began studying part-time while taking on more responsibility in the department. In 1911, he helped to frame the international competition for the design of the new capital city and to process the entries as they were sent from around the world to be judged in Melbourne. The winning entry by Walter Burley Griffin and Marion Mahony Griffin became a formative influence in his life. He was intrigued by the Griffins' capacity to integrate the planned city so fully into the landscape, and he grasped the symbolic importance of the great triangle at the centre of the plan, which linked the civic, governmental and cultural aspects of the planned federal capital. He made a close study of the winning design and also of Griffin's later plans which were prepared after Griffin visited Canberra in 1913 and moderated some of his initial ideas.

Daley saw the Griffin plan as a great design worthy of its high purpose, to inspire the building of a federal capital where the country's laws might be debated and enacted free from local interests and in the best interests of the nation. It was a design, in Minister Hugh Mahon's words, 'not only for the present but for all time'.[3] But Daley was also closely acquainted with the routine demands of management in the public service. Building projects had to work to a deadline, find and employ a reliable workforce and managers, keep within a budget, satisfy departmental rules and regulations and keep ministers and their electorates happy. While admiring Griffin's plans, he also saw that in the straitened economy after the war, they were incapable of being realised.

He saw the sense in the Advisory Committee's recommendations that the building of the city proceed in three stages: first, the building of a provisional Parliament House and offices and the transfer of a core of public servants; second, the transfer of the remaining public service from Melbourne and the building of appropriate infrastructure to support a growing community and workforce; and third – at an indefinite time in the future – the construction of Griffin's monumental buildings and of the formal lake that would be the city's centrepiece. Meanwhile, the design philosophy that would guide the planners was that of the Garden City movement which was so influential in the early twentieth century. The slums, overcrowding and chaotic sprawl of older industrialised cities would be replaced with communities supplied with parks, gardens and open spaces and good transport systems; neighbourhood centres would provide shops, schools, churches and other community facilities.

The Federal Capital Commission continued this approach, and while it paid lip service to the gazetted plan, in reality the layout of Canberra in, say, 1930 was dramatically different to that which Griffin would have envisaged. (The only part of Griffin's plan that was in evidence was the layout of some of the major roads, a project that Griffin had carried out during his brief time as Federal Capital Director.) Two small groupings of suburbs lay on either side of the winding Molonglo River, its flood plains still home to grazing cattle and pasture crops. A few larger buildings stood out, none of them placed in positions which Griffin had chosen. The provisional Parliament House and office blocks were placed at some distance from Griffin's governmental groupings, with the understanding that their placing would not interfere with the later permanent buildings. The greening of the capital city was taking place under the skilled hands of the first Director of Afforestation, Thomas Charles Weston, and the bare Limestone Plains, ravaged by drought, rabbits, ringbarking and overgrazing, were gradually softening in outline and providing a more welcome and restful environment for newcomers. Weston's ideas were not Griffin's and in fact the two men differed markedly in their approach to horticulture, Weston being the more knowledgeable and more practical in his response to the challenges of landscaping the new city.

The Federal Capital Commission was disbanded during the Depression as jobs were lost and austerity measures set in place throughout the country. C.S. Daley became the chief administrator of the territory in a move that was a professional promotion but that brought little professional satisfaction. He was forced to oversee the dismissal of many valued men and there was little scope in those lean years for constructive action. The building of the city came to a virtual standstill. As the Depression deepened, the government made more cuts to the administration of Canberra, dividing management of the territory among three Commonwealth departments and giving Daley the task of management of civic affairs. In this role, he was responsible for such local matters as building regulations, payment of rates and control of stray dogs. It was dull, necessary work performed by – in the public eye – dull, decent public servants. A common perception of C.S. Daley arose at this time as people saw him delivering speeches at school assemblies and at the opening of rural bridges or new sewage treatment works. He seemed the consummate public servant, obedient, efficient, colourless; someone who would always take the official line; who made long speeches (school children grew restless when sitting through his end-of-year addresses in hot school halls). He was in the public eye, but lacked the charisma or the bravado that would have made him a figure of interest.

Others remember him differently: as a gentle, quietly spoken man who performed many unacknowledged acts of kindness. Private letters reveal a man with a gift for friendship, whose writing often displays wit and good humour. He was also remembered for his probity and integrity: 'he never forfeited his principles, for any reason whatsoever…' a friend recalled.[4] The Chief Archivist of the National Archives saw him as a man 'who by any yardstick must be judged as one of the most remarkable public men of his time…'[5]

The post-war years saw Canberra emerge from the doldrums to receive new recognition under Prime Ministers Chifley and then Menzies. The Commonwealth would begin to play a major role in education, economic reform and social welfare; and the development of Australia's federal capital would at last be taken seriously. C.S. Daley, nearing retirement age, found a new and active role in promoting the establishment of a national university in Canberra that would attract historians, scientists and economists to undertake fundamental research; he was a member of the Interim Council of the Australian National University which was established by law in 1946.

These later years also gave Daley the chance to convey to a new generation the importance of Griffin's city plan and to urge those in power to defend its principles. Called upon to report on the city's history to post-war bureaucrats and politicians, Daley made clear that not enough had been done to protect the Griffin legacy, though he also acknowledged that there had to be provision for change to suit a changing world. Daley saw himself as one of the last witnesses left from the early years in the building of the city. His contributions to the newly formed Canberra & District Historical Society and his regular newspaper columns in the *Canberra Times* became a rich source of information and anecdote for many Canberra residents.

A common thread running throughout Daley's life was a love of music: this was the world where he felt most at home, both as a gifted pianist, a partner with others in chamber music and as a creative force in the young city's musical life. In the troubled years of the thirties and forties, when so many spurious forms of nationalism threw the world into chaos, Daley felt that the sharing of music could help overcome other barriers and create a more peaceful world.

Any references in the text to 'Charles Daley' can be assumed to apply to C.S. Daley. If a reference is made to his father, it will be as 'Charles Daley senior'.

Imperial forms of measurement are used throughout the text. Metric equivalents are 1 mile = 1.60 kilometres; £1 = $2 (in the year of currency conversion 1966). In 1910, the average weekly wage of a factory worker was about £3, and of a clerical worker, about £5.

'The boys called their father "Pater".
They must have been aware, from
their teenage years, that he did not
really fit the common mould.'

The Daley family, C.S.Daley top left.
Courtesy Mrs G. Daley

C.S. Daley was born in 1887 in Maldon, Victoria. He was the eldest son of a country schoolmaster, so he and his brothers had an itinerant childhood, attending the local school wherever their father, Charles Daley, was sent. Daley began his teaching career in 1878 with an appointment as pupil-teacher at State School no. 1976 in Bendigo. From there he was moved to a succession of small schools around Victoria in accordance with the policies of the Education Department. The new century saw him appointed to State School no. 502 at Stawell, in the goldfields north-west of Ballarat.

Daley had married in 1886, at Maldon, and his first son, Charles Studdy, was born there a year later. Three more sons followed: Harold, born 1889, Frank, born 1891, and Edward, 1901. During the years after Frank's birth, Mrs Daley had a baby girl who did not survive.

The boys called their father Pater. They must have been aware, from their teenage years, that he did not really fit the common mould. Charles Daley senior had a passion for self-improvement and new knowledge, and a great curiosity about the world around him. He gained his Bachelor of Arts degree through part-time study at the University of Melbourne while the boys were still young. He also led an active life in the outdoors. We would now call him a keen bushwalker, with extended, often solitary walking trips, sometimes accompanied by a packhorse, through some of Victoria's most rugged mountain country and coastal bushland. These excursions left Daley with a lasting appreciation of the Australian bush, from the mountain ash forests of East Gippsland to the still untouched ferny gullies and waterfalls of country within reach of Melbourne. Through his membership of a number of field naturalists societies, he became a lifelong advocate of nature conservation. After he retired from teaching in 1924, Daley gave a series of popular radio broadcasts on station 3LO, each session describing a nature ramble in a local area, with commentary on some local history and on the plants and bird life to be observed. He sometimes included references to Aboriginal sites of significance – not a mainstream interest in the 1920s. A recurring theme of his broadcasts was the need to protect and care for the rich botanical heritage of the bush in the face of unthinking development or deliberate destruction.

His scholarly interest in Aboriginal culture saw Daley collecting and carefully drawing stone tools which he found on his walks, tools which he later donated to Castlemaine Historical Museum. In 1910, he sent his small publication *Remains of the Stone Age* to the British Museum of Natural History and in 1911 he gave a talk on 'The Artistic Sense of the Aboriginal' to a gathering of scientists in Melbourne. The richly varied flora of the bush were a great attraction, and Daley often returned from a ramble or extended walk with many specimens to be sent for identification to the Victorian Department of Agriculture or to Ferdinand Von Mueller at the Royal Botanical Gardens in Melbourne, where they would be added to the national collection.

There were other scholarly interests: a contribution to the *Australasian Encylopedia*; a series of lectures on Victorian history at the Public Library of Victoria; editing the *Geelong Naturalist* and the *Historical Journal*. As well he was actively involved in helping organise and run the Melbourne branch of the Australian Association for the Advancement of Science conferences in 1921 and 1935 (by that stage an amalgamation had meant it was now ANZAAS – the Australian and New Zealand Association for the Advancement of Science). His wife was an associate member at these congresses.

Public recognition in the form of official awards came to Charles Daley in his retirement: honorary membership of the Royal Australian Historical Society; appointment as Honorary Park Ranger with the Victorian Forest Commission; election as Fellow of the Linnean Society; inclusion in the Coronation Honours List for leading citizens in 1937.

Charles Daley's life was conventional enough on the surface, but with strong intellectual interests and engagements that enriched it. After Daley's death in 1947, Sir Robert Garran recalled his 'honourable and useful life, full of many interests'.[1] The pattern of such a life must have left its mark on his sons, who were all high achievers in their various fields. Harold Daley worked with the Dalgety company in developing sheep and wool production in Victoria. He died quite young, in 1942, as the result of a tick bite. Frank, a mechanical engineer by training, was eventually appointed Director of Ordnance Production during World War II and later, returning to his role in General Motors Holden, was involved with the research, development and production of the first Holden cars. Edward, after a medical training, served with the RAAF as senior medical officer and became Director of Medical Services for the RAAF during the war. Created a Commander of the British Empire (CBE) after the war, he became director of the Victorian branch of the Royal Flying Doctor Service and served on the board of the Australian Red Cross.

Music was important in the family life, and the boys were encouraged and expected from an early age to study the piano. Both their mother and father were competent players, and in a *Who's Who* biography Frank and Edward cited music as one of their hobbies. In 1904 at a Grand Military Concert and Gymnastics Display in Stawell Town Hall, Mrs Daley conducted the band and seventeen-year-old Daley and his father played a piano duet.

Family photograph albums show C.S. Daley sharing the outdoor pursuits of his father: catching trout in mountain streams; camping out on field naturalists weekends; bushwalking trips to the high country; or day excursions into the snow. Community life played an important role for the family, with Charles senior's involvement in local sports, church and cultural organisations. That set a pattern which his eldest son was to follow.

After his secondary schooling, C.S. Daley began a diploma to train as a metallurgical chemist and assayer at Stawell Technical College. The early years of the century saw a decline in mining activity in Victoria (one of the effects of the 1890s depression) and in 1905, in the second year of his course, Daley gave up the diploma and applied to enter the new Commonwealth Public Service as a junior clerk in the Public Works branch of the Department of Home Affairs.

Home Affairs was one of the seven original departments established in 1901 when the colonies united to form the Commonwealth. The department's reach was Australia-wide. Among other things it had responsibility for old-age pensions; people of special races; acquisition and control of property and railways; astronomical work; census and statistics; elections; and public works for the federal capital. The department began in a modest way under its first minister, Sir William Lyne, its work being conducted in just two rooms by Lyne and his secretary. But the volume and scope of work soon expanded. In 1901, a senior Defence officer, Colonel Percy Owen, was appointed as Inspector General of Works to oversee all the architectural and engineering work that the new commonwealth departments would require. Three years later, Owen was appointed Director General of Works, retaining his military title after service in the Boer War, as was customary at the time. He was to play a large part in the future career of the young Daley. Owen's connection to the federal capital began early when he was investigating possible capital sites and reporting back to parliament.

Owen was an astute manager of men and of large-scale engineering and construction projects. He recognised in Daley a keen and ambitious young man who, with the right training and experience, could give good service to the new Commonwealth. He encouraged him to seek further education. In 1907, Daley won an Open Evening Scholarship which paid for his study at the Melbourne Working Men's College. He spent three years there studying part-time in the Commerce Department: auditing, accountancy, economics and – surprisingly – modern languages, where he excelled at German. He was praised for his growing skill in translating a text into 'good English idiom'. He later studied part-time at Melbourne Technical College in architecture and building construction, drawing and some engineering subjects. From 1911 he was given time off to study for a degree in Arts, making up the time missed as required. In February 1914, Owen personally congratulated Daley on the award of BA at the University of Melbourne – an award still rare enough in the general population to warrant special notice. By that stage, Daley had been promoted to serve as Owen's personal assistant or secretary, and in that role was to gain first-hand experience of some of the construction projects that the Commonwealth was undertaking.

The most prestigious of these early projects was the building of Australia House during World War I. This palatial building in the Strand sat at the very heart of Imperial Britain. Its marble columns, gleaming bronze fittings, chandeliers and polished floors, its sculptures and works of art announced a country that considered itself worthy of a central place in the affairs of Empire. Its role was to further Australian interests by promoting its industries and manufactured goods, by encouraging British settlement and investment, and by being a point of contact for visiting

Australians. In August 1918, its basement was fitted out as a club for members of the AIF on leave in England.

The building was designed by two Scottish architects, A. Marshall Mackenzie and his son, A.G.R Mackenzie, with a Commonwealth architect, John Smith Murdoch, later taking on oversight of the project and saving the Australian government about £80,000 in capital costs. Local firms were employed in its construction, but as far as possible, the raw materials were obtained from Australia by the Works Branch of the Department of Home Affairs. Charles Daley was given responsibility for the requisition and dispatch of building material for the project. This included a variety of beautiful timbers chosen from each state, with the flooring made from the black bean timber of Queensland. White marble came from Angaston in South Australia and a dove-coloured marble from the quarries of Buchan in Victoria. Altogether there were fifteen consignments of Buchan marble shipped over in 1916 and 1917, as it was to be featured in the grand staircase and columns of the main public rooms. Marble of a consistent colour was particularly requested, but even though the government geologist arranged for the opening up of fresh quarries, they could not promise to send consignments that were uniform in colour.

Charles Daley was proud of the role he had played in this project, which was beset by the challenges of wartime shipping disruptions, escalating costs and labour shortages. As well there was the difficulty of acting on urgent requests sent from half a world away. Many years later, Daley had the opportunity to visit England and see Australia House for himself, paying a visit to the High Commissioner, Sir Thomas White. Always a stickler for historical accuracy, Daley was able to point out a number of factual errors in the official account of the building project, and White provided a secretary to make a note of the corrections.

Australia House was officially opened by King George V on 3 August 1918 (though from 1916, the High Commissioner and his staff were provided with temporary offices there). It became a popular venue for patriotic and official gatherings by Australian visitors from then on. In Australia, views about the building were divided. Many people muttered about the cost: nearly a million pounds (counting the purchase of the land). It had opened with much pomp and ceremony near the end of a four-year war that had taken thousands of Australian lives in the course of fighting for the Empire. That was bound to seem a tragic juxtaposition to people of more radical views (a small but vocal minority in Australia at that time).

When war broke out in August 1914, many of Daley's contemporaries rushed to enlist, including some of his friends at Ormond College, a residential college of the University of Melbourne, where Daley was boarding. In October 1916, he applied for exemption from military service on medical grounds. He suffered from time to time from severe neuritis, a condition where nerves became inflamed, sometimes from overuse or bodily stress. This condition had accounted for a number of months' absence from work during his part-time study. He had begun a law degree part-time in 1915, but a breakdown in his health forced him to give up the study until some years later. Walter Bingle, acting head of the department, wrote a letter in 1916 requesting his continuing service in the department.

> Daley is the Senior Clerical Officer in the Public Works Branch. His duties include the supervision of clerical staff and the handling of all correspondence, much of which is of a technical nature. It is essential his service be retained, as the department deals with many defence works, including extensions to the cordite factory, drill halls, Ordnance stores and military hospitals.[2]

Both Walter Bingle and John Murdoch, Commonwealth architect, were by that time heavily involved in matters to do with the new federal territory. They watched Daley's career with interest, both of them perhaps sensing that his future must lie with the new city being built in Canberra. Bingle had sent Daley a New Year's greeting in 1910, with a postcard showing the tents and wooden huts at the federal capital survey camp. Murdoch was also something of a mentor to Daley, who served as his administrative assistant for ten years and who in later life wrote,

> I found him a man of wide culture and human sympathy, and he inspired me to undertake studies in architecture and town planning. He was a bachelor and gave me much of his time, frequently walking with me around Melbourne to analyse the features of the more important buildings – setting before me a high standard of values in conception and practice.[3]

In 1913, while Murdoch was travelling overseas in connection with the new capital, he entrusted Daley with oversight of his mail, as he was sending valuable papers and building samples back to the department for study and safekeeping.

*

Australia House has survived and prospered as a heritage-listed building which proudly welcomes many of Australia's most prestigious overseas visitors. Another Commonwealth building project that Daley was associated with in the early days had far less happy associations.

In 1908, the inland town of Lithgow was chosen as the site for a small arms factory to equip the newly formed Commonwealth defence force. Already an industrial centre, Lithgow was considered the ideal site because of the availability of coal and steel and the existing rail link to Sydney. As well, the Lithgow Progress Association had lobbied hard for its establishment. Building began in 1910 and it was officially opened in June 1912. Between 1913 and 1918, around 100,000 rifles were produced at what was considered the most advanced factory in Australia.

Men flocked to Lithgow. There was work aplenty for unskilled men, operating the manufacturing machines designed by the contractors, the American firm of Pratt & Whitney. Skilled tradesmen were also in demand, for making new tools and precision measurement gauges. Percy Owen, the Director General of Works, had initial oversight of the project, but he passed the building project on to the department's Sydney office under George Oakeshott, NSW Director of Housing. This included the construction of houses for the managerial staff; three substantial houses were built for them, on a rise above the factory. However, there was ongoing argument over the form of heating to be used. The manager, Arthur Wright, insisted that in Lithgow's notorious winters a system of central heating was needed to warm the houses. Owen disagreed; why couldn't open fireplaces be installed in each room? And besides, the central heating hadn't been budgeted for. In the end, the steam-heated systems were installed after the Minister for Defence, Senator Pearce, supported Wright's request. These handsome houses are still standing today.

There was a less positive outcome for the workers on the factory floor. In May 1916, Arthur Butler, secretary of the Small Arms Factory Association, wrote to the Minister for Home Affairs, King O'Malley, about the housing crisis in Lithgow. Men eager for a job found they could rent a single room but would have to leave their family behind in Sydney, effectively paying two lots of rent. The alternative was for two or more families to share the one cottage. Butler said that 25% of the houses in Lithgow were occupied by two or more families. He pointed out to the minister the stresses that this involved: men on shift work trying to sleep in a house full of young children; women sharing the same kitchen; and more gravely, serious outbreaks of typhoid fever, measles and scarlet fever because of insanitary and overcrowded dwellings. Cases were known where men slept under a bridge in the bush for want of accommodation. Butler had a proposal for the minister: could the government resume a piece of land on the boundary of the factory, subdivide it into allotments, and arrange with the Commonwealth Bank to give loans to people to build their own cottage on their piece of land?

The government had other priorities in 1916, not least the need to find replacement troops for the Western Front, and a looming referendum on conscription. No action was taken on Lithgow housing shortages until near the end of the war, when action came too late. The Commonwealth acquired 130 acres adjacent to the factory, which were subdivided into about 400 allotments, with provision for roads, playgrounds and gardens. In August 1919 a tender was accepted with a contract to build 100 houses; the Lithgow Council agreed to provide roads, footpaths and accessory services. A board of control was set up in 1920 to oversee the management of this new workers' village. The board consisted of Mr Ratcliffe, the manager of the Small Arms Factory, John Goodwin, the Surveyor General, and George Oakeshott from NSW. Charles Daley was asked to be secretary of the board.

The new village was to be known as Littleton, named in honour of Littleton Groom, the current Minister for Home and Territories (formerly Home Affairs). It was to be a garden suburb, modelled on an enlightened social experiment taking place in Sydney at Daceyville, about three miles south of Sydney's CBD. This was Australia's first public housing scheme. Built by the state's first Labor government, it was the outcome of a Royal Commission in 1909 that found that most working-class dwellings in inner Sydney were dilapidated, overcrowded and unsanitary. The Housing Act passed in 1912 enabled the government to be both builder and landlord, a move the opposition condemned as a step towards socialism. Inspired by England's Garden City movement, the planned suburb would have its own tramline, schools and shops, and plenty of parks and open spaces for families to enjoy, with sewerage connection, curbed streets and electricity laid on. The architect, John Sulman, who was to be an important figure in Canberra's development, was one of the designers of the attractive cottages.

But the ending of the war brought changes. Enlightened town-planning policy became less important than the pressing need to house thousands of returned soldiers and their families. The Nationalist Party introduced a new housing policy that gave loans to those who wanted to buy land or purchase an existing house, with the inevitable fragmentation of the planned suburb and its well-designed enclaves. By June 1920, just 315 of the intended 1,473 cottages at Daceyville had been built. These days, the district has been absorbed into surrounding suburbia. However, most of the area is still in government ownership and there have been some well-designed infill projects that blend in with the older dwellings.

The planners of Littleton also intended their project to be a model of good town planning. Goodwin noted that

> recreation plays an important part in the health and well-being of a community. At Lithgow it is especially important to provide leisure grounds and also a recreation hall for dances and technical instruction of young employees. Blocks should be large enough to give privacy and scope for gardens.[4]

Thomas Weston, in charge of afforestation for the Federal Capital Territory, submitted a planting layout for the village reserves, with trees and shrubs sourced from the nurseries he had established in Canberra.

A number of factors contributed to the failure of this model. By an ironic turn of events, the village was planned at the very time when the Department of Defence was winding down the contracts for small arms. What would be the factory's future now that war had ended? There were gloomy headlines in the newspapers: 'Further dismissals at Lithgow'; 'Dismissals at Small Arms factory – maimed Anzacs included'.[5]

During the war, the factory had worked continuously and employed about 1,500 men, but by 1923 there were only about 300 men employed, and much of the machinery was lying idle. It was in this demoralised climate that the creation of Littleton village went ahead, and it seems to have affected the town council in particular. The council failed in its promise to connect the village to the town's gas supply, so the residents of Littleton had to depend on kerosene lamps for lighting, and the streets remained unlighted. When electricity came to Lithgow in late 1923, again the Littleton residents missed out on this convenience until the Commonwealth intervened in 1924. Roads, kerbing and guttering and drains were all to be undertaken by the council but this they also neglected.

George Oakeshott had drawn up the specifications for the erection of cottages in May 1919. On paper, it is hard to fault the design: they were all to be of brick construction with terracotta or cement tile roofs, all with indoor toilets and proper drains. But the unseasonable rainfall in the autumn of 1921 turned the village site into a swamp and the unsealed roads into a muddy quagmire. In March 1924, the Commonwealth Joint Committee of Public Accounts visited Littleton, commenting that 'the housing scheme could not be said to have served its purpose'.[6] The committee was struck by the neglected and unattractive appearance of the settlement. Their inspection confirmed what the residents had told them of inadequate supervision during construction. The houses were located on a storm swept slope; tiles had been placed on the roofs in an unworkmanlike manner and there was already a large bill for repairs and maintenance. Most of the planned gardens and playgrounds were still dreary patches of waste ground, this in spite of the fact that Weston reported on the successful planting of 15,000 pines as a shelter belt, and fifty-two ornamental trees on the reserves. A passionate horticulturalist himself, it saddened Weston to see the apathy among many of the tenants. He felt that a sense of ownership and enthusiasm would come in time if there was official encouragement by such means as annual garden competitions.

But the inhabitants of Littleton had more pressing matters to cope with. Gordon Reid, a section hand at the Small Arms Factory and secretary of the Littleton Vigilance Committee, made sure that the residents' grievances were placed clearly before the parliamentary visitors, who were to recommend early action to improve the appearance and amenities of the settlement. They also recommended that a trust fund be set up to manage the scheme on a strictly commercial basis.

One is left not knowing where the blame might lie for this failed public project. A demoralised town council? Shoddy contractors? Inadequate supervision by the government? Perhaps a combination of all of these. In his evidence to the Joint Committee, Percy Owen admitted that the dwellings at Littleton had been planned as cheap cottages and that though work had been carried out according to specifications, it wasn't a gilt-edged job.[7] While inferior to workers' cottages being built in Canberra, he regarded them as equal to cottages rented elsewhere. It is doubtful that his defence would have been much comfort to the families living in that bleak environment.

In 1927, the Department of Works and Railways transferred all the Littleton Estate lands still owned by the Commonwealth to the War Service Homes Commission.

*

In July 1916, a secret cable was dispatched to the High Commission in London from the Minister for Defence, George Pearce, on a matter of some urgency. The cable asked whether Mr Arthur Leighton, Controller General of Munitions Supply but at that stage employed with the British Ministry of Munitions, would come back to Australia to take on the position of general manager of a new arsenal, one to be established in the federal territory.

While Lithgow's small arms factory was producing rifles during World War I, the explosives needed for warfare were produced at the cordite factory in Maribyrnong, Victoria. The government now proposed to embark on a plan to extend and centralise the manufacture of all munitions of war. In 1915, Colonel Owen led a deputation to India to study a number of factories there. On his return, planning began for this new venture.

The rationale behind establishing a large arsenal in the federal territory was that it would ensure that the Commonwealth had proper oversight of the country's arms production. It also meant that savings could be made by combining small arms production and munitions production on the one site. A number of sites in the federal territory were identified as suitable. One was north of the city and another on the Molonglo River to the south-east of Canberra. Then there were two sites on the Murrumbidgee River, one near the village of Tharwa and one in the Tuggeranong Valley, both of these being south of the planned city and separated from it by a number of hills (a factor to be considered in the event of an explosion). The site which received endorsement was Tuggeranong, a rambling sheep station which had been in the hands of the Cunningham family for many years. The Commonwealth had already taken steps to acquire it as part of the ongoing acquisition of lands in the new federal capital, with a final handover of the property to the Commonwealth in March 1917.

Walter Burley Griffin, who was at that time Federal Capital Director of Design and Construction, had already been pressed into preparing a model of the proposed township, though he had strong reservations about placing the arsenal in his planned federal capital: he felt it would change the character of the city as well as making it a target in wartime. He was also dismayed at the final choice of Tuggeranong, where the arsenal 'would occupy the most attractive land of the Territory, land that is needed for a National Park...'[8]

The township he designed would sit in a beautiful amphitheatre sheltered from the arsenal by a large hill, with views across the river to botanical gardens. Griffin contended that it was the best site for the township from both a scenic point of view and for the health of its residents. The total cost, including a rail link to the factory site, was estimated at three million pounds. Such a cost was not politically acceptable and Griffin's plan was shelved.

But groundwork at the Tuggeranong site continued. In January 1917, Leighton had made a request for a most careful survey to be made of the region, both of the factory site near the river and of the planned township, to be sent to him in England as soon as possible. Arthur Percival, one of the original border surveyors of the federal territory, surveyed the proposed rail link between the Cooma–Goulburn line and the factory down in the valley. Other surveys were done along the Murrumbidgee River. In February 1918, Surveyor General Goodwin forwarded to the Department of Defence twenty-five sets of the arsenal site plan. Defence had left arsenal matters up to the Home and Territories Department, but it is clear that by this stage in early 1918 they were getting anxious at what they regarded as the slow rate of progress of the scheme. But Goodwin merely cautioned them about frugality: 'It will be necessary to exercise the greatest economy in connection with these plans as the supply of suitable paper in Australia is almost exhausted.'[9]

A committee was established in August 1918 to prepare a new layout of the arsenal town. It was chaired by the former Professor of Engineering at the University of Queensland, Major A.J. Gibson. Colonel Owen and John Goodwin were also on the committee, and Griffin was taken on as one of the consultants. The committee asked for Daley's services as secretary. The committee worked hard from August to December that year, preparing a design for the arsenal township, with an estimated population of 15,000, and considering various schemes for the management of the town.

Daley was asked to investigate a scheme of cooperative control of supplies, whereby residents of the town could become shareholders of a society which provided all the basic goods and which returned dividends to its members. Professor Meredith Atkinson of the University of Melbourne was a strong supporter of the scheme which he had seen operating successfully in England. He advised Daley and the arsenal committee that such a system of cooperative supply

> would cultivate civic progress, and divert to the development of self-government a great deal of that Australian energy which at present finds its outlet in industrial and political strife.[10]

Enthusiasm and expectations for the arsenal township were high.

> This is the first occasion when a town has been begun by the Federal Government on absolutely virgin ground. So it is an opportunity to establish a 'model town'. Contented men, who spend two thirds of their living hours outside the factory walls, will need pleasant surroundings...[11]

Victorian town planner James Morrell was charged with the actual design of the township, but other experts played an important role in advising about the site, including Ernest De Burgh, chief water engineer for NSW, and G.D. Delprat, General Manager of BHP. Griffin's planned town had been placed south of the factory site, but Morrell placed his town about a mile or so north of the factory, separated from it by a park belt. The town featured bowling greens, playgrounds, parks and reserves, tennis courts and a cooperative store. There were churches, Sunday schools, a hotel, banks, offices and hostels for single men and women. The Tuggeranong Homestead, once home to the large Cunningham family, was to become quarters for staff. Goodwin summed up the feelings of the committee with his views that

> Money spent on the comfort and well-being of employees is not wasted... so the mess house, club house and amusement hall should receive first consideration. When a man leaves work he shall be entirely free from official control and encouraged to take part in the government of the town... Maintenance of pleasure grounds and libraries etc could be by an elected committee, with sanitation, hospitals etc under Federal territory administration.[12]

These were fine plans that were never to be realised.

Men heard that there would be work at a big new construction site south of the capital city and a small union deputation met Owen in Melbourne: would they be receiving award wages as per the 1912 award rates? Owen explained that the initial clearing of the site was mainly being done with mechanical excavators. When construction began and buildings were pegged out, he assured them that there would be work then for members of the Builders and Labourers' Federation.

A program of tree planting began on the grazed valley floor, and by November 1918 plans were well advanced for water supply, sewerage, stormwater, roads and pathways and electricity supply.

The end of the war brought a wave of jubilation everywhere, but left the arsenal committee with demoralising news. All work at Tuggeranong was to be suspended in view of the ending of hostilities. Six months later, official statements still talked about the arsenal project being 'in abeyance'. Technical staff were thanked for their contribution to the project and sent home to Melbourne or Sydney. The Tuggeranong Valley returned to its quiet rural ways, its splendid views to the mountain ranges unimpeded by construction works. The rambling homestead in its copse of English trees lay empty, the Cunningham family having moved further south to Lanyon on the sale of their Tuggeranong property to the Commonwealth.

The only evidence of the grand plans that had occupied senior bureaucrats for over two years was a few concrete survey posts fixed in the ground and a thick bundle of maps, technical reports and memoranda filed in government offices.

Charles Daley was given the task of compiling the Arsenal Town Committee's final report. In later years, he talked about 'the frustrations suffered by responsible public servants in devoting time, thought and energy to projects that have come to nothing'.[13]

By November 1919, Tuggeranong Homestead had a new tenant. Surveyor General Goodwin arranged for the homestead to be handed over to the Defence Department, who were to rent it to the official war historian, C.E.W. Bean. The homestead paddock of sixty-five acres was to be cleared of the stock owned by the current lessee, the old woolshed was to be demolished and Bean and his staff were to travel from Melbourne to take up residence by the end of the year. Bean and his projects, especially the creation of the Australian War Memorial, were to play an important part in Charles Daley's story in the coming years.

'Their labours were heroic...'

'...there are few cities in the world where such a magnificent supply of fresh water is available from an absolutely uninhabited catchment...'

Camp at 'Westerman's' on South boundary of Federal Capital Territory.
From the collection of the National Archives of Australia

The young C.S. Daley was to find his professional life linked from the outset with the fortunes of Australia's new capital city, which in 1905 was still only an idea on paper, but whose final shape would be administered by the Department of Home Affairs.

The decision to establish the federal capital in the Yass/Canberra region could have been taken in 1901 in the parliament's first sitting. In 1899, the Lyne government had appointed a Royal Commissioner, Alexander Oliver, President of the NSW Land Appeal Court, to report on the merits of twenty-three possible sites in the state. Oliver had recommended three sites: Bombala/Eden, the Orange district and Yass/Canberra. For the first three months of 1901, the Minister for Home Affairs, Sir William Lyne, was also the Premier of NSW, the state which a constitutional referendum had determined would host the capital city.

In 1901, Lyne expressed the hope that federal parliament would meet in the 'new Washington' in three to five years, though he would have liked to see it established in Albury or Tumut, which were in his own electorate.[1] In fact, it was to take twenty-six years for his hope to materialise, and the first decade of the new century was marked by a series of squabbles between competing interest groups who all wanted to see the capital established in their locality.

When Daley entered the Department of Home Affairs as a junior clerk in 1905, the department was embroiled in an ongoing controversy between the Commonwealth and the state of NSW over the chosen site. In August 1904, the Seat of Government Act had determined that the new capital would be within seventeen miles of Dalgety, a small village on the banks of the Snowy River. However, the government fell soon after that and the legislation was put on hold. The NSW Premier, Joseph Carruthers, expressed the feelings of many of his constituents in opposing the Act. He argued that Dalgety was too remote from Sydney, which was after all capital of the Mother State: its southern boundary virtually placed it on the Victorian border. There would be heavy expenditure for rail access; the soil was unproductive; and the costs for building and maintenance would be high. As well, its bleak winter climate would have little appeal for those required to live there year round.

John Norton, editor of the scurrilous Sydney paper *Truth*, told his readers, 'I would rather see Federal Parliament retained in Melbourne than stuck down in that territorial appendix, that cul-de-sac of hills and gullies in Dalgety.'[2]

In December 1904, Carruthers, speaking in the NSW Legislative Assembly, hoped for a speedy settlement of the matter in terms favourable to NSW. Unless the matter was settled, he argued, '...the federal capital would remain in Melbourne for years and Parliament would be dominated by the Melbourne press.'[3]

Heated correspondence passed between Carruthers and Prime Minister Alfred Deakin. Carruthers threatened to cancel the reservation of Crown lands in Dalgety which had been gazetted in 1904 for the Commonwealth, and he prepared to accuse the Commonwealth of trespass if moves were made to survey the region. In response, Home Affairs sought the legal advice of the Attorney General, Robert Garran. Garran made clear that the Commonwealth, not the state, had the power to determine the capital site, and the state's proprietary rights over the region were to be ceded to the Commonwealth without compensation.

In July 1905, Littleton Groom became the new Minister for Home Affairs. His predecessor, Dugald Thomson, commented wryly, 'I am afraid I have left my successor, Mr Groom, with a fight on his hands.'[4]

The Commonwealth went ahead with its plans for Dalgety despite vocal NSW opposition. Crown lands in the vicinity of the village were reserved from sale or lease pending their acquisition, and NSW Surveyor Charles Scrivener was co-opted to make a survey of the site. Colonel Owen, as Director General of Works, accompanied him on his journeys and made careful studies of water flows from the Snowy River. The Bill to establish Dalgety was passed in August 1904 but the government fell two days later and the legislation failed to receive assent.

In May 1906, Deakin promised the Governor General that the question of the capital site would be brought before Parliament in the coming session and every effort would be made to resolve the question.

In June 1906, Carruthers (still hoping to secure a site nearer to Sydney) offered to fund a series of visits by parliamentarians to a number of sites, including Canberra, Dalgety and Lake George. Further parliamentary visits took place to the final two contenders, Dalgety and Canberra, in

August that year. About twenty MPs accepted the invitation, including former Prime Minister Chris Watson. They arrived in Canberra on a splendid winter's day of sunshine and clear skies. John Gale, the owner of the Queanbeyan paper *The Golden Age*, was their guide on a walk up the slopes of Mount Ainslie, which commanded extensive views over the Limestone Plains and beyond to the western snow-capped range of mountains.

In the winter of 1907, further parliamentary visits followed, with John Gale as their guide. The visitors could not fail to be impressed by what they saw. On Watson's suggestion, Gale was later to write a pamphlet on the superior attractions of the region compared to Dalgety. These visits and the pamphlet (distributed to every senator and member) proved decisive in the final vote and earned Gale the honorific 'Father of Canberra'.

In October 1908, after a series of nine ballots, the House of Representatives voted in favour of Canberra over Dalgety, as did the Senate the following month. The *Seat of Government Act 1908* repealed the 1904 Act and determined that the capital city site was to be in the Yass/Canberra district. In December 1908, Charles Scrivener's services as a surveyor were again requested and in February 1909 an advisory board was formed to consider the survey results when they were ready. Board members were Scrivener, Owen, David Miller the Secretary of the Department, and Walter Liberty Vernon, NSW government architect. Hugh Mahon, Minister for Home Affairs, directed Scrivener to bear in mind that

> the Federal Capital should be a beautiful city, occupying a commanding position with extensive views and embracing distinctive features which will lend themselves to a design worthy of the object, not only for the present but for all time.[5]

Scrivener was instructed to do a preliminary reconnaissance of the whole region, including all the river catchments, and to do a close contour survey of ten square miles of his preferred city site. A detailed contour survey would be needed before the design of the city could be prepared.

The site Scrivener chose for the city lay in an amphitheatre of lightly wooded hills, with an outlook north-east over open grazing country through which the Molonglo River meandered. Scrivener and his assistants – the first government officials to take up residence in the

Molonglo Valley – set up a tented encampment on the northern slopes of Kurrajong Hill (henceforth known as Capital Hill) in March and later that month began a preliminary contour survey of the valley and environs. Their labours were heroic: sixteen-hour days, seven days a week for two months. Surveyors often did 3,000 observations a day and then their computing of data at night. In 1910 a concrete bunker was built to house precious maps and survey equipment.

In February 1909, Home Affairs proposed a base camp at the Molonglo River to allow senators and members a chance to inspect the country chosen for the new capital, with Scrivener as their guide. In March, Home Affairs approached the Department of Defence with a request to man the camp, provide sleeping tents and latrines, barrack room tables, washstands and a field kitchen. A chef from Parliament House in Melbourne would cook their meals on a fuel stove set up in a galvanised hut. A flagpole was to be erected to show the official nature of the camp, with an Australian flag, not the Union Jack: this was Australian Commonwealth territory. While many parliamentarians were curious about the site, few were willing to accept the invitation in view of the difficulties of transport: all-night train to Yass, then a tedious journey of thirty-five miles by horse and buggy to Canberra. The alternative was an eighteen-hour wait at Goulburn to connect with the Cooma train to Queanbeyan. Hugh Mahon feared that, 'under such conditions, many of the members may hesitate to make such a personal sacrifice'.[6]

About a dozen members accompanied Mahon on the first visit, with further visitors planned. Senator Neild proposed to visit but was anxious on one point: would it be necessary for him to bring his own supply of whiskey or could a little be obtained there? Evidently the availability of alcohol did not prove a problem, as the parliamentarians brought their own supply. Mrs Sullivan, who lived at Springbank on the Molonglo River, collected two pillowcases of corks after their camp; they had held a party outside her fence.

Later distinguished visitors to the survey camp included the Governor General the Earl of Dudley and his wife, who stayed overnight in their railway carriage at Queanbeyan station and viewed the region by motorcar and on horseback (Lady Dudley in specially designed trousers and covering skirt).

The territory they visited was not the bleak wilderness that its detractors in Melbourne liked to imagine. Paintings from the early years of the century show a settled, pastoral landscape. The willow-fringed Molonglo River wound through an open valley where cottages marked the properties of small landholders who had lived in the Canberra region for a generation or more. They grew crops on the river flats and grazed their sheep on the drier grassy slopes and stony uplands that ringed the valley. The larger pastoral estates had grander dwellings.

Duntroon, named after an ancestral castle in Scotland, was a fashionable Gothic mansion, surrounded by a cluster of buildings for the workers on the Campbell estate. The spire of St Johns was a landmark in that open valley: Robert Campbell had given the site to the Church of England and had built nearby a schoolhouse for the estate children. At the western end of the valley, another member of the Campbell clan owned Yarralumla, the centre of a wealthy pastoral operation.

Charles Scrivener would have shown the visitors the main features of the site: the river and its flood plain; the surrounding hills that might provide shelter from the prevailing winds; the possibilities for water supply and modern sewerage for the planned city. He would have described for the visitors the more remote areas of the territory to the south-west, including the upper reaches of the Cotter River: an area of 'heavy, steep rugged hills of granite formation so rough and unfit for settlement that some parts of it did not appear on the maps of the state'.[7]

The parliamentary visitors might have heard reports about the wonderful purity of the new city's potential water supply. In 1908, NSW engineers Ernest De Burgh and William Corin had prepared a report for the NSW Legislative Assembly that stated, '...there are few cities in the world where such a magnificent supply of pure water is available from an absolutely uninhabited catchment...'[8]

Scrivener himself was not convinced of the feasibility of sourcing water from the Cotter catchment, believing it would involve prohibitive expense; he favoured supplies of water from the Queanbeyan River, if the catchment could be protected from further deforestation and over-grazing. (The final boundaries of the territory were to exclude Queanbeyan, but NSW was still required to manage and protect the catchment as it would flow through the Federal Capital Territory.) *The Bulletin*, always hostile to the idea of the federal capital, had a ludicrous view of the Cotter catchment, condemning the river as 'mainly manure and diseased cow'.[9]

By May 1909, Charles Scrivener had completed his survey of thirty-five square miles of the region, showing the site he was recommending for the city, a choice which the Advisory Board supported. Two hundred lithographed copies of the survey maps were forwarded to Melbourne for federal parliament, and Colonel Owen and other members of the Site Advisory Board received three copies each.

In December 1909, the Seat of Government (Surrender) Act and the Seat of Government (Acceptance) Act allowed the Commonwealth to accept from NSW an area of nearly 1,000 square miles, including access to the sea at Jervis Bay.

Daley was still a junior clerk in Owen's department, studying part time at night and during time off from office work. Intelligent and ambitious, he was keen to play a role on a wider stage: his imagination was fired with the idea of being associated with the planned federal capital. Working with Owen, he became familiar with Scrivener's maps and was to follow closely the development of the city from then on. Early in his studies, Daley had gained qualifications as a shorthand writer, a very useful skill at a time when all information had to be recorded manually, before twentieth-century technology had transformed office life. Within a year of entering the department, he was assisting at commonwealth conferences as stenographer, and thus he began a close observation of policy making at a high level. In 1906, he accompanied John Murdoch to the Transferred Properties Conference in Melbourne, which laid down the principles for valuing property and equipment for transfer to the Commonwealth. (Murdoch was secretary to the conference.) The compulsory acquisition of property and the compensation offered to landholders were to prove long-running points of contention between the government and individuals in the story of the federal capital.

The Commonwealth began the process of compulsory acquisition of property within the territory in 1910 with the acquisition of Duntroon. The house and 370 surrounding acres were leased from their owner, John Campbell, and eventually acquired outright in 1912. Campbell received a generous compensation of £141,000, but the tenants received nothing, as they were on short-term leases that eventually expired. Duntroon was to become the home of the Royal Military College in 1911, the first Commonwealth establishment to be built in the territory. The property had been chosen by the Defence Department for a national military college because it was well away from 'the distractions and temptations of a large city'.[10] Initially, the Tuggeranong Valley had been proposed as a suitable site for the college but it fell out of favour when the Defence Minister George Pearce visited it on a day of cold westerly winds and found the site too exposed.

Daley, acting as stenographer, was present in Melbourne at meetings of Major General Bridges and other senior military officers with Colonel Owen and chief government architect John Murdoch as they planned the Duntroon establishment. Bridges' austere but effective leadership at the college was to end with his death at Gallipoli four years later. Many letters home from young cadets were to lament the spartan regime of cold showers, plain food and strenuous physical demands. Bridges had made clear at the planning meetings that he was going 'to send the cadets dog-tired to bed every night'.[11]

Daley learnt valuable skills about town planning working with John Murdoch as the Victorian-era estate was transformed into a modern military college. Every detail on the site had to be planned from scratch: barracks, homes for the commandant and officers as well as the teaching staff; stables and a shoeing shed, laundry, hospital; and a fire alarm tower. Timber for the new buildings, as well as for the temporary buildings at Acton, had to be brought up from the densely forested slopes near the Clyde Mountain. A timber mill at nearby Monga sent loads up by bullock dray, a trip which took a week in each direction. Henry Rolland, a young architect working on the Duntroon project, recalled the thrill of seeing 'a fourteen bullock team with its timber loaded wagon slowly wending its way across the Limestone Plains'.[12]

Plans for the new college had to be prepared for every installation, whether this was the electric light fittings, the tables in the library, cabinets in the dispensary or the setup of the rifle range. Plans were signed by either George Oakeshott, NSW Director of Works, or by P. Owen. There was a degree of urgency in the planning, as the first contingent of cadets arrived to start their four-year course in June 1911. Daley's signature appears from time to time when he was a witness to building contracts, including a beautifully drawn plan, dated June 1913, of an observatory which was to be set up on the site. The observatory was built and remained in use until 1954 when it was demolished.

On 1 January 1910, Scrivener formally began his duties as Director, Commonwealth Lands and Survey, with three survey teams, a draughtsman and clerk plus local men to work as chain-man and axe-man. He set up office on 8 January at the Capital Hill site, accompanied by Owen, who spent some days in preliminary investigation on water supplies. Together with a team of engineering surveyors, he collected stream flow data from the Molonglo River and its tributaries.

In 1911, the Acton estate on the northern banks of the Molonglo River was acquired from the Brassey family, who had been leasing it from absentee owners. Acton became the first workplace of Commonwealth officials arriving from Melbourne. At first, everyone was housed in tents until a cluster of wooden buildings was erected for administrative, surveying and engineering staff, including a barrack-like building for the unmarried officers that became known as the Bachelors' Quarters. The new administrative offices were occupied on 22 August 1912. The old Acton homestead was occupied by Charles Scrivener and his wife. His two daughters, who came down for holiday visits, remembered it as a wonderful episode in their teenage years.

One of the men who lodged at the Bachelors' Quarters was the young geologist, Thomas Griffith Taylor. A member of the Federal Geological Department, he had come up from Melbourne in September 1912 to work with D.J. Mahony of the Geological Survey of Victoria. They were to map the geological formations of the territory and seek out sources of brick-making clay and good quarrying sites.

Taylor had already visited the territory. In 1910 he climbed some of the local hills in the company of Professor T.W. Edgeworth David, who had come down to Canberra to study the site's geology. Pressure of work at the University of Sydney led David to decline survey work in Canberra, and the geology of the area immediately around the city site was to be surveyed by Edward Pittman, NSW Government Geologist.

Taylor stayed on and decided to explore the territory, 'traversing it in all directions' on foot and by pushbike. Percy Owen recalled seeing him leave the survey camp early one morning, 'his pockets bulging with newspaper packets, bread and cheese…he said that he intended to cross the mountains of the Cotter River via Tharwa to Brindabella… A few days later he returned, bike and all. I have been over that country and to this day I do not know how he did it…'[13] One outcome of this first visit was a relief model of the city site which Taylor created and which was used by the administration as part of the information for entrants in the city design competition.

Taylor was to enjoy an influential career as a geologist both in Australia and abroad. He is also remembered for his role in Robert Scott's doomed expedition to the Antarctic in 1911–12. As a member of the scientific staff, Taylor was not in the party that set out for the South Pole, and he returned safely to Australia in April 1912, unaware, as was the rest of the world, that Scott's party had all perished on the return trip to base camp.

While staying in Canberra in late 1912, Taylor wrote letters to members of that ill-fated company. He wrote to their leader, Captain Scott, hoping to hear soon of the success of the expedition. To Titus Oates, he wrote about his journeys exploring the southern part of the territory and his ascent of the highest peak, Bimberi, where he met a girl who had climbed it on a pony. On their journey, they came across a huge granite tor that had tumbled down and blocked the track. Too heavy to move, it was systematically undermined by the party till it lay level with the ground and the track could pass over it.

Taylor recalled writing these letters sitting on a deckchair outside the Bachelors' Quarters, the very Australian quality of the scene a poignant contrast to that world of snow and ice where his colleagues now lay buried. He recalled 'the western wind sighing through the gum trees and the moon rising over Mount Ainslie, reminding me of her climbing over Erebus, a mountain so similar in outline'.[14]

In Melbourne, the workload of the Department of Home Affairs increased. Written memoranda shuttled to and fro between Melbourne and the post office at Queanbeyan on the Cooma mail train, with telegrams being delivered to Acton by a boy on a bicycle. (A post office was established at Acton in 1912.)

In Melbourne, an army of clerks worked long hours in offices in Spring Street, just down from the imposing bulk of Parliament House. There were also large offices in nearby Russell Street, and perennial overcrowding saw more office space acquired in buildings dotted around the city. David

Miller, the departmental secretary, had complained as early as 1903 of unhealthy crowded conditions, especially for men 'required to work well beyond ordinary office hours'.[15]

In March 1907, there were more complaints of cramped quarters in the Spring Street offices, with light so poor that gas lighting was needed in the middle of the day. In 1912, the minister, King O'Malley, announced plans for a large new four-storey building to house Treasury and Home Affairs, near the peaceful expanse of the Treasury Gardens. Designed by John Murdoch, this was to be the first block of offices built specifically to house Commonwealth departments.

In August 1912, Colonel David Miller moved up to Canberra to take up the position of Administrator of the Federal Capital Territory (FCT). He had to make do with a timber cottage until his own quarters were built – an imposing two-storey residence on the hill above Acton, made of cement blocks from local limestone deposits.

Miller became a controversial figure in Canberra's story until his retirement from the position in 1917 and his return to military duties. He had been secretary to the Department of Home Affairs since 1901 after his return from the Boer War. With a military background and used to command, he did not always fit easily into a civilian workplace. The surveyor, Arthur Percival, found him 'gruff and frightening'.[16]

'Like others,' recalled Daley, 'I was often irked by his strictures, but found him scrupulously fair. Behind his apparent austerity, he had a sense of humour, and he was ready to give kindly advice and encouragement when genuinely needed.'[17]

Together with Charles Scrivener, Miller had oversight of the territory in the early years.

The process of acquisition of land continued, and by Christmas 1912, all of the area encompassing the modern city of Canberra was in Commonwealth hands. By February 1910, the site had been fixed for an astronomical observatory on Mount Stromlo, midway between the eastern and western boundaries of the FCT. This allowed the survey teams to begin precise demarcation of territory boundaries and water catchments.

Compulsory acquisition of the church land where St John's stood was gazetted in July 1912. The registrar of the diocese was quick to protest, claiming that the church's title to the land was inviolate. It had been solemnly consecrated and set apart for its present purpose over seventy years before. Interference with this piece of land, with all its sacred and human associations, would be an outrage to the community.

The government at first offered a ten-year lease to the church, with the warning that no more interments could take place in the graveyard there after the city cemetery was established. The church insisted that the land be permanently dedicated to their trust and that compensation be paid for loss of freehold title. Matters were not resolved until 1926 when at last a Church of England Lands Ordinance authorised dedication of the church and compensation of £2,000 was finally paid.

Frederick Campbell was another disaffected Canberra resident. On receiving notice in August 1912 of the acquisition of his Yarralumla estate, Campbell wrote a forceful and bitter letter to Scrivener. 'I note that the Commonwealth by notification has resumed my land and wish they had gone elsewhere for their Capital.' A further letter to Scrivener in September 1912 had a request to make. Campbell wished to retain 626 acres of land he owned just over the border in NSW, part of an original grant to the explorer Charles Sturt in 1837.

> It is my Ewe Lamb, and I hope the Commonwealth Government will be satisfied to leave me that much of Sturt's 5,000 acre grant and not drive me altogether out of my native land.[18]

The Commonwealth allowed Campbell to retain that portion of land: in any case, it was freehold land in NSW. Portions of the Yarralumla estate were leased to Selwyn Miller, David Miller's son. The Campbells left the district quite abruptly. The valuation of Yarralumla was completed in April 1913 and the family were given five weeks to pack up and leave their home. They moved to Goulburn.

Unsure what to do with the rambling homestead, the government used it for the next twelve years as a guest house for visiting dignitaries. The extensive grounds provided a convenient venue for summer camps for the cadets at the new military college.

Many small landholders in the district – there were about 200 at the time – had looked forward to the benefits they would enjoy when Canberra became the capital. They assumed that their land would be greatly enhanced in value, and they anticipated positive improvements in roads and infrastructure. So it came as a shock when they learnt the terms of acquisition.

With regard to any private lands within the territory, valuation would be based on the worth of the land on 8 October 1908, the date of passage of the Seat of Government Act. This proviso was built into the legislation to thwart land speculation, and was broadly supported within the Commonwealth parliament. It was felt that the rise in land values generated by the development of the capital should be enjoyed by the whole nation, not just a few local landowners. All lands within the territory would be leasehold, so in reality all were owned by the Commonwealth, to be leased out for short or long-term periods.

A further cause for discontent among locals was the loss of any voting rights. It was clear that they could not now vote for the NSW parliament, but they were also to be disenfranchised at a Commonwealth level. The government had decided that the Federal Capital residents – about 1,500 in number – were too few in number to warrant a seat.

In March 1911, a public meeting of landowners was convened in Queanbeyan to discuss these grievances. A Vigilance Association was formed with local shire councillor, Jeremiah Keefe, as president. Keefe was a small-scale farmer and grazier but he had the support of prominent graziers like Frederick Campbell and Jim Cunningham of Tuggeranong. All were affected by the new legislation and knew it would be difficult to appeal to the High Court; they needed a local tribunal to settle the issue of compensation speedily and fairly.

Over the next decade, the association lobbied hard to get a better deal for landowners from the Commonwealth. A delegation visited Melbourne and presented a petition signed by 165 local landowners, but King O'Malley, the Minister for Home Affairs, proved unsympathetic. The need for a better appeals system was acknowledged but nothing eventuated, and even into the 1920s valuation was still based on 1908 values. Meanwhile, land prices in NSW were escalating, making it very difficult for an FCT resident to buy an equivalent farm elsewhere. There were many sad farewells as local landowners settled with the government and moved away to try and start a new life elsewhere. Others stayed on, in a kind of limbo. They did not feel warranted in making big plans or improvements to their property, as they knew that sooner or later all land with the territory's boundaries would be acquired.

*

In Canberra, Owen was keen to begin work on the city's infrastructure. Water supply, sewerage, electricity and building materials were all prerequisites for the establishment of a modern city. It was said that a million pounds had been spent in Canberra before the city began to show any shape at all. There was some degree of truth in this. Most early development took the form of vast excavations and tunnels for sewer and water schemes, reservoirs, drainage, the grading of roads and levelling of building and plantation areas. Almost a quarter of a million pounds had also been spent on the acquisition of land.

Canberra was to be a truly modern city, wholly powered by electricity. At that stage, even Melbourne and Sydney only had electricity on a restricted basis. Priority was therefore given to the construction of a power house. Designed by John Murdoch, this imposing, utilitarian building began its working life in August 1915 with the supply of public electricity to Duntroon and Acton. A year later it was also providing power for the brickworks and for the pumping station at the Cotter River which delivered Canberra's water to a reservoir on Red Hill. A large proportion of the Power House load in the early days was to work these pumps. Murdoch designed the Cotter pumping house in 1912; the pumps were brought over from England and the motors were purchased from General Electric in the United States. During the 1920s, the water supply needs of Canberra's population (about 5,000) could be met by pumping one or two days a month. One or two technicians travelled up from Melbourne for the job, enjoying a novel excursion away from their boss and their everyday work.

The Power House – always graced with capital letters to acknowledge its importance to Canberra's story – was constructed from unreinforced concrete, made from river gravel. It was sited next to the Molonglo River, where a small dam provided a source of cooling water for the condensers of the steam generators. A railway branch line was constructed from Queanbeyan to bring coal down from Lithgow to heat the water.

The Power House was to become the focus of a small community as associated structures grew around it: a sawmill and pipe-making plant; a fitters' workshop, railway siding and workers' camps. The Power House made ice, packed in sawdust, which was delivered by horse and dray to

46

the offices at Acton. On hot summer days, the dam above the weir was a popular swimming spot. In years to come, the starter and lunchtime whistles became reliable signals for local residents. The Power House supplied the needs of Canberra and Queanbeyan until 1927, when electricity was obtained from the Burrinjuck hydroelectric works.

Adequate sanitation was a priority for the new city. There was still wide public awareness of the human suffering caused by disease: as recently as 1900, bubonic plague had broken out in the crowded tenements of the Rocks area in Sydney; and typhoid fever still carried off young children in the Queanbeyan district, where contaminated water from pit toilets drained into the Queanbeyan River.

In 1914, Owen's department undertook to design the broad features of a modern sewerage system for Canberra. A main underground sewer would be driven west from the city site south of the Molonglo River to meet an intercepting sewer from the north. The sewage would be discharged by gravity at a treatment plant at Weston Creek outside the city boundaries.[19] The main outfall sewer is still a vital part of the city's sewerage system.

An alternative form of sewerage, with shallow sedimentation tanks and local dispersal of sludge – a kind of septic system – had been operating at Duntroon and Acton up to that time, but a large-scale adoption of this scheme would have been impossible with a growing population. The city's future designer, Walter Burley Griffin, favoured a different scheme again, which was to prove one of many points of difference between Griffin and the department's engineers. He favoured a disposal of sewage effluent within the city by means of specially constructed tanks that would send the treated water back into the

or the ornamental lakes system. This would have been much cheaper than the construction of three miles of outfall sewer but Thomas Hill, the departmental engineer advising Owen on costs, warned that there were serious difficulties with such a scheme and supported the original gravitation system.

The Cotter Dam and the brickworks were two other projects that Owen supervised before the war. In October 1910, Owen met NSW geologist, Edward Pittman, on the federal capital site where they inspected shale sites for possible brickworks. Samples of shale were sent to Melbourne to test the suitability of the material for brick making.

By July 1911, Owen had settled on Shale Trig as a likely source of material for a brickworks. He made a rough contour plan of this hillside and asked for a large scale map to be prepared. Shale Hill was part of Frederick Campbell's Yarralumla property and Owen urged David Miller to approach Campbell for permission to open a trench on the site to test for shale. Further action on the site was suspended at the end of 1911 as the Commonwealth acted to acquire further privately owned lands in the territory. By August 1912, Home Affairs could announce that Yarralumla had recently been acquired by the Commonwealth.

In February 1928, Prime Minister Stanley Bruce gave an address at the Institute of Engineers Conference – the first such institution to hold its annual conference in Canberra, at the newly built assembly hall which came to be known as the Albert Hall. In his speech, Bruce lauded the often unacknowledged and unseen achievements of engineers.

He pointed out,

> In all the criticism of the Federal Capital which has been hurled at it from its inception and which covered every phase of the idea itself, its location, its layout, its expense, and its hopeless future, not one word of criticism has been heard against the work of its engineers... The great engineering foundations of this city have been well and truly laid.[20]

As a demonstration of the triumphant modernity of the new city, the Federal Capital Commissioner, John Butters (himself an electrical engineer), arranged a demonstration of radio broadcasting, sending radio greetings to fellow engineers in Great Britain and the United States.

'He had expected to be given scope to achieve a great and unique work and to be associated with it in history.'

Walter Burley Griffin.
Reproduced with permission of Canberra & District Historical Society

By December 1909, the creation of the federal capital, the Commonwealth's first major building project, was underway.

Three men were effectively in control of its direction: David Miller, Administrator, Federal Capital Territory; Charles Scrivener, Director Capital Lands and Survey; and Percy Owen, Director General of Works. In theory, they were all answerable to the Minister for Home Affairs, but the first decades of the century saw fourteen ministers come and go, with consequent erratic and confusing changes of policy. This was especially so in relation to the federal territory, which continued to prove a controversial issue in public affairs. Each of these three men, decisive, practical and hard-working as they were, put their own stamp of authority on significant areas of development in the national capital.

By 1912, both Miller and Scrivener were permanently based in Canberra with their families, as the survey and acquisition of federal lands took place and crucial development projects got underway. Owen was still based at his headquarters in Russell Street, Melbourne, but his life for the next decade saw him commuting frequently between Sydney, Melbourne and Canberra, with long overnight journeys by train or by vehicle over indifferent roads. Much of the work in Canberra was outdoors, inspecting sites with Scrivener or engaged on field work with one of the surveying teams. It was a working life whose demands would have taxed a less robust person. Owen came to rely on his assistant, Charles Daley, for efficient record keeping, management of his Melbourne office and the preparation of ministerial briefings and reports to Parliament on federal capital matters.

In May 1911, the international competition for a city plan was launched. The architect, John Sulman, had advocated the idea for such a competition, which had its genesis in the growing professional and public interest in town planning. Sulman had given an influential paper on 'The Laying Out of Towns' at the 1890 meeting of the Australian Association for the Advancement of Science. Then in May 1901, the first conference on city planning held in Australia was staged in Melbourne, timed to coincide with the first session of the Commonwealth Parliament. Many of the papers addressed the ideal of a 'City Beautiful', where monumental buildings, grand piazzas and sweeping vistas through extensive parklands created a truly civilised urban setting. Whether a young democratic nation like Australia was ready to embrace this ideal was another matter.

The historian Lewis Mumford observed that

> Democracies are often too stingy in spending money for public purposes, for the citizens feel that the money is theirs. Monarchies and tyrannies can be generous because they dip their hands freely into other people's pockets.[1]

Another strong influence on town planning was the Garden City concept, where the slums, speculative building and crowding of so many older cities was replaced by a city whose overall design, transport system and parks and gardens provided a healthy and comfortable life for all classes of citizen.

Owen and his department played a central role in the design competition, which became the object of international interest. The competition guidelines and conditions, which were detailed and comprehensive, were prepared by Owen, Scrivener and Miller with the help of Walter Vernon, NSW Government Architect. Daley was an assistant in the process. Advertisements appeared in newspapers throughout the world inviting prospective entrants to apply. The information kit contained a detailed description of the site, topographic maps and copies of panoramic paintings that had been specially commissioned. Included in the kit was a list of major buildings and institutions that competitors needed to include in the plan; a decorative water feature was also considered desirable. Contour models of the city site, prepared from Griffith Taylor's relief model, were displayed in London, New York, Washington, Chicago, Paris, Berlin, Ottawa, Cape Town and Wellington. Built into the competition were two conditions: the chosen design would become the property of the government for its unrestricted use either in whole or in part; and the government would give effect to the adopted design using its own officers.

Throughout the summer of 1911–12, the designs arrived in Melbourne, where the judging was to take place. The large parcels were variously marked for delivery to 'The Department of Home Affairs', 'The Hon

King O'Malley', 'The Prize City Committee', or simply 'Insured Parcel'. They came on ships arriving from Europe, from India, New Zealand, South Africa, Canada and the United States. Of the total of 137 entries, forty-two were from Australia, and forty-one from the UK. Some of the designs arrived in large wooden cases, carefully packaged and registered. Some, alas, suffered mishap on the journey: one was received in January 1912 from India in a dilapidated condition. A parcel from Vancouver arrived stained with grease. Another, damaged, case, unloaded from the SS *Wyreena*, had been hopefully valued by its owner at $100,000.[2]

Anonymity was an important part of the design competition. The authors of the design were not allowed to attach their names to any part of their submission but instead were required to send their personal details attached in a separate, sealed envelope. Any attempt at disclosure of the author's identity led to the disqualification of his design.

The closing date for the competition was 31 January 1912, but this was extended to 28 February when it was clear that many competitors were hampered by factors beyond their control: shipping delays, maritime strikes and the vagaries of the weather. One entrant from Canada delivered his parcel on 21 December to an express train, 'to reach Vancouver for the next steamer due to arrive in Australia on 21 January. But owing to the rush of Christmas packages, the company would not promise it.'[3]

The dispatch of what was to be the winning entry from Chicago was itself a dramatic, last-minute event. Marion Mahony Griffin describes it thus:

> …toward midnight on a bitterly cold winter night, the box of drawings, too long to go into a taxi, was rushed with doors open, and the men hanging out without their coats – no time to go back up the twelve storeys to get them – across the city to catch the last train for the last boat to Australia…[4]

That package, identified as entry twenty-nine with sealed enveloped accompanying it, arrived safely in Melbourne. Inside the five-foot square box were Marion Mahony Griffin's drawings of a splendid new city, rendered on fabric and mounted on frames.

*

The future fate of these designs for the capital was to be closely linked to the career of one particular Minister for Home Affairs, King O'Malley, who held two periods of office: April 1910 to June 1913, then October 1915 to November 1916. Charles Daley, as one who was required to work for several years under his regime, distrusted and disliked him. Daley's memoirs paint an alarming portrait of this 'fustian [clownish] figure… whose wild shock of hair and full beard and extravagant style of dress drew attention to him at once. His speech was a heavy drawl, with reliance on reckless exaggeration…'[5]

O'Malley's early history remains obscure, with many details based on his own unverified claims. Claiming to be a Canadian by birth, his early history included tales of founding a religious sect before coming to Australia for his health. He entered state parliament in South Australia as an Independent Christian Socialist, losing the seat, he claimed, due to his opposition to the liquor lobby. He was later elected as an Independent in the first session of the Commonwealth Parliament in 1901.

In 1909, before his accession to office in a Labor government, he was vehement in his opposition to Canberra, and talked about the proposed federal capital legislation as '…a crime unparalleled in history'. He condemned the proposed site as '…a district which at times is so dry that a crow desiring to put in a weekend vacation there would have to carry its water-bag'. He also chose to capitalise on Melbourne's hostility to the new capital and the reluctance of most MPs to leave it. 'Why should we leave a healthy, prosperous, successful city like Melbourne, where the rents are low and the people healthy and intelligent?'[6]

To public astonishment, O'Malley obtained office in 1910 by a vote of the Labor caucus, becoming Minister for Home Affairs. Seeing now in Canberra's development some fine opportunities for his own career, O'Malley became its ardent supporter, boasting that '…Canberra will be a city to rival London, Athens and Paris'.[7]

O'Malley often sought influence and personal publicity at the expense of wise policy making and he constantly meddled in departmental affairs. During his time in office, he directed that all departmental work was to be carried out by day labour, not by the award of contracts. This meant that departmental officers had to carry out all the many functions of a contractor: purchase of materials, stock-keeping, transport, timekeeping, payment of wages and detailed supervision of workers. This applied not just in Canberra but Australia-wide. In Melbourne, where the Commonwealth offices were being built in 1912, the use of day labour led to significant budgetary blow-outs and the condemnation of the system by the Master Builders Association. Daley recalled occasions in Melbourne when he had the 'unenviable task' of finding jobs for large numbers of men who, having voted for O'Malley, came looking for work.

It was no uncommon thing to receive an order from the Minister to discharge an efficient foreman, and replace him by a poorly-qualified but militant unionist... Again, against the advice of the Permanent Head, O'Malley often appointed 'consultants' at high fees, whose reports the department never had the advantage of perusing.[8]

Daley recalled other aberrations: O'Malley's office tantrums; his flamboyant speeches in Parliament; his extravagant use of public money; his constant interference in financial and administrative matters within the department. Daley observed that the Head of Department, Colonel Miller, found proper administration under his minister a great difficulty; '...he was glad to leave the mounting chaos and take up his post as Administrator for Canberra' in August 1912.[9] Even there he did not escape O'Malley's influence, as the minister travelled frequently to the territory to check on progress. Arthur Percival recalled him visiting the survey camp and interrupting the weary men at their nightly paperwork with requests for their views on O'Malley's plan for a Commonwealth Bank.

One of O'Malley's first duties as minister was to launch the international design competition in May 1911. Against the advice of his department, he insisted upon appointing himself as the final adjudicator with a board of assessors to report to him about the designs. This decision outraged the professional bodies who were taking a keen interest in the competition. The Royal Institute of British Architects and the Royal Australian Institute of Architects boycotted the competition when they discovered that O'Malley – a man with no architectural training or background – was to be final arbiter of the winning design. O'Malley's intransigence in this matter led to strong comment in the journal of the Royal Victorian Institute of Architects in July 1911.

It is well known that the Minister soars infinitely above his officers and loses no opportunity of belittling them in public… It cannot be expected that he should accept their recommendations, because his own sense of assurance is so pronounced… We know full well some of the difficulties of his professional staff, and sympathise with them in their awkward position.[10]

The appointment of the assessment panel was only made after the competition closed. The assessors were John Coane (chairman), a Fellow of the Victorian Institute of Surveyors; James Smith of the Victorian Institute of Engineers; and John Kirkpatrick, a Sydney architect. Their deliberations extended over several months but they failed to reach a unanimous decision. None of the three premiated (winning) designs recommended by Smith and Kirkpatrick were mentioned in Coane's minority report. O'Malley adopted the majority report, announcing the winner with due ceremony on 23 May 1912, in a speech that was calculated to appal his critics and to muddy the waters for years to come:

I am satisfied that the best design has been selected. We will begin to build right away…we will not be actually restricted to the winning design…we may use all three designs: a park might be taken from one, a boulevard from another and a public square from another…[11]

John Sulman spoke for many experienced architects when he wrote,

If the Minister for Home Affairs thinks that he can obtain a satisfactory result by allowing officials without town planning experience to compile a new plan from those selected, he is utterly mistaken, and the result one that Australia will in the future deplore.[12]

In fact, the assumption that the government could make unrestricted use, either in whole or in part, of the designs, had been built into the competition conditions.

Undeterred by widespread criticism, O'Malley referred the three premiated designs to his department for a report. David Miller was reluctant to undertake the review but in the end was appointed chairman of a departmental board. Other members were Percy Owen and Charles Scrivener. John Murdoch and the Commonwealth Directors of Works for Victoria and NSW, Thomas Hill and George Oakeshott, were co-opted as members. The departmental board found that it could not recommend any of the premiated designs and produced a plan of its own devising, which O'Malley accepted in November 1912. After Cabinet approval in January 1913, this became the official plan for the new capital city, and the one which was in place when the official naming of the city as 'Canberra' took place on 12 March 1913.

*

Canberra's story over the next decade had elements of a dramatic stage play. The main players were a number of radically opposed and strong-willed individuals, motivated variously by idealism, ambition or a strong sense of public duty. The conflicts and misunderstandings that grew out of this clash of personalities form the background to events after the judging of the city design competition. Charles Daley remained a close observer of these events but was soon to take on a central role as defender of Walter Burley Griffin's plan.

The design which Griffin and his wife submitted made its mark and won it first prize in the competition partly because of the brilliance of Marion Mahony Griffin's drawings, which rendered in dreamlike colours of gold, grey and blue their 'ideal city'. The drawings were mounted on frames which were packed individually but re-assembled to form a series of illustrated perspectives of the city over 360°. One drawing depicted the city as viewed from the northern eminence of Mount Ainslie, looking south across the Molonglo Valley to the distant Brindabella Mountains. Those with a trained or sensitive eye recognised in the Griffin plan a feeling for landscape – for the particular layout of the Molonglo Valley – that put it ahead of its competitors. Griffin's own description of the site was written in October 1913 to further explain and clarify his design. It was couched in theatrical terms: he saw the site as an irregular amphitheatre with the top galleries formed by three northern hills, Black Mountain, Mount Ainslie and Mount Pleasant. The slopes down to the water formed the auditorium; the formal expanse of water created by damming the Molonglo would be the arena; and the southern slopes rising to Capital Hill would be the stage. It was these southern slopes that Griffin chose for his 'governmental' structures: the judiciary, Parliament and administrative buildings, all set in monumental fashion around a large pool, and rising tier on tier to the pre-eminent building of the city, the Capitol. This would be a place for national gatherings, perhaps an archive of the nation's history, a public space that symbolised and celebrated the Commonwealth as a democracy. Beyond Capital Hill rose other hills, Mugga Mugga and Red Hill, and beyond them, the blue and distant ranges, snow-capped in winter, forming a theatrical backdrop to the city scene.

A grand axis running south to north could be drawn between Capital Hill and Mount Ainslie, below which Griffin placed a 'Casino' – a place for outdoor entertainment and public recreation. The east–west axis intersecting this would be formed by the lake, sketched as a series of formal basins and two extensive lakes east and west of the city proper. Along the northern shore of the lake Griffin envisaged a broad avenue along which he arranged the cultural buildings of the capital. The marketing centre and railway station would lie at the eastern end of the main boulevard and the civic centre at the western end. Residential blocks of European-style terraces would be set back from the main thoroughfares and trams would be the principal mode of city transport. Most citizens would be living at some distance from the city centre in residential enclaves with their own parks and playgrounds, shopping centres, schools and churches.

Apart from the major public buildings like the Capitol, most of Griffin's planned architecture stressed a 'horizontal mass' (as opposed to high-rise American cities), which would allow better conditions of fresh air and sunlight. A general simplicity of outline was aimed for, without columns and other useless decorative features. Griffin's preferred building material would be reinforced concrete.

A strong theoretical and symbolic structure underpinned Griffin's plan. Its formal geometry expressed his ideas about the workings of democracy. At the apex of a great triangle stood the people's palace, the Capitol. Below it lay the institutions representing and serving the people: the judiciary, Parliament and government administrative buildings. Across the lake, the parks, museums and galleries of the city's cultural life formed the base of the triangle which extended from the Civic Centre of business to the market and railway centre representing the mercantile and trading life of a busy city. At the terminus of each broad avenue there would be views of the hills and ridges surrounding the capital.

The layout of the city showed that Griffin and his wife had closely studied the series of panoramic paintings by Robert Coulter which competitors had been sent. These panoramas clearly showed the significance of hills and long connecting vistas in the geography of the valley. Marion Mahony Griffin's rendering of the imagined city as seen from Mount Ainslie is astonishing in its accuracy, considering she had never visited the site. The only feature she got wrong was the distant Mount Bimberi, its flattish summit the territory's highest point, which she drew as a pointed cone.

When Griffin first visited Canberra in August 1913, he must have felt gratified to see the correspondence between the site itself and his plan. What he was not prepared for was the light: the strong upland clarity of mountain country, the high clouds and splendid sunsets over the western ranges. This landscape would truly be a dramatic setting for his creation, 'the most beautiful city in history'.

What did the departmental board make of the Griffin plan? These men were surveyors, engineers and public officials. They knew what it meant to work within a tight budget and to a deadline. They were worried by a number of features of the Griffin plan. Its expense: how could you build a new city simultaneously on two sides of a flood plain? That would mean double the expense of all the basic services for roads, power, sewerage and landscaping. Then there were the effects of climate. Griffin's city site would be exposed to all the excesses of that southern region, freezing south-westerlies in winter and hot, dust-laden north-westerlies in summer.

The board was also critical of Griffin's separation of the government grouping from the business centre and railway depot, which they saw as inefficient and uneconomic. Other aspects of the plan that came in for criticism were the railway route, which would require expensive earthworks to take it through the city, and the road plans which seemed at times to have too steep a gradient.

The plan which the board prepared took these concerns into consideration. They located the city centre south of the river in a more sheltered area; the north side was to be used only for institutions. Griffin's three formal water basins were considered too expensive and the board substituted water areas which followed the natural outline of the flood plain. Other changes to Griffin's plan resulted in a rather confused network of roads that did not have any overall symmetry.

In Australia, the professional response to the publication of the board's plan was muted. Overseas journals were crushing in their criticism. The layout of the plan reminded the *British Town Planning Review* of a 'third-rate Luna Park'.[13] The board members were judged to be 'utterly untrained in the elements of architectural composition'. The lack of cogent criticism from professional bodies in Australia may have been evidence of limited knowledge of city planning, though John Sulman thought that the Griffin plan was the only one 'in which the designer possessed an artistic grasp of town planning'.[14]

The Journal of the American Institute of Architects had this to say:

> The plan appears to acknowledge but one principle of town design, that of dotting every rising point of ground with a building...the cathedral jostles the capitol, a police barracks shadows a school... The road plotting is too grotesque for serious criticism, and appears to be largely the result of an office boy's amusing himself with a pair of bow-compasses.[15]

O'Malley, enthusiastic about putting the board's plan into operation (even though he had voted for the Griffin plan), arranged a ceremony in Canberra on 20 February 1913, where he drove the first peg into the ground for the setting out of the plan on the site. Meanwhile Griffin, having received a copy of the board's plan, was shaken to discover that his own premiated design had been put aside and that the new plan claimed to embody many of his own ideas. He wrote a long letter to O'Malley, suggesting that if he made a personal visit to Australia and had further consultation over the details of his plan, this would resolve the issue. While the letter was circumspect in tone, it still leaves one with a sense of his distress and anxiety at this reversal of fortune.

There is no record of any acknowledgement by O'Malley of Griffin's letter. But O'Malley's influence ended with the defeat of the Labor government in June 1913. The new Prime Minister, Joseph Cook, appointed William Kelly, Minister without Portfolio, as effective Minister for Home Affairs and, amid growing criticism of the board's plan, Kelly arranged for Griffin to receive an invitation to visit Australia and consult further about the city design. Griffin had already decided to come to

Australia. John Murdoch had visited Griffin at his Chicago office in 1912, and had suggested he come out to present his case in person.

Griffin arrived in Sydney on 19 August 1913 and went down to Canberra to inspect the site in the company of Owen, Scrivener and Murdoch, staying with Miller at the Administrator's new residence in Acton. Owen's and Miller's first impressions were of an effete and rather ineffectual man, with boyish features, a floppy bow tie and a head of thick wavy hair – a decidedly unmilitary character. Inclined to patronise this newcomer, they were soon to learn that Griffin had a tenacity and will-power equal to their own.

Kelly was impressed by Griffin, seeing him as 'a man with a mission in life', and he instructed the board that they were 'to consult with Mr Griffin on the basis of his original plan with such recommendations for amendment as they could make'. Sensing their resentment of this order, which in effect, invalidated their own planning work of the last months, Kelly issued a terse warning to the board members: 'I expect from you every loyalty in carrying out my decisions.'[16]

Discussion over the next few weeks between the board and Griffin led to a stalemate. It was clear Griffin did not intend to make any major alterations to his design. At this point, Kelly called the board together, thanked them for their labours and disbanded them. A few days later, he appointed Griffin as Federal Capital Director of Design and Construction on a part-time basis. Griffin was entitled to maintain a private practice in Sydney and Melbourne, and would receive from the government an annual stipend of 1,000 guineas, which was more than the annual salary of either Miller or Owen. Of course they were resentful and must have had a strong sense of personal humiliation. Scrivener, too, who had put a significant part of his working life into the survey of the capital site and had thought deeply about what plan would best serve it, was convinced that Kelly had made a bad decision. He was offended by Griffin's belief that surveyors were less important than designers in building a city. He had run out of patience with Griffin, who on some occasions had blamed him for survey inaccuracies and delays and implied that the older surveyor was incompetent. Scrivener took early retirement from public service in November 1915, finding little pleasure in these harassing times and with the territory's biggest project – the border survey – nearing completion.

Griffin's new contract included among his duties 'directing the details and execution of works', thus usurping Owen's role as Director General of Works. From the start, Owen interpreted Griffin's responsibilities as applying only to the city site and not to the engineering works beyond the city site required for roads, bridges, railways, water supply and sewerage. Survey and design investigations for all these works continued after Griffin's appointment and many were started. At the same time, the acquisition of property and general administration of the territory progressed under David Miller, who saw his own role as central to the city's future.

Griffin prepared a revised plan, known as the 'Preliminary Plan', taking into account some of the board criticisms, but then he left for overseas. He had been given six months' leave of absence to arrange his business affairs in Chicago and to make arrangements for an international board of assessors for a design competition for Parliament House. He returned with his wife to Australia in May 1914, to face more conflict with the department.

Full of ideas from overseas inspections, Griffin wanted to see the latest Imhoff system of sewage treatment used (locating the treatment works in the city and using treated effluent for irrigation and to replenish the lake). Owen would not agree to these ideas and had technical advice which supported him. In any case, he believed that projects like these were of no concern to the city designer.

In June 1914, the Parliament House competition was launched but the declaration of war in August led to its withdrawal. By that stage, a new government was in power and a new minister in charge of Home Affairs. William Archibald was a burly, tobacco-chewing ex-wharf labourer from Port Adelaide. Indifferent to the building of the national capital, Archibald also developed a strong antipathy to the soft-spoken American, whose aesthetic interests and circle of friends aroused Archibald's hostility. He had no wish to be bound to carrying out this man's projects. He sought advice from the Attorney General's Department and told Parliament that there was no legal obligation on him to be bound by Griffin's directives or wishes.

David Miller, anxious to proceed with the city's construction, pressured Griffin on his return to Australia to produce a detailed city plan:

his Preliminary Plan was inadequate as a basis for construction. When the amended plan was finally presented in March 1915, Percy Owen was quick to assess it and to point out that Griffin's lake proposal was still not feasible, requiring expensive earthworks that were beyond the resources available to the department. In any case, with Australia's commitment to support England's war effort 'to the last man and shilling', any plans for further development of Canberra came to a halt, apart from ongoing construction at the Power House, the Brickworks, the Cotter Dam and Mount Stromlo Observatory.

Griffin's contract would need to be renewed in October 1916. Meanwhile, Miller and Owen adopted an attitude of passive resistance to Griffin and his plan, believing – given the conflicts and delays already experienced – that his contract would end and they could restore the board's plan. Griffin's credibility had sunk further in their estimation after he announced a plan for an 'inland lake' whereby the waters of the Murrumbidgee River could be impounded to form a lake thirty-five square miles in extent with 100 miles of deep water. His motive for airing this plan was to discredit Owen's plan for a sewage treatment plant outside the city, which Griffin asserted would be drowned if such an inland lake was built. This plan ignored all of Scrivener's advice about the needs of the new Burrinjuck Dam near Yass, but Griffin's airy statement that such a lake could be built for a million pounds was taken up by the newspapers and became another statistic to wield by those hostile to building the new capital.

Griffin's contract might not have been renewed if Prime Minister Fisher had not resigned on 17 October 1915 to assume the office of High Commissioner in London. Billy Hughes formed a new Labor government and King O'Malley returned to the Home Affairs portfolio. Keen to hold further sway over the fortunes of the new capital, O'Malley appointed himself Administrator of the Capital Territory: in January 1916, Miller had transferred to the Department of Defence and became commandant of AIF camps in NSW.

At this point, Griffin and O'Malley formed an alliance which Charles Daley was to attribute to Griffin's 'sinister influence' over his American compatriot.[17] They had become close friends, with O'Malley extending hospitality to the Griffins on their arrival in Melbourne in 1913; later,

Griffin designed a house for O'Malley and his wife in Sydney. Championed by O'Malley, Griffin was given full command of federal territory works and took up part-time residence in the Yarralumla Homestead, his contract having been renewed for a further three years from 14 April 1916. O'Malley also promoted Miller's deputy, a clerical officer named James Brilliant with no engineering qualifications, to authorise all territorial works. This was a deliberate slight to senior professional officers in the field, especially Owen and Thomas Hill, Chief Engineer of the department. However Owen, as Director General of Works, found himself involved in a number of military projects during the war years. National attention – and government funds – shifted away from the new capital and Griffin's ambitious plans for the city.

The most important work which was carried out under Griffin's direction in the war years was the survey and site pegging of the entire city, thus laying down the essential framework of his plan. This included extensive earthworks to form two major roads, Adelaide Avenue and State Circle. Several small sections of the lake embankments were formed, to remain untouched until they were drowned with the filling of the lake some fifty years later. As described previously, Griffin's plans for the arsenal township were also abandoned.

*

From August 1914, men left the district to enlist. Country boys from the big stations went to Sydney to join the Light Horse; clerks and officers from Acton and men from the work camps around the territory were lining up too to join the AIF battalions. June 1916 saw the start of the Somme offensive. In Canberra, the quiet winter days progressed with little to disturb them, but a political storm was brewing in Melbourne over the role of Griffin and the fate of the national capital. In the face of growing criticism of slow and expensive progress in the building of the city, a commission under King's Counsel Wilfred Blacket was set up on 14 June 1916. Blacket's brief was to hold an enquiry into expenditures on the federal capital and to air grievances against officials in the Department of Home Affairs – grievances which Griffin had brought to O'Malley's attention.

The commissioner's findings were overwhelmingly in favour of Griffin. He found that Archibald and members of the departmental board had endeavoured to set aside his design in favour of the board's design, and that necessary information and help had been withheld from Griffin by departmental officers. Blacket also found evidence of 'carelessness and incompetence' in dealing with and accounting for Commonwealth moneys and that expenditure had been wasteful.

The Hughes government responded to these findings in several ways. Griffin's plan was formally approved and his role in its construction confirmed. Griffin had made a number of alterations to his original 1912 design. His final plan, completed in January 1918, prepared by Scrivener's team and printed that year, became the official city plan. Charles Daley was the man responsible for the choice of the 1918 design as the official one. Given his long familiarity with the city project, he was asked to review all of Griffin's plans and choose the one which seemed most capable of realisation. In the 1918 plan, Griffin modified his original lake design to make it less expensive to build, and also made provision for a 'temporary' town centre at Kingston, south of the Molonglo River.

The official City Plan was printed in the *Commonwealth Gazette* on 14 November 1925. Henceforth, the plan could only be varied after due notice to both houses of parliament, when members would be given an opportunity to disallow the change.

As a result of the Royal Commission, the Department of Home Affairs was restructured. The Works branch became a new Department of Works and Railways, responsible for the execution of works in the federal territory; Home Affairs took on a new name as Department of Home and Territories, which would deal with the planning and administration of Canberra. There were hopes that this restructuring would lead to more efficient administration, though this was never really put to the test with the virtual cessation of building activity in the territory for the duration of the war.

The Minister for Works and Railways, William Watt, obtained advice about the Blacket report and concluded that no further action was warranted. Owen stayed on as Director General of Works, and was to oversee crucial development in Canberra in the inter-war years.

From October 1919, after the expiry of his second term as Federal Capital Director, Griffin's contract was renewed at quarterly intervals at the direction of the new Minister for Works and Railways, Littleton Groom.

Groom, a Queenslander, was a firm supporter of the federal capital project and believed strongly that extended Commonwealth powers were needed to promote the country's development after the war. He had been Minister for Home Affairs in 1905–6, when the idea of an international design competition was first adopted and he admired Griffin's city plan. In 1919, some of Griffin's supporters were lobbying to have Griffin appointed as sole commissioner to direct and control Canberra's development, but Groom doubted that Griffin had the administrative capacity to lead such a program. While he favoured an independent commission to run Canberra, he knew that the Australian public would be hostile to such an idea, seeing in it shades of autocracy or, at the least, a lack of accountability. Instead, Groom proposed the establishment of an advisory committee of experts to prepare a plan for transferring Parliament and the seat of government to Canberra within the next decade. Knowing of Charles Daley's work under Owen and Murdoch, Groom offered Daley the position of secretary to the new committee.

Groom anticipated that Griffin would be happy to serve as a consultant on the advisory committee, thus safeguarding the integrity of his plan. But in this he misjudged Griffin's character. He did not make allowance for Griffin's stubborn refusal to compromise; he underestimated the man's unshakeable belief in the rightness of his cause. Griffin would fight to be recognised as the sole architect and director of the city project, not merely a consultant on a government committee. In defending his cause, he drew on reserves of energy that came from a mix of egotism and passionate idealism. Throughout the summer of 1920–21, memoranda passed to and fro between Griffin and the department. Griffin's main concern was with the make-up of the committee, especially when he learnt that the Director General of Works, Percy Owen, would be a member. He did not trust Owen, knowing that he had been associated with the departmental plan that had for a time replaced his own. Griffin feared that if he were to join the committee as a mere consultant, his name 'would be associated with almost inevitable failure' and he 'would be entirely without power to avert it...'[18]

When pressed to make a decision one way or another, before staff left for the Christmas break, Griffin prevaricated. He asked for more time to consider his position, and requested a personal interview with Prime Minister Hughes to press his case at the highest level. But Hughes was out of the country. When back in Melbourne, Hughes declined to meet Griffin, feeling no useful purpose would be served by it. Griffin prepared an altered draft contract, giving himself more executive powers on the committee and the right to take to Cabinet any committee decisions he disagreed with. Neither Groom nor the cabinet would accept this.

Griffin's final memorandum to the department came at the close of the year, on 29 December, when he once more rejected Groom's offer of a consultancy position on the new board. This final message reflects his sense of bitterness and failure. He had expected to be given scope to achieve 'a great and unique work and to be associated with it in history' but instead, he had been deprived of title, status and function as director of the city project. The proposed board would have no executive power, which instead would lie with the Works Department, 'which has been consistently hostile to me, my plan and my procedure...'[19] He felt a deep sense of humiliation in this public dismissal of his worth, a dismissal which, to his professional brethren, would mean that he had been tried and found wanting.

In January 1921, Groom sought legal advice from Robert Garran, the Attorney General, who advised him that the government was under no obligation to renew or continue Griffin's appointment. Griffin accepted this advice with great reluctance, writing that he was compelled, under protest and with great regret, to bow to the minister's decision to terminate his engagement.

So ended Griffin's involvement with the building of Canberra. While he attracted a circle of like-minded people and devoted followers, Griffin did not have the political insight to negotiate or seek compromise with those who disagreed with him. His architectural practice in Melbourne, and later in Sydney, continued to flourish and produce some enduring bodies of work, but his years in Canberra left no legacy of important or monumental buildings. The lake which bears his name is actually closer to the design which Scrivener and Owen prepared, with the lake following the natural contours of the river basin instead of contained by formal edges as Griffin had wanted.

One physical structure survives: the grave of Major General Sir William Throsby Bridges, first Commandant of the Royal Military College at Duntroon. After Bridges' death at Gallipoli in May 1915, he was honoured with a state funeral and his body was interned in a grave on the hill called Mount Pleasant, overlooking the college and the Molonglo Valley beyond. Griffin, who had given advice on the construction of the college buildings while he was Director of Design and Construction, was given the task of designing a suitably impressive grave.

One other small piece of work can be attributed to Griffin's Canberra years. In June 1920, the Prince of Wales visited the territory to lay a foundation stone. (He was to remark that the city seemed to consist of little else but foundation stones.) The ceremony took place on Capital Hill, near the site of the present Parliament House, on 21 June 1920. Afterwards, Littleton Groom presented the Prince with a souvenir of his visit to Canberra: the wooden mallet he had used to 'tap' the stone into place. It had been designed by Griffin, who explained that the mallet, and the decorative box in which it was enclosed, had been made of native timbers, 'to convey an idea of the richness of the resources of the Commonwealth. No polish or stain were necessary to exaggerate the true colours and varieties of the timbers used.'[20] The mallet was made of blackwood, with the handle covered with fine carved representations of banksias. The wooden case was made from Tasmanian pink myrtle beech. The panels on the sides represented the several states, each with twenty-one panels of woods selected from each state. Over fifty native timbers were used, all told, all listed on an accompanying page with their botanical and common names. It is clear that Griffin loved Australian trees and timber, as did his wife. Both of them were attracted to the aesthetic qualities of these trees, which also symbolised the botanical richness of this old/new country. Griffin's horticultural work, and his involvement with Thomas Weston, the Director of Afforestation, will be discussed in the next chapter.

*

At the official opening of Parliament in the provisional Parliament House on 9 May 1927, there were only meagre references to Walter Burley

Griffin. An official commemorative booklet referred to the 'idealist [who] sketched out the plan on which Canberra was eventually to be modelled'.[21] Griffin attended the ceremony as a bystander but would have found little to celebrate or enjoy on that occasion. This young democratic nation – whose energies and achievements he had praised some years before – marked this coming of age with an event that had a distinctly royalist and martial air. The very centre of attention for everyone present was the figure of the Duke of York, second in line to the throne, and his wife the Duchess. Dame Nellie Melba sang the national anthem on the steps of the House, before the Duke ceremoniously opened the building with a gold key and proceeded to the Senate chamber, where he gave an address to members and invited dignitaries.

Before the event, Griffin wrote an article for the *Melbourne Herald* on 7 May about the ideal city he had planned, which had become in the hands of bureaucracy an arbitrary place, the result of several conflicting interests. Addressing a Theosophical Society meeting in Sydney in April 1928, and in an article in the society's journal, *Awake! Australia*, Griffin again pronounced his judgement on a grand experiment that had not been realised. His final words on the city appeared in the *Canberra Annual* of 1934, shortly before he left for an architectural commission in India.

Griffin's name was never widely known to the general public and he faded from public consciousness in Australia for nearly twenty years. In European circles, his plans and achievements must have been more widely known. A young architecture student in Rome during World War II recalled seeing Griffin's plan of Canberra and being fascinated by its beauty. It remained in his mind when all around there was so much destruction. The young student's name was Romaldo Giurgola, and he was later to win the competition to design the new Parliament House. After its completion, he stayed on in Canberra, responding to its particular landscape as Burley Griffin had done before him.

After Griffin's death in India in 1937, Marion Mahony Griffin hoped to honour her husband's memory with publication of her book *The Magic of America*. In January 1947, an Australian friend of Marion approached King O'Malley with the suggestion that he sponsor the book's publication, 'Your intimate association with Canberra's beginnings would make it peculiarly fitting that you should be associated with the publication of a book on Walter's work in Australia.'[22] O'Malley, though a wealthy man, appears not to have responded. Marion's book was eventually published online.

In August 1951, at a town planning conference in Canberra, Charles Daley gave a paper describing Griffin's plans for the city and what had become of them. Daley's own official engagement with the story of Canberra was to end in 1952 when he retired from public office, but for many years he had been the principal, sometimes the sole, defender of Griffin's plan. The talk he gave in 1951, as Canberra entered a new half-century, brought Griffin's story and his legacy to a new and influential generation of town planners and public officials.

'With so great an area of
absolutely bare country to treat,
the loss of a year is a matter
of great importance.'

Horse and buggy.
Reproduced with permission of Canberra & District Historical Society

By the early twentieth century, land in the federal territory – as in much pastoral land in NSW – was showing signs of serious degradation. It was suffering from the multiple assaults of drought, overgrazing, ringbarking and invasion by feral pests. Only the great alpine ash forests in the western part of the territory remained relatively untouched. In the settled areas, many of the wooded hillsides had been thinned or cleared by farmers, and the watercourses, stripped of vegetation and with nothing to hold their banks in place, crumbled into dry, eroded gullies after heavy rain. Of the invasive pests, the most noticeable were the rabbits. They swarmed over the land, destroying grass cover and regrowth in the open valleys of the territory. One observer described the invasion:

Australia's capital site was simply honeycombed with warrens. [Rabbits] had already built their Federal city, and in the evening dusk crowded in their myriads upon their piazzas.[1]

David Miller, the territory's first administrator, saw the urgency of the problem. The ripping and destruction of rabbit burrows in the environs of the city site was one his earliest priorities. To this end, he appointed James Brackenreg as Inspector, Federal Capital Lands. This hard-working officer was to play a crucial role in the management of the territory for the next twenty years.

Another urgent appointment was that of a competent man to oversee the afforestation of the city site and the wider environs of the territory. In July 1912, Minister O'Malley approved £70 for ploughing and fencing a site at Acton for an experimental nursery. Thomas Weston, head gardener at Government House in Sydney, made several visits to the federal capital site to provide advice on the establishment of the nursery. Scrivener, impressed by what he saw of Weston, recommended that he be engaged at once and begin work at Acton to prepare the ground and supervise construction of the nursery. 'With so great an area of absolutely bare country to treat, the loss of a year is a matter of great importance,' he stressed.[2]

As a young man, Weston had worked as a gardener on large country estates in Scotland. In 1896 he emigrated to NSW, where he joined the staff of Sydney Botanic Gardens under its director, Joseph Maiden. In November 1912, he was promoted by Maiden to be Superintendent of Campbelltown State Nursery to the west of Sydney, but he was not to be there long. In January 1913, Maiden was told that the NSW government had agreed to the Prime Minister's request for the transfer of Weston to Canberra. If Weston saw this as an attractive idea, it was not a view shared by most experienced horticulturalists. None wanted to work in Canberra; the commonly held view – and one promoted by papers like the *Bulletin* – was that the territory was a wasteland, devastated by rabbits, without reliable sources of water and inhabited mainly by sheep and flies.

Weston arrived in Canberra on 5 May 1913, with a permanent appointment as Officer-in-Charge, Afforestation. He had a rare combination of gifts which were to be fully exercised in his work in Canberra: a gardener's attachment to the soil and a love of cultivating plants; an ability to work hard to overcome challenges; and a passionate and scholarly interest in matters botanical. He continued to broaden his knowledge through research, reading and experiment throughout his working life.

Weston's interests weren't restricted to the growing of plants but extended into the wider area of urban renewal and improvement. He was a member of the inaugural council of the Town Planning Association of NSW, which was chaired by John Sulman. Through this association, Weston became aware of the urban renewal project at Daceyville in South Sydney. While employed in Canberra, Weston was also given the work of landscaping the new village of Littleton in Lithgow, as described in chapter 2.

Weston's initial appointment in Canberra was to develop the nursery at Acton which would in time provide plantings for the hills surrounding the city, both for protection from the westerly winds and to help overcome erosion. As Scrivener came to know and respect Weston, he thought of further initiatives: the planting of the city site itself and afforestation projects further afield.

While Weston established a productive nursery at Acton in 1913, he saw it as a temporary site. Looking around for a larger site to serve the future needs of the territory, he found such an area on the Yarralumla property to the south of the Molonglo River. After inspecting the site with Weston, David Miller moved to have the area withdrawn from its current lease. First work on the Yarralumla site began in October 1913. One of Weston's former employees in Sydney, John Hobday, accepted a transfer to Canberra to become foreman of the new Yarralumla Nursery.

Weston hoped to bring his wife and daughters down to Canberra and sought an allowance to cover temporary accommodation for them until a house was built for the family at the Yarralumla nursery. But the war intervened, building activity slowed right down and Weston's permanent home at the nursery never eventuated. He lived first with the unmarried officers at the Bachelors' Quarters then moved into a primitive two-roomed hut next to the nursery at Acton while his family stayed in Sydney. For nine years, he saw them only when they visited Canberra on school holidays or when he made trips to Sydney. In 1922, he was at last allocated a family home in Acton, where homes for senior public servants were being built.

Weston's years in Canberra were highly productive but were marred by his continuing struggle for professional recognition for his work. Scrivener (until his retirement in 1915) and Miller both recognised Weston's valuable work and Miller tried to get his position reclassified, without success. The Public Service Board, who were responsible for employing Commonwealth officers, had little understanding of the scope or responsibilities of Weston's work, and did not consider him worthy of the professional recognition given to architects or engineers. In fact, it could be argued that Weston's contribution to the federal capital was more significant and more long-lasting than that of any other individual at the time. The citizens of Canberra live surrounded by his legacy and enjoy a city landscape which has retained the tree-lined avenues, wooded hillsides and parklands which he created.

The Acton nursery where Weston began his horticultural work had a propagation nursery and tool shed and a large testing area surrounded by a shelter belt of fast-growing trees. This is where Weston and his staff began planting trials of a range of indigenous and exotic tree species to establish which would grow well in Canberra, with its harsh climate, poor soils and low rainfall. Before the era of plastic, plant pots were made of cardboard or hollow reed. Seeds and plant material were obtained from a large network of suppliers in Victoria and NSW as well as overseas, and Weston also began building up a reference library. His colleague, friend and mentor, Joseph Maiden of the Sydney Botanic Gardens, was a respected horticulturalist and the author of a number of standard reference books on Australian flora. The two men corresponded regularly and Weston often sent plant material to Sydney for Maiden to inspect and identify. Weston had a special interest in hybridisation of plants. Maiden claimed, 'I look upon [Weston] as one of the most advanced horticulturalists I know in regard to Mendelian work.'[3] In 1919, Maiden told the Royal Society of NSW that Weston was the first man to make a successful cross-pollination of a white gum and a yellow box eucalyptus.

By 1917, the Afforestation Branch was well established and employed twenty-eight men. After Yarralumla was established, nursery work at the Acton site still continued for many years and in time the area was home to many beautiful specimens of exotic trees.

The Yarralumla site included a sheltered area for propagation and testing, an open nursery for holding and 'hardening off' trees before planting, and a 300-acre area set aside as an arboretum, a place of 'beauty, interest and education' for the public where in time they could view over 200 different species of conifers, deciduous hardwoods and native Australian trees. One hundred years later, the arboretum, known as Westbourne Woods, is a shady and beautiful sanctuary on the edge of Lake Burley Griffin, beloved by Canberrans of all ages, who can walk or cycle through the area. It is the oldest arboretum in the territory.

The arboretum was located on rock-hard soil on what was known as Shale Ridge; sometimes Weston had to resort to gelignite to dig holes before planting. The shale provided good material for making bricks at the brickworks that were established nearby. Water for the nursery was pumped from the Molonglo River; Yarralumla was only connected to the town's water supply in 1921. The nursery buildings were completed in early 1915 and in May that year the stock from Acton was brought over. In August 1915, John Hobday moved onto temporary accommodation at the site with his new bride, though his cottage was not completed until 1924. He and his wife raised their children among the trees he had helped plant; he died soon after retiring from Yarralumla in 1944.

The experimental orchard at the nursery was soon producing abundant crops of fruit, which were supplied to government hostels and other institutions like the small hospital at Acton. There were 123 different varieties of apple as well as pears, peaches, almonds, apricots, plums and persimmons. The orchard also attracted many observant locals, both small boys and men from the nearby work camps, who clambered over the fences at night and filled their pockets. John Hobday reported on one theft of a quantity of peaches, 'hob nail boots were worn and their tracks led towards the Brickworks'.[4]

Weston was happiest engaged on the outdoor work which he found so absorbing. He had the ruddy complexion of an English farmer and, as was the custom of the day even in rural Australia, he wore a tie and coat as a matter of course. (Labourers wore coats and waistcoats, but no tie.) A typical day would see Weston out in the field, maps or charts tucked under his arm, legs clad in leather gaiters, and a plan for the day's planting spread on a board held at arm's length as he scanned the rows of seedlings set out before him. He asked the department to provide the branch with a motorbike and sidecar, which had heavy and constant use along the back roads and tracks of the territory until 1919, when Weston saw that after a number of breakdowns its usefulness was nearly at an end. By 1920, he had persuaded the department to issue the branch with a Ford car.

Canberra poet Geoff Page, in *The Forester*, his tribute to Thomas Weston, addresses him as he moves among his seedlings:

> Measuring the stems and weather
> you quietly start to savour distance,
>
> your minister down there in Melbourne,
> the world that rattles in each day
> by Cooma mail from Sydney.
>
> Towards the end you walk among them,
> Some knee-high, a few to the shoulder.
>
> You have the forester's assurance
> That everything you plant outlives you.[5]

Weston knew that large-scale plantings in this untried environment would only prove of long-term value if careful records were kept of their progress. The original card filing system which he established documents the history of each planting, from the date and location where seed was collected to a record of the plant's performance. There are records for trees, shrubs, flowers and pasture grasses. Joseph Maiden believed that Weston's 'methods of keeping records are quite in advance of planting records in Australia and probably most other countries', a view that the director of Kew Gardens in London supported.[6]

Among the nursery's very first stock was the batch of seeds from Roman cypress (*Cupressus sempervirens*) which Weston brought with him from Campbelltown. The first seedlings were raised in the nursery in 1915 and planted out in Westbourne Woods and Greenhills, on high ground to the north of the Molonglo River, in 1917–18. Progeny from these trees was then collected to raise more seedlings in the nursery. In 2003, after the bushfires that destroyed a great swath of western Canberra, these seedlings were planted out to regenerate the burnt-out Greenhill slopes. In this way, Weston's early work and careful record keeping have left their own remarkable legacy for generations to come.

The seeds stored at Yarralumla, and now given full heritage protection, lie on shelves in rows of old glass jars, reminiscent of a countrywoman's pantry. This humble setting disguises the great scientific and historical significance of the collection: it is a storehouse of the seeds of most of the plants grown in Canberra and surrounding countryside over the past 100 years.

While seeds were ordered from Weston's network of suppliers, many seeds were sourced locally, and their provenance tells a story of wide-ranging expeditions by Weston and Hobday into the mountains, country roads, scattered farms and large estates of the territory. Weston gathered plant specimens from many places including Booroomba, a lonely mountain property in the shadow of the Tidbinbilla range; from the verges of the road between the mining hamlet of Captains Flat and Queanbeyan; and along the Cotter River, where T.G. Taylor had first seen the beautiful river oaks (*Casuarina cunninghamii*) and urged their protection. Weston's records allow the researcher to match the seeds collected with their progeny: casuarina seeds collected near the bridge over the Cotter River in November 1920 provided six seedlings which were planted in Telopea Park, near the suburb of Kingston, in August 1922. In 1918, Weston gathered the seed of the white brittle gum (*Eucalyptus Mannifera ssp maculata*) on the slopes of Black Mountain and today the visitor to the Australian National Botanic Gardens on that site is welcomed at the entrance by a large brittle gum from that seed bank. The tree which Joseph Maiden had discovered and bears his name, *Eucalyptus maidenii*, is one of the native trees that was given pride of place on King George's Terrace in front of the new Parliament House in 1927.

The large estates of Gungahlin, Duntroon, Yarralumla, Tuggeranong and Lanyon yielded a wide variety of exotic seeds. These properties had all been planted in the nineteenth century by landowners with strong attachments to their family homes in England and Scotland, and their gardens reflected these attachments. Oaks, elms, cedars and other conifers had pride of place along the gravelled driveways and bordering the lawns; willows lined the creeks and helped keep erosion in check; climbing roses, lavender, lilies, spring bulbs and flowering fruit trees all brought memories of northern springtimes and summers to the dusty Limestone Plains.

Duntroon was a favourite site for Weston because of its established garden which the Campbells had planted years before. Weston gathered pine cones from the magnificent Atlas cedar in its grounds and also germinated thousands of seedlings from a Roman cypress tree on the property. These trees were to become part of the plantings to enhance the surroundings of some of the public buildings of the early city – the Albert Hall and Hotel Canberra – and were to border some of the main roads as set down in Griffin's official plan for the city.

Weston took up his Canberra appointment in May 1913 and a few months later Walter Burley Griffin arrived in Australia to champion his winning design and to defend his right to carry out the planning of the city. As Federal Capital Director of Design and Construction, Griffin had oversight of the work Weston was doing and for the next six years the two men shared responsibilities for the creation of a garden city.

Griffin and his wife were both keen seed collectors and were to send thousands of specimens to Weston's office. They collected both exotics and natives on expeditions in Sydney and Melbourne and country areas. Marion Mahony Griffin's renderings of native trees in her architectural drawings show how much she loved the stately *Angophera* of the Sydney region.

Griffin's 1918 plan included an ambitious design for a Continental Arboretum that would extend from the slopes of Black Mountain across the planned lake to the Yarralumla area. Five different areas of ground would, corresponding to their relative position on a world map, represent the continents of Europe, Africa, Asia, the Americas and Australasia, and would be planted with species native to these continents.

Weston would have had serious doubts about the viability of such a project; his own planting schemes proceeded after careful experimentation and consideration above all of the need for shelter if plants were to survive in Canberra's unforgiving climate. However, he complied with Griffin's directions to establish Australian and New Zealand species in the area of his own arboretum. The rest of Griffin's project was never realised. Griffin never acknowledged the existence of Weston's own arboretum, which pre-dated his. That is surprising, but perhaps in keeping with his intense focus on realising his own plans.

Another planting scheme of Griffin that was never realised was his plan to clothe the hills surrounding the city site with contrasting colour: yellow foliage on Mount Ainslie, red on Red Hill, white and pink on Black Mountain and white on Mugga Mugga. The only plantings that were made that have survived are a collection of red bottlebrush (*Callistemon sp*) on Red Hill.

Weston complied with Griffin's insistence on a large plantation of Californian redwoods (*Sequoia sp.*) which were planted at Piallago to the east of the city site. Out of 120,000 trees, only 400 were alive sixty years later. The drought of 1918–19 and the lack of shelter contributed to their failure. Weston considered, after experiments with the species, that it could be grown as an ornamental tree but would fail as a forestry plantation. He was able to successfully plant individual Sequoia in sheltered sites at Westbourne Woods and Telopea Park.

Griffin was also keen to plant a cork oak forest in Canberra with the hope of starting a commercial industry. He secured cork acorns (*Quercus suber*) from Spain and from the Melbourne Botanic Gardens with the help of Mary Masson, the wife of Orme Masson, Professor of Chemistry at the University of Melbourne. From 1917, the nursery propagated thousands of trees from acorns procured by Griffin. By 1920, 9,600 cork oaks covered twenty acres of Greenhill Reserve. The intended industry was never founded but the cork oak forests survive as part of Canberra's new arboretum and provide visitors with a fascinating walk through a landscape that in Griffin's plan would have stood on the border between Europe and Africa.

Griffin's enthusiasm for native Australian plants led him to advocate their widespread use in the planting of the new city streets. He did not appreciate the need for deciduous trees which could provide sunlight in Canberra's cold winters and shade in hot summers. In July 1919, Joseph Maiden paid a visit to the territory to report to the government on Griffin's planting scheme for the city. He wrote a seven-page report in which he made some forthright criticisms of Griffin's choices. He felt that some of the eucalypt and other native species Griffin proposed were unsuitable and their adoption could 'only result in disaster'. He commended Griffin's enthusiasm but saw that he had not had the time or opportunity to obtain more than a superficial knowledge of Australian plants. Weston 'can make a far better selection and I recommend that he be instructed to push on with the planting… I would suggest that he be not given too many detailed instructions…' He is

a loyal, hard-working man with abundant imagination and professional knowledge, and I am prepared to stake my reputation that he will not fail. My recommendations imply no disloyalty to the beautiful design of the Director, I want our federal city to be one of the most beautiful cities in the world, indeed I want to help him carry it out, but I do not want to hinder this by bungling the planting.[7]

Aware of the political climate at the time and the widespread uncertainty about Canberra's future, Maiden stated that the planting of the city 'should be placed in the hands of a man whose knowledge and experience will reduce the anxiety of the government to a minimum'. The new Surveyor-General, John Goodwin, took Maiden's advice to heart. After initially saying Weston had to obtain ministerial approval for all plants, he recognised the impracticability of this and told Weston that the class and nature of trees was up to him to decide.

Charles Daley came to know and respect Weston after Daley's appointment as secretary of the Federal Capital Advisory Committee in 1921. The committee, under John Sulman's chairmanship, was impressed by the wonderful resources that Weston had assembled and the extensive and successful plantings already underway. Seeking to establish a comfortable living and working environment for the planned city, the committee took Weston's advice that extensive belts of trees be established to protect the city from strong north-westerly winds. As a result, Weston and his staff planted Haig Park, a long windbreak extending east to west across the northern city area. They also planted additional shelter at Yarralumla and the Power House and established a beautiful park, Telopea Park, to shelter the southern area of the city. Tests undertaken in 1952 at the Forestry School, Acton and Duntroon indicated that wind pressure in those areas had dropped by 25% as a result of this far-sighted program.

Weston was also much engaged in restoration of the rural landscape, where farming practices had led to extensive ringbarking, and lopping of trees for firewood, fencing and fodder. T.G. Taylor's geological report for the government had condemned the wholesale cutting and clearing of timber. Weston himself, in strongly worded terms, talked of a 'holocaust of destruction'[8] when viewing Mount Majura, one of the local hills whose natural cover of mountain pine (*Callitris* and *Casuarina sp*) had all been removed as fodder for stock and only bare earth remained, with no regeneration due to rabbit activity.

After the war, some of the big properties in the territory had been divided up for soldier settlement blocks, whose owners often struggled to make a decent living on blocks that were too small. Drought, a lack of capital and little farming expertise saw them overstocking their land and using up its timber resources in a few years. In February 1920, Goodwin asked Weston and Brackenreg to inspect soldier settlement blocks to prevent wanton destruction of useful timber.

Weston was trying to change traditional land management practices in the territory and from 1919, the Timber Protection Ordinance gave him legislative backing for his work. But he also became known as a wise counsellor and good friend to many people on the land or in villages and small towns in the district, providing free horticultural advice and arranging for generous free issues of plants from his nurseries.

He often visited Tuggeranong Homestead, where he received a warm welcome from its new incumbent, the war historian Charles Bean, who had moved there with his staff in late 1919. The property, its main house and outlying cottages would be their home and workplace for the next six years. Bean wanted to maintain the gardens which Mary Cunningham had established there in the early years of the century and which were renowned for their beautiful roses. The garden was also graced by an almond tree which Charles Bean believed was at least eighty years old, and which still bore heavily. In 1914, the Cunningham family had vacated Tuggeranong and moved to their sister property, Lanyon, but Mary Cunningham arranged for the almond crop to be harvested during the war and the boxes of almonds were sent to the troops overseas. Weston arranged to collect seed from the old almond tree, and cones from the Monterey pines that bordered the long driveway to the homestead. The pine seedlings were later planted out in the pine forest being established on Mount Stromlo, and Mary Cunningham was given for her Lanyon garden a dozen almond seedlings that were progeny from the original tree.

Weston provided dozens of fruit trees and flowering shrubs for Tuggeranong, including for the caretaker's cottage, which was now home to one of Bean's staff. Bean's letters to Weston reveal the warmth of their friendship.

I'd be very glad to see you some weekend if you'd care to stay with us. Now that you have your car, we'll expect you out here quite often; and promise not to talk floriculture or horticulture or any other sort of culture...[9]

The municipal council at Queanbeyan gave Weston permission to collect seeds from any tree in the district, and in return he was generous in sharing plants with a wide range of householders. These included John Gale, the venerable editor of the *Golden Age*, who had a long association with the federal territory. Sister Brigid of St Benedicts Convent in Queanbeyan approached Weston in 1920 for advice about where to buy a lawnmower, and in the next few years she was the grateful recipient of trees and shrubs for her convent. One-teacher schools in the district discovered that Weston was very ready to help them with issues of climbing roses, pine shelter belts and wattles. Children had been encouraged since federation to celebrate Wattle Day on the first day of spring, as a way of developing patriotic sentiments but also a love of their native flora. (In March 1917, Weston had discovered a wattle on Mount Jerrabomberra near Queanbeyan which Maiden identified as *Acacia pycnantha*; he recalled distributing the seed of the tree to every public school in the colony thirty years before.) Frank McGee of Tuggeranong Schoolhouse encouraged his pupils to see the value and beauty of the trees of their district. In February 1918, McGee helped them compose a carefully written letter to the District Surveyor, Percy Sheaffe, requesting him to stop the ringbarking of old eucalypts that bordered Tharwa Road, where they walked or rode on their way to school. Not only did the trees provide pleasant shade and relief from the summer sun, but they were home to numerous small creatures who relied on the shelter they provided. 'We regarded those trees as our friends, for they made the road beautiful.' Sheaffe sent a courteous reply promising to protect the trees.[10]

In 1921, Weston was given dual responsibility as Officer-in-Charge, Afforestation and as Director, City Planting. His days might be spent overseeing the destruction of noxious weeds in plantations; inspecting telephone lines for interference from ornamental trees; instructing forestry work camps about disposal of rubbish; and advising householders and landowners about spraying fruit trees. While Yarralumla House was being refurbished as the Governor General's home in 1925, urgent requests would come for an extension to the size of the asparagus bed in the gardens there, or requests for annuals to be planted in time for 'a floral display next Christmas'. There were requests for flower arrangements at church bazaars and official functions; and Weston, as founding member of the Canberra Horticultural Society, never refused an invitation to judge the floral displays at local fetes.

The issue of free plants was regarded from the start as a useful public relations exercise in the district. As well, politicians who requested them could obtain free plants (whether for their electorate or their own properties was never quite clear). But from 1932, the issue was to be restricted to rate-payers of the territory.

Weston's most significant planting projects were to be carried out on hillsides that had been stripped of timber and needed massive afforestation. Once the grazing leases were revoked, rabbits eradicated and the areas fenced, plantings were made of a number of species that Weston had found to be hardy, both eucalypts and exotic conifers. Mount Stromlo was an early priority for afforestation, as that was where the new observatory was being built, and it was important to achieve a dense tree cover to keep down dust. Though a major drought in 1918–19 led to heavy losses at most of the plantations, the Monterey pine (*Pinus insignis*) proved durable on Mount Stromlo and became the main species for planting in the lower Cotter catchment and the basis for a local timber industry.

In October 1921, Charles Scrivener, by then running his own sawmill in the Blue Mountains, returned to Canberra at the invitation of the government to inspect areas of native timber that might also serve as the base of a future industry. Accompanied by Weston and Goodwin, he rode out into the rough country of the Tidbinbilla range, and also inspected the western watershed of the Cotter River, where the tall stands of alpine ash and mountain gum grew. While he judged the ash as a beautiful timber for furniture, Scrivener considered that this western region of the territory was too inaccessible to be a payable proposition for a timber industry.

The remote south-western corner of the territory was to play an invaluable role in protecting the purity of Canberra's water supply, the Cotter River. Early foresters and scientists recognised the magnificence of the region's stands of native timber, and part of the area was set aside as a nature reserve in 1979. Namadgi National Park, including the upper and middle sections of the Cotter River catchment and covering nearly half of the federal territory, was declared in 1984.

While in Canberra, Scrivener visited Weston's nursery and suggested a couple of trees indigenous to the Blue Mountains – a lilly pilly and a wattle (*Acacia melanoxylon*) – as possibly suitable for Canberra, as they were quick growing and could 'stand up to a furious gale'.[11] He also talked with Percy Owen about the timber that was to be used for decorative purposes in the provisional Parliament House.

In 1918, three separate reports by independent forestry experts had assessed the state of the territory's forests and the prospects for a future timber industry. All the reports strongly supported Weston's afforestation and conservation work.

Weston fully understood the symbolic importance of trees for human communities, especially those who were mourning. He helped propagate many seeds brought back from the graves of AIF men who had died on the Western Front and on Gallipoli. The shrubs were planted on the approach to the Australian War Memorial but none remain, having been replaced by rows of eucalypts.

Weston helped the small hamlet of Nimmitabel on the edge of the

Snowy Mountains to plan and plant their small war memorial. In 1919 he helped plan a peace park at the small village of Hall in the north of the territory, advising on a mix of deciduous and evergreen trees; 'the springing into life annually of the deciduous trees' was important for those who would regularly visit the site. One of his employees, Private Malcolm 'Mac' Southwell, had been killed in action in France in November 1916. Southwell described himself as 'a ganger'. His calling: 'Afforestation'.

*

In nineteen sixteen (Pozierès)
you're setting down the pines at Stromlo.

And then for two more ticking years
the plantings at Shale Ridge continue
as do those other ones in Europe.

Until at last on the eleventh
you would have heard
St John's one bell
insistent there across the river

and looked up, sweating, from a seedling
to see in saplings on Shale Ridge

the foliage of a future.[12]

5
Transition

'Canberra resembled a huge, scattered construction site.'

Canberra road construction.
Reproduced with permission of Canberra & District Historical Society

Many of Griffin's supporters, in looking back on those early years of Canberra, have felt that his vision for the city was compromised or betrayed by the Federal Capital Advisory Committee (FCAC), the group of experts that was appointed to advise on the development of Canberra after World War I. Their view does not take into account a number of factors that influenced the committee. There were the many constraints on government spending after the heavy burden of the war; and there was a degree of urgency in their planning to ensure that Parliament could meet in Canberra within the decade. But politicians continued to capitalise on anti-Canberra sentiments; some felt the infant city should be abandoned and handed back to the squatters. There was continual harping in Parliament on the theme. Senator Guthrie, in debating the budget allocation for the territory for 1921–2, blustered about it being a 'criminal waste of taxpayers' money to consider expenditure of £500,000, away out in the bush'.[1] The prevailing climate in democratic Australia meant people were suspicious of grand bureaucratic plans at taxpayer expense. The Advisory Committee developed a useful, workable plan to serve the needs of the time; Griffin's 'City Beautiful' would be left for later generations to worry about and to pay for.

John Sulman, architect and town planner, was chairman of the new committee. Other members were Ernest de Burgh, the chief engineer for water supply and sewerage for NSW; Herbert Ross, a practising Sydney architect; Colonel Percy Owen as Director General of Works; and John Goodwin, Commonwealth Surveyor General.

De Burgh's name is not well known to modern Canberrans. But it was de Burgh who first investigated the potential of the Cotter River as a water supply for Canberra. He had had a distinguished career as an engineer, associated with the major irrigation and water storage projects of Burrinjuck, the Murrumbidgee Irrigation Area and Sydney's major dams. He built important bridges over the state's major rivers, and he supervised the building of Canberra's well-loved Tharwa Bridge in 1895. The bridge provided a vital link for the isolated farms on the west of the river with the town of Queanbeyan, the railway line and roads to

Goulburn and Sydney. It is still the link between the city and the western regions of the Australian Capital Territory, most of which is now included in Namadgi National Park.

Charles Daley was appointed as secretary to the FCAC in January 1921, having been personally approached by Littleton Groom to take on the position. He had come to Groom's notice for his work in assisting both Owen and Murdoch with their Commonwealth responsibilities. As well, he was an officer who possessed all the qualifications insisted upon by Sulman: competence as a shorthand writer (full records of meetings would be essential in such a politically sensitive area); a knowledge of the capital city project; and knowledge of the technicalities and terminology of architecture, town-planning and engineering.

The committee was to proceed with their planning on the basis of the acceptance of Griffin's city plan. This posed some dilemmas for the committee members. John Sulman, while he had admired Griffin's original 1913 plan, had not really wanted to get involved in the politically charged question of building the city. He was also concerned about the siting of Griffin's city out on the flood plain of the Molonglo River with no protection from the prevailing winds. But as chairman of the FCAC, he took a positive approach. He expressed the confidence that this problem would be resolved in time by a large-scale planting program.

Sulman had agreed to chair the committee on a pro bono basis, with the understanding that his services might afterwards be acknowledged with a knighthood. His wife and he had lost a son in the Royal Flying Corps during the war, and Sulman felt that the honour of a knighthood might give his grieving wife a new connection with life.

Ernest de Burgh also had a number of concerns about the Griffin plan. He felt there needed to be 'some elasticity in order to develop the plan, by making rational minor alterations'. For one, he was concerned that Griffin had made no provision for sports grounds, such an essential feature of every Australian country town and city. And there were many minor problems, such as road layouts, that had not been solved in detail and that Griffin himself might have modified on closer consideration. Home and Territories Minister R.W. Foster agreed with de Burgh's proposal, put to him in April 1922. This meant that minor details of the city plan could be changed without recourse to parliamentary approval.

Following on his 1907–9 surveys of the Cotter catchment, de Burgh confirmed to the committee his support for Canberra's future water supply. 'It is impossible to imagine a catchment from which a purer water supply could be obtained.'[2] The newly built Cotter Dam would provide enough water even in times of drought; and there were other sites upstream that were suitable for more dams as Canberra's population grew. At that time in the Cotter catchment, there were two properties, one of which grazed cattle and sheep, which de Burgh recommended be acquired by the Commonwealth as soon as possible. De Burgh and Corin had recommended a dam be built upstream and gravity feed to the city but Owen felt the cost of this scheme would be prohibitive and he persuaded the government to choose a dam sited below Canberra with water being pumped by electric power up to a reservoir on Mount Stromlo, where it was fed by gravity to Red Hill and other points of consumption.

De Burgh also submitted to the committee a report on Canberra's future sewerage scheme. Up to that time, there had been ongoing controversy about this, as Griffin's plans for large treatment works within the city had been supported by Calder Oliver, an engineer retained by King O'Malley at a high fee. The Royal Commission of 1917 had also recommended Griffin's Imhoff tanks proposal. De Burgh, on reviewing the evidence, concluded that most expert witnesses supported the proposals for an outfall scheme, with gravity taking the sewage by pipe for treatment outside the city. Because of the controversy, work on the sewerage scheme had been at a standstill since 1917. De Burgh recommended immediate resumption of the project after he and Owen submitted plans for the main sewer in June 1921.

The task handed to the FCAC by the government in January 1921 was to appraise all the existing data, plans and works relating to the capital – an accumulation over ten years – and then devise a scheme for establishing the seat of government in Canberra at an early date. This had to be done within financial constraints that excluded any works or features of a monumental character, while ensuring that there was no departure in principle from the city plan.

Charles Daley, still based in Melbourne, was given the task of unearthing and assembling all the relevant documents and plans from the office of the Federal Capital Director. Griffin had worked here for the six years of his tenure, with his own staff and with very little contact with departmental officers apart from correspondence. This lack of contact was due in part to the atmosphere of mutual distrust and suspicion that clouded relations between the two groups in those years. There were many occasions when departmental officers did not release plans that Griffin had requested; it comes as no surprise then that Griffin himself would have kept data in his office that might have been of use to the department.

Among the papers that Daley uncovered were plans for the layout of the city and boulevards; for the brickworks and lime kilns in Yarralumla; for the subdivision of allotments at Civic; and for the completed railway line over the Molonglo to Civic. Daley also found plans that Griffin had drawn for projected buildings at Duntroon, and the design for Major General Bridges' grave on Mount Pleasant. There were also plans for a simple artisan's cottage. This design was never tested in Canberra, a fact that many of Griffin's later supporters have regretted. Daley comments that the design was not considered suitable for Canberra conditions. The committee looked at Griffin's design but on Owen's recommendation the designs used for the workers' cottages at Littleton at Lithgow were adopted instead, and became the first cottages built at 'Neighbourhood 1' in the north-east of the city. Though called workers' cottages, they were in fact built to house the first influx of middle-income and lower-income public servants that would be coming from Melbourne. Similar cottages were soon to be built near the Power House and the Brickworks to house staff. The workmen themselves who were building the cottages would be housed in moveable tenements – or barracks – which could be taken from one building site to another as work progressed. The labourers working on the big construction projects like the sewerage pipes or in earlier years the Cotter Dam, the Brickworks and the Power House, lived in tents supplied by the government or, if they were married men, they could construct their own dwellings out of galvanised iron, timber and hessian. The story of these early worker communities has been fully researched and faithfully recorded by Canberra historian Ann Gugler.

Daley brought the drawings and plans he had found to date in Griffin's office to the third meeting of the FCAC, which was held in Canberra at the Works office at Acton on 31 January 1921. The committee had been given offices on the fourth floor of Customs House at Circular

Quay in Sydney, but they came down regularly to Canberra to inspect existing works at the city site. These included the Power House, the Cotter Dam and reservoirs, roads, bridges, temporary buildings of all kinds like the hospital, workers' camps, stores and manufacturing sites like the brickworks. As well, there were large stores of timber, building materials, machinery and equipment that had been assembled and lay waiting assessment for their future usefulness. At these visits to Canberra, Thomas Weston became a respected source of advice about the city plan, accompanying the committee to advise on tree planting for the Civic area and along Commonwealth Avenue, one of Griffin's main axial lines from Capitol Hill to the Civic Centre.

The committee meeting on 28 February 1921 was to be pivotal in the future deliberations of the committee and in the planning of the city. At that meeting, Sulman 'emphatically' recommended a 'compact, easy to build and easy to work city, in contrast to a scattered, expensive and hard to manage settlement to the north-east of Civic'.[3]

At this point, Owen reminded his colleagues of their government's commitment to developing the city in accordance with Griffin's plan. This required the Civic area to be developed north of the river and the governmental area to the south; they were all integral parts of that great triangle which was at the centre of Burley Griffin's concept of the city. 'Once we depart from Griffin's plan's essential features,' he warned, 'we might as well cast it to the winds.'[4]

Griffin would have been surprised that his former enemy was now proving to be a strong defender of his plan. Perhaps Owen, a military man used to both the exercise of authority and obedience to a higher authority, accepted the government's decision on the city plan as binding, requiring him to give his best efforts to bring it to fruition. In fact, Owen was to devote the best part of twenty years of his professional life to Canberra's development.

On 20 May 1921, the committee met at the Residency, the rather grand two-storey home that had been built for the Administrator David Miller and now served as the headquarters in Canberra for the FCAC. The preservation of historic records came up for discussion. It was resolved that tracings be made of the original city plan (one inch to 200 feet map as approved by King O'Malley) and that heliographs be made from the tracing. The committee knew that Griffin's plan was a valuable document which needed to be stored in a safe and permanent place. To their pragmatic eyes, it was 'the result of many thousands of pounds of engineering and survey expeditions'.[5]

Because the FCAC was advisory in function, a copy of an 'interim report', prepared by Daley and Owen, was forwarded to the minister after each committee meeting. The minister could either approve or reject the works recommended, or refer them to the Joint Parliamentary Committee for Public Works, which had to review every works project costing over £25,000.

By July 1921, the committee had prepared its first General Report to be presented to the Minister for Works and Railways. On 18 July, Daley returned to Melbourne on the overnight train to attend to the final printing of the report. It summarised the progress to date in the construction of Canberra and advised on future building requirements: cottages and a school; hostels for Commonwealth officers and politicians; a conference hall which would serve as a provisional Parliament House; the continuation of the sewerage scheme and network of roads; and further afforestation of the city site. The committee also outlined their proposals for the city's future development. They envisaged the building of the city in three stages. In the first stage, Canberra would be built as a garden town, with simple, pleasing and unpretentious buildings. During this stage, a limited number of staff from government departments would be transferred from Melbourne and parliament would meet for the first time in the federal capital. In the second stage, the remainder of government departments would be transferred and appropriate infrastructure for the growing population put in place. Griffin's monumental city, with its ornamental lakes and great public buildings, would be the third stage, not to be built for decades to come.

While the FCAC had proposed expenditure of £417,400 for the first stage, Parliament only voted £220,000. To meet the government's desire for employment for returned soldiers, the committee had to allocate a considerable amount of this reduced budget for unskilled work, mainly road construction. Over the next few years, the returned servicemen's organisation continued to press for more returned men to be employed at Canberra in areas like the workshops. Owen explained that trained fitters who had finished their apprenticeship in engineering works were very hard to come by. He pointed out that one returned soldier had been taken on for this work but he was 'addicted to drink' and had to be discharged.

In July 1922, Owen and Daley worked together to prepare the second General Report, outlining further construction work carried on during the year. A new project came to the committee's attention in July that year. Charles Bean wrote from Tuggeranong to their Sydney office suggesting that Canberra should be the future home of a National War Museum. A year later in September 1923, he addressed the committee in Canberra at the Residency to outline in more detail what he had in mind. He pointed out that Australia could not hope to compete architecturally with the great memorials of other countries but whatever was done, he felt, should be a gem of its kind. Discussion took place as to where such a memorial could be built on the city plan. Mount Vernon, a small hill to the south of the Civic Centre, was suggested; but Owen, again proving to be Griffin's defender, spoke against identifying a war memorial with the civic functions of business and commerce. He proposed instead the area below Mount Ainslie, originally to be the site of Griffin's Casino. The committee inspected the site, striding out over the grassy slopes below Mount Ainslie and taking in the extensive views across the river to the distant mountains. They also viewed the site looking north from the area below Capital Hill, their gaze directed along the great axis that Griffin had designed to lead from the governmental buildings towards the centres of commerce and culture. Owen had already made quite clear at earlier committee meetings that Griffin's main axis must stand, and that the provisional Parliament House should be located on that main axis. Likewise, shopping facilities to be developed on the southern side of the river to serve the likely influx of workers and public servants should remain limited on the understanding that the main commercial activity would be in Civic. The first General Report had recommended a cooperative system of shopping in the early stages as there was a reluctance to encourage private enterprise in Canberra until there was the infrastructure in place to service shops and businesses.

In the early 1920s, Canberra resembled a huge, scattered construction site. The roads in the city area that were taking construction traffic were heavily gravelled but most other roads remained dusty, or potholed after heavy rain, until 1928 when the spraying of tar over blue metal came into wide use. A narrow bridge with white timber trusses spanned the Molonglo River from Commonwealth Avenue to the city site; two vehicles could pass if they drove cautiously. Heavy loads trundled across the bridge carrying building materials from the Brickworks to the city site. A light railway had also been built to cross the river at the Causeway, near the Power House, to carry construction materials to sites in the city. Heavy rains and flooding in July 1922 totally destroyed the Causeway bridge and also damaged the white timber bridge, which had to be urgently reinforced as it was the only traffic link with north Canberra.

For road making and construction, quarries were established at Mugga Mugga (the hill to the south-east of the city), on Mount Ainslie and on Red Hill. The excavation scars are still in evidence at the first two sites. Photographs of the time show the continued use of horse-drawn drays and manual labour with pick and shovel; but throughout the 1920s there were moves to tractors, steam-powered shovels and traction engines and tip trucks.

Construction of the sewerage system re-started in 1921 with the digging of the main outfall sewer. This ran from near Commonwealth Avenue for five miles out to Western Creek [sic] beyond the city limits. Tunnelling began from the western end and proceeded beneath the Yarralumla fields and under the hill called Stirling Ridge to Commonwealth Avenue. The men recruited for the work lived in tented encampments at Westridge or at Westlake, a pleasant grassy woodland sloping down to the southern banks of the Molonglo River. Some of the men had travelled from the gold mines at Araluen to find work at the sewer after the gold ran out.

The work was strenuous, dirty and often dangerous. A workman died, accidentally electrocuted while drilling in the sewer tunnel. The men were sometimes working underground in water up to their waist, as Stirling Ridge has many natural springs. The Molonglo Valley is called the Limestone Plains because of its underlying geology; T.G. Taylor had reported on limestone caves and hollows near the river at Acton. Certainly the workmen struck so much cavernous limestone during the driving of the tunnel that they believed that the planned system of lakes would never hold water.

A cage connected to a belt worked by a steam-powered traction engine lowered men 200 feet down one of the access shafts to the tunnel. The cage was also used to raise mullock from the tunnel, which was then spread in huge dumps around Stirling Ridge. A story is told of Miss Margaret Morrison, collecting funds for her church, who was lowered in a bucket to collect from the sewer workers in the tunnel. When the Hotel Canberra, facing the main thoroughfare of Commonwealth Avenue, opened in December 1924, great piles of slag were heaped right along on the central strip of the road. These came from the sewerage tunnels being constructed underneath.

By 1923, simple wooden cottages had been built at Westridge to provide more solid accommodation for workers and their families. One man recalled putting cotton wool in his children's ears at night to allow them to sleep through the midnight explosions in the tunnel below.

Other camps were scattered around the building sites of the territory and at the forestry operations in the Brindabella range and on Mount Stromlo. At the Cotter River, camps were constructed for dam workers in 1913 and by late 1917, following completion of the dam, they were disbanded. During their lifetime, a 'tent school' was set up to cater for the children of workers. There would have been very little at the Cotter settlement to show its members they were part of a nation-building project. Dust, noise, hazardous physical work; no recreational facilities and remoteness from settlement; and the assaults of a harsh summer climate and an even harsher winter one: it was a hard and unrewarding life.

Many men left the territory during the war, either to enlist in the forces or to seek work elsewhere when Commonwealth construction stopped. The early 1920s saw early intimations of the Depression, with high unemployment in many parts of Australia. Returned soldiers came looking for work in the federal territory, but some were embittered by the experience. The Anzac Buffet Employment Bureau in Melbourne was responsible for sending 200 returned men to Canberra for construction work in 1922, to help in the building of a road up Mount Pleasant, near Duntroon. When they arrived, there were no blankets and three men were expected to share two-man tents.

John Howie, a successful building contractor in the territory, made a point of looking after his workers. He was given the contract to build

Hostel No 1 (the future Hotel Canberra) and his men needed to live nearby. Howie erected twenty-five two or three-bedroom timber cottages for married men and at least eighteen timber huts for single men, on the ground above the Molonglo at Westlake. The settlement had halls as well, one for mess and recreation, the other for church services and recreation. These settlements were never seen as permanent by the government. Some were removed before the opening of Parliament House in 1927 but others were still there in the 1940s. By 1927 the Commonwealth had adopted its own policy of replacing tents with more settled accommodation for single men as well as families. In fact Howie's cottages became the model for the design adopted by the government architect Henry Rolland in 1923.

After the war, a large settlement of timber huts and barracks became available for the Commonwealth to use in Canberra. They came from the Molonglo Internment Camp. The camp had been built over a twelve-week period in the early part of 1918 in an atmosphere of great secrecy. The camp, a Department of Defence project, was built at the request of the British government and was intended to accommodate some 3,000 German nationals then interned in China. They did not arrive and the camp was used instead to house Austrian and German families who had been interned at Bourke and Berrima.

Charles Daley recalled clearly the day early in 1918 when the secret cablegram from the British government arrived in Melbourne. Percy Owen, himself an ex-soldier, took on the challenge posed by the urgency of the job – and by its appeal to his patriotic attachment to Britain in this final stage of the war. He confirmed that his department would take on the job, even though there was a serious shortage of staff, skilled labour and materials at the time. John Murdoch designed the layout and buildings for the scheme, with four Sydney contractors sharing the construction load. The engineering works and military buildings such as barracks and lookout tower were erected by the department, with some buildings being moved from the Duntroon military college, transferred by lumbering traction engines and bullock drays to the new site. Electricity, sewerage and water were all connected within the time, and a railway siding connected the camp to the Queanbeyan–Kingston line.

The families arrived in early winter 1918, travelling from Bourke by train to Queanbeyan and then to the Molonglo siding. They were to be housed in a collection of wooden tenement blocks fanning out from the central buildings; each tenement block faced a small unit housing shared bathroom, toilets and laundries. There were butchers' and bakers' shops on the site, a fire station, public school, teacher's residence, hospital and assembly hall. The camp looked down towards the Molonglo River over treeless, windswept paddocks.

What could have been an unrelentingly bleak and hostile environment was softened for the inmates by an enlightened and liberal regime, with the officers under the leadership of Brigadier General Spencer Browne doing their best to make this time more comfortable for the families. Browne encouraged community life at the camp, with music making, a library and sporting competitions with locals from Queanbeyan. The inmates were allowed to have shopping excursions to Queanbeyan, and their children were taken on picnics to the river.

The main complaints of the inmates were at the lack of privacy in the tenements and the lack of insulation in the huts. There were of course other sources of distress. It was after all, a time of both exile and imprisonment for them. Many of the men had been merchants, professional men, planters and naval captains in the Far East before their capture and deportation to Australia. When the war ended, they were released from the camp and repatriated directly to Germany. They become lost to our history after that, but one wonders what the next decade brought for these men and their families. Frau Hurtzig's diary noted, 'January 1919: The Kaiser is gone. What kind of government will come to power? Will we be able to live in our home, and will there be enough money, food and bread for everyone?'[6]

As arrangements for the closure and dispersal of the camp were put in place, the internees sold many of their personal effects in the face of an uncertain future. A collection of white tropical suits, sewing machines, cameras and tool chests – and a number of German violins – were among the items which Queanbeyan residents were able to purchase at auction.

In Canberra, the government was faced with the challenge of what to do with this 'model township'. A Molonglo Camp Trust was set up (with Charles Daley as executive secretary) to report to the British government and to consider what to do with these valuable assets. In the early 1920s, nearly half of the tenement blocks and some of the store buildings were sold to the NSW government to use as barracks at water conservation and irrigation projects. Some buildings were removed to various locations in Canberra, including camps at Eastlake and at Westridge near the Brickworks. Some furniture for the use of the war historian C.E.W. Bean at Tuggeranong was requisitioned from Molonglo.

By mid-1921, almost all the camp's buildings and fittings earmarked for removal had gone. Charles Daley mourned the destruction of the excellent camp library with its beautiful editions of standard German literature. The whole library, being in the German language, was burnt by a sergeant in charge of a clean-up detachment.

The remaining twelve tenement blocks and some nearby military buildings were transformed into a settlement for building workers and their families who came to Canberra for construction work under the Federal Capital Advisory Committee. The camp hospital was converted into a public school and the commandant's home became the teacher's residence.

By the beginning of 1922, there were twenty-six families renting Molonglo tenements. Single workers were also accommodated in an area away from the married quarters. The six barracks for the single men were divided into a number of cubicles each shared by two men. The walls dividing the cubicles did not reach the ceiling, so the space was filled with fencing wire to curtail the common practice of throwing bottles over the partitions.

During the Advisory Committee's years (1921–24) the population of the Molonglo camp was about 200 and was to increase in the following years to nearly 800, making it the largest workers' settlement in the territory. Records show that there was a strong sense of community, with sports teams and an active progress association. Its continuing story will be told in the next chapter.

*

During the 1920s, the Commonwealth continued the process of acquiring land in the territory. The whole of the FCT outside the city area – with the exception of the Cotter catchment and the areas reserved for forestry – was to be acquired then leased for grazing or agricultural purposes. Landowners were to be compensated for the loss of their property in two ways. The unimproved value of their land was fixed at 1908 values; the improved value of the land was estimated by a government valuer as of 1 January preceding the acquisition of the property. Until a property was acquired, the owner could still treat it as freehold land and sell it or improve it as he thought fit.

The reality was that no one wanted to buy land over which the owner had no secure long-term rights. In 1921, a number of properties were put up for auction and passed in with no bids at all.

In October 1921, the landowner John Noone approached the government for information as to when his land would be required by the Commonwealth. John Goodwin wrote back, in a letter notable for its bureaucratic stiffness, that

> Your property is not at present required for Commonwealth purposes. I do not feel justified in incurring any expenditure in obtaining a report on its value. The Commonwealth is under no obligation to have a valuation made or to disclose its contents.[7]

Further difficulties awaited men like John Noone. A landowner could not obtain advance from banks, who would not lend any money until the Commonwealth made known its valuation of his property.

Many of the old residents of the district wished to retire but they were compelled to remain on their land until the Commonwealth was ready to acquire it. The Tiernan brothers farmed land at Freshford, on the western banks of the Murrumbidgee River near the village of Tharwa. They wished to sell the property so their beneficiaries would receive their legacy, but they could not find a buyer. They had recently bought more stock and were now heavily in debt as there was a slump in the market. They appealed to Goodwin in late 1921, could the Commonwealth purchase their land? Goodwin replied, '…there is no reason special provision should be made for Commonwealth acquisition; he was not prepared to purchase the property at present.'[8]

In 1923, the Department of Home and Territories gave an undertaking not to acquire two large pastoral properties, Booroomba and Lanyon, for ten years, with the reservation that any portion of the land could be acquired by the Commonwealth for road purposes

One property of particular interest to the Commonwealth was

Lambrigg, further up the river from Freshford. The property had been the home of the late William Farrer, who had done so much for the wheat industry in Australia in developing a rust-free strain of wheat. His small laboratory still stood in the homestead grounds and looked out over a paddock where he had experimented with growing different strains of wheat. Goodwin was keen to acquire the property.

> There is no doubt that as the Capital proceeds, the resting place of William Farrer will be of considerable interest. The property could, at a later date, be used in connection with the Afforestation department, as Headquarters for a forest ranger.[9]

In 1922, Farrer's widow, Henrietta Farrer, negotiated with the Commonwealth to sell the property and lease it back to her. She especially desired to maintain the beautiful orchard facing out over the river, and to ensure that her husband's grave, on a rocky knoll behind the homestead, was left undisturbed. Mrs Farrer agreed to an offer of £4,500 and to pay a rental of £100 per annum for the homestead and forty acres of land. The Minister for Defence, George Pearce, later agreed to accept a 'peppercorn rent' for the house and land in question, 'in view of the services rendered to the country by the late Mr Farrer'.[10]

*

In late July 1923, Parliament approved the erection of a provisional Parliament House. Owen had moved permanently to Canberra by then as the city was now his chief responsibility. Daley was still travelling up from Melbourne to Sydney and Canberra for committee meetings and inspections, as well as managing departmental work in Owen's absence. His life must have had a frantic pace at that time, as he had married in 1917 and already had three young children. In August 1923, Owen put a strong case to the Public Service Board for an extra allowance for Daley.

> Mr Daley has accumulated a knowledge in regards to all questions bearing on Canberra which is probably unique, and he is constantly being referred to from all quarters for information and advice. When any matter affecting Canberra is before Parliament he is required to be in attendance to advise

the Minister. In fact departmentally the Minister deals with him direct. He works two or three nights a week at home. He is not a mere secretary to the Federal Capital Advisory Committee, but really a member of it, taking part in all discussions, deliberations and decisions.[11]

Daley's allowance was to be £200 but the Audit Office knocked it back to £150. Walter Bingle, Secretary of Works and Railways, had tried earlier to gain extra pay for Daley, pointing out that most FCAC reports were actually prepared by him because of his extensive technical knowledge. His memo hinted at some of the stresses the family were under: 'Daley has had to engage a private companion for his wife while he is away.'[12]

One of Daley's tasks in Melbourne was to collect data to predict forward numbers of population in Canberra. He approached the various Commonwealth departments to obtain information on the numbers of their officers to be removed to Canberra, the size of their families, and the office space or working areas required for each department's activities. Very few of the departmental heads cooperated. 'I may as well tell you, that my department will not be moved to that place,' Robert Ewing, head of the Customs Department in Melbourne, warned Daley.[13] In a number of cases, Daley had to obtain a Cabinet direction to require heads of department to cooperate in providing information. This did not win him many friends among his Melbourne colleagues, who mocked him as 'Mr Canberra'.

Daley took the role of government official seriously but he made a point of steering clear of the perks that came with high office. While staying in Canberra for FCAC meetings, he occupied a room in Colonel Owen's suite of rooms at Yarralumla House. Finding he had been undercharged on his bill as a member of the official party, Daley told Owen he would prefer to pay the full rate, as he had a specified travelling allowance and should use it as such.

His work in Melbourne for the FCAC included gathering data on the likely number of tradesmen, professionals and businessmen who would come to Canberra as the population of public servants grew. Daley investigated numbers in towns with populations of 4–5,000, like Cowra, Casino and Wellington. He also provided estimates of official accommodation needs and their likely cost for stage 1 of the city's development.

In February 1924, Daley prepared a summary of arguments in favour of a provisional Parliament House, to provide background for parliamentarians who would soon be moving there. His report was designed to reassure members that they'd made the right decision, and to provide them with some accurate information, which the Melbourne press was reluctant to do. His readers, used to the nineteenth century Victorian ambience of the Parliament House in Spring Street (albeit with its antiquated plumbing and heating), needed to be reassured that they would not be moving into an unsightly galvanised iron structure as had been canvassed, but 'a brick building of commodious and comfortable character' which could be ready within three years.[14] Daley put forward an eloquent case to his readers that, on all counts, they had made the right decision. 'This building represents the central idea and justification for the city's construction – a place where Federal legislative activity may be conducted, free from local interests and in the best interests of the nation.' The provisional scheme was the right one for their time; 'no scheme which loads the present generation with an additional economic burden is acceptable'.

The provisional Parliament House was to be built on Griffin's main axis, 2,000 feet north of Camp Hill, the site he had chosen. Any buildings to be associated with this governmental group were to be strictly temporary in nature and clear of the site for permanent buildings as laid down in the city plan. John Murdoch, as chief architect for the department, would design the building. This was to be a public works project, not the outcome of an international design competition; that would have to wait for when the country was ready to fund the monumental buildings of Griffin's plans. Murdoch also designed two administrative buildings to serve the provisional Parliament House; they would be placed clear of the permanent structures in the city plan. At first Owen submitted a plan for temporary buildings constructed of timber and corrugated iron. The Public Works Committee could not approve of important public documents being housed in such structures so both administrative buildings (later known as East Block and West Block) were to be two-storey buildings of brick or concrete.

While everyone agreed that the country could not afford to fund the permanent building at that time, there were strongly held opinions about what should be done in the short term. This was revealed in evidence given to a parliamentary standing committee enquiring into the project. Walter Burley Griffin was one witness. He strongly condemned Murdoch's plans for the provisional building below Camp Hill; his own plan provided for a water feature on that site, with a series of formal open spaces leading down to a frontage on the lake. To place a provisional building on that site, he claimed, 'would be like filling a front yard full of outhouses'.[15] Other witnesses believed that the nucleus of the permanent building should be erected on Camp Hill, and extended later. Others supported the Advisory Committee's choice of a provisional building below Camp Hill, and this was the choice that was accepted. A further view, however, was expressed by John Murdoch, who thought Parliament House should be built on Capital Hill, the most prominent site on the City Plan. Very few people understood Griffin's concept of a People's Palace and its democratic role; there was never any concerted effort to defend or explain this concept, which was quietly dropped from the official plan.

In August 1923, Murdoch's plans for Parliament House were far enough advanced to allow for an official launch at the building site below Camp Hill. The government, keen to avoid expense, planned a low-key ceremony and no official invitations were issued. But Queanbeyan Municipal Council decided the occasion warranted a half-day holiday for the town and a day off school for the children. On 28 August, many Queanbeyans flocked to Canberra and a holiday atmosphere prevailed. They crowded in to watch the Minister for Works and Railways, P.G. Stewart, turn the first sod of soil, not with a conventional spade, but with a steam shovel. This novel machine – likened to an elephant waving its unwieldy trunk about before biting at the soil – proved a source of great entertainment to both children and adults in the large audience. Stewart, aided by his early seafaring experience with winches, drove it with aplomb.

The press who were there grumbled about the occasion. A reporter from the *Sydney Morning Herald* complained about the 'complete lack of facilities for the press' and noted that a strong wind carrying clouds of dust made the day very uncomfortable.

The locals were more philosophical. They listened to long speeches by three politicians, Stewart, Littleton Groom and Austin Chapman, and then there were cheers all round: for Mr and Mrs Stewart, Mr and Mrs Chapman, the Prince of Wales (remembered for his stone-laying ceremony in 1920), for the Federal Capital Advisory Committee, for the workmen and for all the ladies. Stewart's speech drew on the report that Daley had earlier prepared for Parliament. So the listeners received some reassuring words about the symbolic importance of this event.

A footnote to the story of the building of Parliament House concerns the original competition to design a permanent Parliament House. That competition had been inaugurated in 1914, abandoned during the war, re-opened in 1916 but postponed indefinitely after three months. Some architects had done designs for the competition. The Australian Institute of Architects felt that the government had a moral obligation to acknowledge and reimburse the competitors who had entered the original competition. Sulman proposed that competition designs be called in and compensation paid for work done. In 1924, the government provided £3,000 to be allotted to registered competitors on the basis of the value and quantity of work done towards the design. Daley distributed this money in accordance with decisions by a board, with drawings all being returned and no record kept of them.

6
Commission Rule

'This commission achieved the almost impossible task of building a city from the ground upwards.'

Sir John Butters.
Reproduced with permission of Canberra & District Historical Society

In January 1924, John Sulman was given six months leave of absence by the government to travel overseas and to investigate various forms of commission government, with a view to advising the Commonwealth on the future direction of the federal capital. In June that year, he was knighted by King George V in London.

Sulman prepared a report on 'Commission Government in America' after he had made a close study of Washington DC. Like Canberra, Washington was a city that had been built to house a federal government independent of state interests. Since 1878, Washington had been governed by a commission of three men, two of whom were DC residents, the third an engineer in the US Army. These men were appointed by the President and held office for three years. A Fine Arts Commission under presidential order had the right to veto or pass all plans for government buildings in Washington, thus safeguarding the integrity of its splendid architecture and city landscape.

Based on his Washington observations, Sulman's recommendations to his ministers were radical: '...enlist the services of the best men in the community irrespective of politics, trusting them and giving them a free hand to carry out their work'. He also issued a piece of advice that was to prove prophetic: '...one of the Commissioners should be elected by the rate-paying public, otherwise they will resent "taxation without representation". As soon as lessees' improvements amount to half of total valuation of the city, they should have the privilege of electing one of the Commissioners.'[1]

As early as February 1923, the Advisory Committee had outlined a suggested form of future government for the territory. They believed 'that the future construction of Canberra should be vested in a separate body', and Prime Minister Bruce confirmed that this was the government's intention when he addressed the House of Representatives in March that year.

From the beginning, Canberra had been run on a system of divided authority. In 1923 this consisted of two separate government departments,

Works and Railways, and Home and Territories. There was overlap, duplication of services, difficulties in communication and a great deal of wasted time in the need to refer matters to Melbourne. All projects likely to cost more than £25,000 had to be referred to the Parliamentary Standing Committee for Public Works. Percy Owen spoke from personal experience when he argued that any system where department officers had to refer all matters to Melbourne for consideration made good and effective management impossible.

But the kind of independent commission which Sulman was advocating was 'a touchy and inflammable topic', according to Charles Daley.[2] There was hostility enough towards Canberra among many Australian taxpayers, and the daily papers knew they had receptive readers when they attacked Canberra. *The Daily Telegraph* referred to a 'phantom city of futile foundation stones'.[3] *The Age* wrote of 'how impossible it will be for the Commonwealth to find the money required to make the bush capital habitable for MPs and the vast army of government servants who will have to be housed in Canberra…'[4]

Charles Daley was well aware of the controversy surrounding the capital and the move to a commission style of government. He collaborated with the Parliamentary Draughtsman, Sir Robert Garran, in drawing up a draft bill for this legislation's first reading in parliament. He then prepared the second stage of the bill and helped the minister in the difficult passage of the bill through parliament. The Seat of Government (Administration) Act was finally passed in October 1924 and created a new form of government for Canberra.

In the early stages, Cabinet did not favour a completely independent commission and recommended a body made up of elected parliamentary representatives – the Treasurer and ministers for Home and Territories and Works and Railways – with members of the FCAC as technical advisors. But the commission as appointed by the 1924 Act was to be independent and have wide executive and financial powers.

The Federal Capital Commission was a statutory corporation in which were vested all Canberra's lands and public assets, and it had the authority to raise loans, subject to Parliamentary concurrence, and plan its budget, with budget estimates to be approved by the Minister for Home and Territories. For the first time, a single authority would be responsible for the administration, design and construction of Canberra. This included a clause allowing minor modifications of the city plan.

Its first major objective was the speedy completion of Parliament House and of residential and office accommodation for a small nucleus of public officials: a secretariat, with direct phone contact to Melbourne. Owen assumed that he would be given the role of Chief Executive Officer of the Commission and he thanked Sulman and FCAC members for nominating him for this position. It must have been a bitter blow to him when an outsider was appointed to head the new body.

The outsider was a man with a formidable reputation in the engineering and construction world. John Henry Butters had trained in England as an electrical engineer and, after extensive experience in designing and costing power stations in the UK and abroad, he was consulted for advice on production of electricity in the Great Lake hydroelectric scheme in Tasmania, the first major attempt to harness water power in Tasmania in this way. Butters became engineer-in-chief and manager of the scheme in September 1911, a position he retained when the undertaking became a state responsibility. The scheme was completed in 1923 and earned Butters the imperial award CMG. It established his reputation as a man who could tackle and solve large-scale engineering challenges in the unforgiving environment of the Tasmanian highlands. Butters was known to set and demand high standards – for example, he declared the raw mining township of Miena a 'dry' town with no alcohol – but he was also warmly regarded by his large work force and by the state government, who delegated considerable authority to him. In fact, many people regarded the honorific CMG to stand for 'can manage governments', as Butters had singular success in that field. In October 1924, Butters was appointed Chief Commissioner of the Federal Capital Commission for five years on an annual salary of £3,000. Two other commissioners were appointed on a part-time basis: Clarence Gorman, who worked in real estate, and Sir John Harrison, a successful businessman. Percy Owen was appointed as Chief Engineer to the Commission.

In October 1924, Charles Daley received a letter from a Cabinet minister, Major C.W. Marr.

Mr Butters is anxious to see you, as I wrote to him and suggested he could not have a better man as secretary – you've been connected to Canberra so long. I have heard of at least two officials who are trying for the position…[5]

Daley pondered his options as he saw the Advisory Committee's work coming to an end. He was married with a wife and four young children by that stage, with strong family ties in Melbourne. One choice was to resign from the Commonwealth service and take up work with a Melbourne law firm. Wider horizons also beckoned. In August 1924, he applied for the position of Senior Clerk with the Prime Minister's Department in London, an application that was accompanied by warm references from John Sulman and departmental secretary Walter Bingle. In the end, the prospect of further work in Canberra at a decisive stage of its development influenced his choice. In December 1924, he accepted Butters' invitation to join him as secretary of the new Federal Capital Commission, where he would be 'on loan' from the Department of Works and Railways until a permanent appointment was made in December 1925. Butters was to confess to a departmental officer that Daley's 'experience and knowledge of FCT matters will be of enormous help to us'.[6]

Meanwhile, there was one last demand on his services to the FCAC. At one of the committee's last meetings in Canberra, in October 1924, it was proposed that a full report and review of the Committee's activities should be written. Daley was the obvious man to do the job. In December, his minister 'undertook to make his services available for this'. As Daley began work with the Commission in early January 1925, this meant he must have worked long hours through the Melbourne summer and over the Christmas break to get the job done. In March 1925, he wrote to Sulman, 'I had hopes to have the first draft of the report ready in January but have had to work up to the limit of my capacity on matters connected with establishing the Commission.'[7] In effect, the report was all his own work, though he consulted the committee members in regard to 'any opinion they may want to leave on record regarding Canberra's development'. That summer, Owen write to Daley after seeing the final report, 'My dear Daley. Please allow me to praise you for the masterly way you have drawn up the final report…to thank you and to express my wonder at how on earth you have found the time to do it!'[8]

The completed report was a detailed record of all the construction that had taken place during the term of the FCAC. It was a clearly written account of four years in the building of a city; it also ranged back to the early controversies about the city design and forward to a future where an independent body of experts would take over to administer the territory.

After the FCAC members accepted Daley's final draft, they added a concluding 'acknowledgement', in which Mr C.S. Daley was singled out for 'his absolutely indispensable and invaluable' services.[9] Sulman strongly recommended an honorarium of £500 for his work but this was never paid. In Melbourne, Daley was kept busy selling his house and settling his family in other accommodation. His wife and children were to join him in Canberra once the house being built for them in Acton was ready. Daley arrived in Canberra on 7 January 1925, travelling with Butters; they were both to start work in temporary quarters made available to them at the new Hostel No. 1 (the Hotel Canberra) until the Acton offices were extended.

Ernest De Burgh wrote to Daley from Sydney in a nostalgic mood after the FCAC was wound up,

> I miss the meetings of the old Committee. There was a very pleasant note to our association, no group of men could have worked more amicably under such irritating conditions. So many authorities – and these changing. Frequent alterations of arrangements and dates, which left me in a state of uncertainty and upset my other business. I think the Commissioner will still have plenty of worry, for lack of power in the Act.[10]

One of the largest and most challenging projects for the new Commission was arranging the transfer of staff, their families and belongings, plus government records and archives, in time for the opening of Parliament on 9 May 1927. This date had been chosen to commemorate the opening of the first Commonwealth Parliament in Melbourne on 9 May 1901. This deadline meant that the Commission's work over the next two years was always driven by a sense of urgency; memoranda and letters at the time reveal the stresses and challenges this deadline posed. There were other pressures. The government decided that the secretariat scheme was unsound and reverted to the original scheme to transfer complete staff of some departments. Instead of 200 public servants, there now had to be plans to receive 1,000.

In February 1926, Parliament appropriated £500,000 to meet the cost of transfer. A trusted military officer, Colonel W.J. Farr, was loaned from the Department of Defence to act as Director of Transport Arrangements. The total number of officers to be transferred by November 1927 was 590.

Colonel Farr's records show him to be a man of compassion and common sense with a robust sense of humour. These qualities were needed in abundance in the job he was given. He was aware that the transfer to Canberra would bring 'wholesale uprooting and dislocation of family ties' and he hoped to make the transfer as smooth and trouble-free as possible.

It was resolved that all transfer would be by rail rather than road or ship, and the department obtained greatly reduced freight charges, so families could choose to move their furniture and possessions with them. Farr reported that many families were disappointed when large baulks of timber and galvanised iron from fowl houses and outbuildings were refused cartage. It was the same story with an officer who owned forty prize-winning fowls, and a family with a cow: all such livestock had to be left behind. But one small cage of birds could be packed, and a pet dog could travel on the train with the family.

If officers chose to drive their own car to Canberra, they would be paid an equivalent of the train fares. There would be no payment for wear and tear or petrol. Farr warned that travel by car posed a big risk 'in direct ratio to the rattle-ability of the car'. 'Some might be a week or more on the track', with their office in Canberra left waiting their arrival. 'What about the man who could not afford a car but had a horse and jinker? He would argue that he was just as entitled to his own form of transport as the man with the car.'[11]

Public Service regulations allowed salaried officers of a certain level to travel first class with their families while the rest travelled second class and sat up all night. Labor Prime Minister Jim Scullin roundly condemned these arrangements. 'If a sleeping berth is provided for the wife of one officer it should be provided for the wife of another. It would appear that the Federal Capital is perpetuating the worst kind of snobbery...'[12] In response to this publicity, the Public Service Board advised that all officers and their families could travel first class to Canberra; household servants would travel second class.

Under all this fuss and comedy, there were real issues of loss and grief to deal with. Families were leaving behind a lifetime of attachment: to elderly parents, to neighbours and community, to church and children's schools, to well-loved homes and cherished gardens. They truly felt they were going into exile.

Daley had the job of investigating the costs of removal of household goods and office equipment. Special arrangements would be made for the transfer of the Gold Reserve, and for valuable libraries held at Parliament House, the Patent Office and Attorney General's Office. All departments were to dispose of out-of-date matter to expedite the move. The bulk of the material to be moved was registers, gazettes, field books, parliamentary papers and debates. The Lands and Survey Branch reported that they had 25,000 plans of every shape and size. They also held twelve cases containing the original Canberra designs and eleven boxes of glass negatives of the prize-winning and other federal capital designs. They sent a strong warning to Farr that these would all need careful handling.

It was a far cry from the early days of federation, when Barton travelled from Sydney to Melbourne with all his official papers in one black bag.[13]

The first officials to be transferred – the parliamentary staff – elected to stay in one of the government hostels that had been built ('hostels' because they did not serve alcohol). Yarralumla House was being renovated and furnished for its future vice-regal inhabitants, and Miller's former home, the Residency, was also being refurbished to provide a home for John Butters and his family.

In 1923 an architectural competition had been launched to design houses for higher-ranking officials. The houses were to be built at Blandfordia, an area now known as Forrest. The Melbourne architects Oakley, Parkes and Scarborough (the latter a temporary partner) won the competition, and designed a range of attractive one-storey dwellings priced according to features like built-in cupboards and number of bedrooms. They also designed a comfortable family home to serve as a 'provisional' residence for the Prime Minister. An early partner in the practice was a young Melbourne architect, Kenneth Oliphant. In May 1927, Oliphant opened his own professional practice in Canberra and was to design many distinguished homes and public buildings in Canberra in the years to come.

Oakley and Parkes also designed a number of comfortable single-storey homes for senior officials in Acton on a rise of land above the administrative buildings. These homes were built of timber on the understanding that they could be moved as they were not part of the city plan. They are still there today, a valued heritage precinct of the Australian National University. One of them, 20 Balmain Crescent, became the home of the Daley family.

Officers being transferred from Melbourne were to receive financial compensation for their home there, and could arrange to rent a dwelling in Canberra or purchase it with a deposit and payments over twenty-five or thirty-five years. The Commission set up an office in Melbourne to give advice and help to families on their move. Everyone was assured that there would be a suitable home to go to by the time they arrived in Canberra. The Commission published a booklet, *General Notes for the Information of Public Servants*, explaining what facilities were being made available in Canberra; it also included designs of more than twenty homes from which prospective buyers could select one that suited them (and their salary).[14]

At the same time, there was an urgent need for accommodation for manual workers and their families. Henry Rolland, an architect employed by Works and Railways, pointed out that 'respectable artisans and their families' would not be attracted to Canberra unless suitable accommodation was available for them. In October 1923, Rolland had designed a simple cottage of Oregon timber on raised footings, with living room, open fire, two bedrooms and a kitchen and bathroom with indoor toilet. By June 1924, forty of these temporary wooden cottages had been built near Parliament House 'well screened from view' by an intervening ridge; and more were to be built near the Power House and at Acton. The cottages were intended to be temporary and portable, but they were provided with plumbing for sewerage which suggested they would be in place for some years. Owen asserted that sewerage was necessary on public health and safety grounds.

The Molonglo internment camp, now reduced in size and refurbished as a workers' settlement, housed many of the workforce for the major construction sites. The men crowded the Molonglo siding early each morning for the train that took them into Kingston. A strong community spirit grew at the camp, fostered partly by a sense of shared lives and hardships, and by a determination to have their views heard by the Commission.

For people who had grievances, the Commission appeared to be an impersonal and autocratic body which failed to understand the problems of ordinary citizens. A meeting in June 1925 saw some union representatives approaching Butters with a request to adjust their working hours: could they work the forty-four-hour week over five days rather than spread it over Saturday morning? They were keen to have the weekend for rest and recreation or to visit their families out of Canberra. The request was not approved and the men continued to work on Saturday morning. Those who didn't turn up were dismissed.

Butters was conscious that his large work force was living in indifferent conditions, but his approach to the problem was to appeal for everyone's cooperation. He had in mind a large community effort to improve facilities with the Commission's help. In April 1925, he drafted a letter for circulation to all the work camps. 'It must be appreciated by all employees that the living conditions on a construction site are less than ideal – so it is all the more essential that all concerned cooperate to improve facilities.'[15]

This initiative by Butters was well received and groups responded with a host of suggestions: for recreation halls at each camp; for children's playgrounds; for evening classes and libraries; for sports ovals and mothers' circles. A meeting was arranged at Acton recreation hall on the night of 18 May to further discuss all these issues. It was to be a men's evening; Butters would see the ladies at a later date. Motor cars and charabancs were organised to bring along union delegates and camp representatives.

The meeting did not take the form Butters had intended. Many of the men were angry, wanting a chance to air their grievances about living conditions at the camps. The Molonglo men had complaints about muddy roads and drains, draughty timber walls, shared ablution blocks with no privacy, vermin infesting the roofs and eaves of the buildings. Mr L. O'Neill considered 'the Molonglo tenements a disgrace to the Commonwealth'.[16]

Butters was a tough negotiator, with years of experience in addressing the grievances of large bodies of men and in getting the results he wanted. He reminded O'Neill that the Commission had promised to initiate a large workmen's housing scheme of one hundred cottages and a large contract had been let to erect a tradesmen's mess – but such work could not be done in a minute. What was preferable, he asked the meeting: to put up with some inconvenience for a few weeks, or ask the Commission to turn away the fellows who asked for work and send them back to Broken Hill? He also stated quite bluntly the reality of the housing position: 'there is not the slightest hope of every married man being accommodated with a cottage – to do so would take as long as to build 3 or 4 capitals'.[17]

An amended motion put to the meeting accepted the Commission's assurances about housing and proceeded to discuss welfare at the camps. Butters won the move that evening.

Butters had a grant of £15,000 from Home and Territories and at the meeting he promised the Commission's help in getting community initiatives underway. For every pound's worth of effort, one pound would be made available by the Commission up to £5,000. Committees were elected that night to plan projects for recreation (indoor and outdoor), education, libraries and children's and women's welfare. Three members of the Commission staff, James Brackenreg, Harry Mouat and Percy Sheaffe, volunteered their time to assist the committees. By November 1925, a social services association had been elected, run by a paid departmental officer, Mr Waterman.

In the winter of 1925, workers at the Power House and adjacent workshops moved into their newly built wooden cottages and there was strong demand for a local hall to be built as a recreation centre. A Causeway progress association was formed to advance the project.

The building of the Causeway hall was the earliest and the most successful of Butters' initiatives to promote community spirit and improve community welfare in the territory. The Commission provided the materials to build the hall and departmental labour for the interior joinery; it also put on transport for the workers to the site from their camps for the Saturday work party on 29 November. The local community, under the auspices of the Social Services Association, would provide labour to erect the hall. A committee of ladies was organised to provide morning and afternoon tea and lunch on the Saturday. Mr F.E. Priddle, superintendent of building construction at Parliament House, had volunteered to supervise construction and would have exclusive control of the whole undertaking. Feeling the pressure of work at Parliament House, he withdrew from the project, but on a request from the Commission he relented; he would see the hall project through to its completion.

At the last minute, it seemed that the planned community day might not proceed. Butters heard rumours that the unions were opposed to voluntary labour doing the job. On 25 November, Butters sent a terse letter to Mr Brill, president of the local branch of the Carpenters' and Joiner's Union.

> The Commission will not construct halls in temporary locations unless the great majority of workmen are standing behind the scheme. The organisation for Saturday is complete, the women have made all the arrangements for refreshments; it will now rest entirely with the men as to whether the effort is successful...[18]

In the event, the unions did not boycott the project, and after two successful weekends (with progress recorded hour by hour by the Commission's photographer William Mildenhall) the bulk of the construction was completed. Local men came back in their own time, on summer evenings and at weekends, to finish the job.

The official opening of the hall took place on 6 February 1926 and was an event where all sections of the community were represented. Buses brought people from the camps and settlements scattered around the valley: from Ainslie Hotel, White City Camp, the Bachelors' Quarters at Acton, from Red Hill Camp, from Westridge and Westlake and from the Molonglo camp. Public servants and their families came from Blandfordia and Acton. The Canberra City band played lively selections of popular tunes before the 8 p.m. opening and a tableau, 'Advance Australia', was performed by the Causeway children and Boy Scouts. Butters, seasoned administrator that he was, gave a morale-boosting speech

> I have been in quite a number of towns in Australia that do not own a permanent hall as attractive as this temporary one, and I have seldom seem a finer looking and sturdier audience and heard so excellent an orchestra as is here tonight.[19]

From the start, there was a high demand from community groups for use of the facilities. Dances were held to raise funds for the local football club, the Koalas; the Church of England held church services and Sunday schools there; a grand concert by the Canberra Philharmonic Society was to be broadcast on Radio 2FC on 17 July 1926; boxing matches were held in June 1926, organised by the Fire Brigade Recreation Club. (Two of the Federal Capital Commissioners, Sir John Harrison and Mr Gorman, were interested spectators.) Mr William Freebody, who ran the local garage in Queanbeyan, gained the licence to show moving pictures twice a week and drew large crowds who paid to watch such early classics as *The Ten Commandments* and *For the Term of his Natural Life*. In 1927, Freebody took over the licence to show pictures at the newly built Manuka Hall but the Causeway Hall remained a popular venue for dances and social gatherings.

In December 1924, the first auction of residential and business sites was held as the government took the step of including private enterprise in the role of building the city. The first houses were finished and offered for sale in 1925 and a small shopping centre grew up at Eastlake. Further auctions were held in 1926 and 1927. Commission architect Henry Rolland designed a number of standard homes, and small suburban settlements sprang up to the north of the river at Ainslie and to the south, at Eastlake and Blandfordia. Thomas Weston's work in planting avenues of trees, shelter belts and parks gave the garden city its first tentative shape on the Molonglo plain.

In 1927, the Melbourne and Sydney buildings designed by John Sulman were erected in the area that Griffin had designated as the city's commercial and civic centre. The first insurance companies were setting up office in Civic and new banks were operating, besides the Commonwealth Bank which had been established at Acton in 1913. Griffin had envisaged boulevards with shops along their length interspersed with apartment blocks; but the Civic Centre that was built did not follow this European pattern. Sulman in fact had judged that such a city design was foreign to Australian tastes and to the garden city concept. The Civic buildings consisted of two colonnaded blocks facing each other across the main road, surrounded, in the early days, by empty paddocks where a network of footpads through the grass led to the houses of Ainslie. Across the river, a similar network of tracks took workers and schoolchildren on short cuts across Capital Hill to the small shopping centre at Kingston and to the public school at Telopea Park.

On 28 November 1925, the commission was advised that the plan to establish a secretariat had been abandoned in favour of permanent transfers. Instead of 160 officers, as first proposed, nearly 900 were transferred, and office accommodation was in short supply, so premises were rented in the Sydney and Melbourne buildings.

The focus of the Commission's efforts in those years was the construction of the provisional Parliament House. Determined to provide an up-to-date and well-equipped home for parliament, Murdoch designed a building with central heating and air-conditioning, electric lifts and synchronised clocks. A pneumatic tube carrier system would provide instant communication with the printing office near the Power House and the Post Office. The office produced the vast output of printed material generated at parliamentary sittings and also supplied other government printing needs.

From 1923, the building site at Parliament House was a hub of activity. A light railway carried bricks from the Brickworks to the site; at a joinery near the Power House, apprentices and their supervisors created fine interior fittings for the building. Owen had arranged well in advance to acquire seasoned timber from each state of the Commonwealth and the timber was stacked under cover at the Joinery.

At one stage, Owen had to investigate charges of large-scale wastage and corruption at the building site. He was able to refute these charges but he did admit that workmen took timber offcuts for their own use. They thought the offcuts were as much their property as the government's, and they found plenty of use for them in constructing fowl runs and domestic furniture. Windows, some with a fine decorative detail round the border, were ordered in bulk. Some, excess to requirements, were stored and later made available to the public at auction. Hugh McCormack, who had acquired the Tuggeranong Homestead property after C.E.W. Bean's years of residence, acquired some of these windows which were fitted into his 1950s woolshed and still have pride of place there.

The first administrative building to serve the provisional parliament was opened in 1926 and became known as East Block. A post office with a 2,000-line automatic telephone exchange was established there in 1927, providing an essential service for the functioning of Parliament and also for the convenience of Canberra residents. Before that, the only telephone lines were at Acton Post Office, where long queues of men waited to make trunk calls to their families in Sydney or Melbourne.

At the opening of Parliament on 9 May 1927, the government arranged for all eastern capital cities to be linked by landline to Canberra so they could hear the Duke of York's speech and Dame Nellie Melba singing the national anthem. It was judged a striking success, though the overseas coverage was less so. *The Times* reported from London that the broadcast failed, as nothing intelligible was heard. But the event received extensive and positive coverage in the national press and in England as well. *The London Daily Telegraph* commented that 'Canberra will undoubtedly be one of the finest capitals in existence, to which a distinctive Australian character will be given by the prevalence of the single-storey type of house which is general throughout the Commonwealth.' *The Times* announced that 'the curtain is now being unrolled on a very great stage'. *The Sydney Morning Herald* referred to 'brilliant ceremonials'. Even the Melbourne press dropped its usual combative stance towards the new capital. *The Argus* devoted two full pages to the ceremonies, calling it 'a brilliant pageant'.[20] It reported that the federal offices in the city had all stopped work to listen to the full proceedings and, throughout Melbourne, many municipal town halls set up loud speakers to convey the ceremony to assembled crowds.

Charles Daley was responsible for organising an evening concert in the Senate chamber during the festivities. He arranged for three singers to come down from Sydney to perform, as well as a local group of musicians with Daley as pianist. The program was broadcast by Sydney radio station 2FC. (Another successful radio broadcast took place on 5 September 1927, when 2FC transmitted an address by Prime Minister Bruce and a musical program which was heard by several millions of British people and by millions in India.)

Prime Minister Stanley Bruce and his wife Ethel took up residence in the new Prime Minister's Lodge a few days before the opening of Parliament and provided hospitality and a bed for a number of visitors including Lord Somers, Governor of Victoria, and his wife, Lady Somers.

Eirene Mort, a well-established Sydney artist, offered the Commission a series of her Canberra sketches to have on display during the celebrations. Eirene, who often stayed with her Crace cousins at Gungahleen, a property north of Canberra, had been intrigued by the mix of old and new in the territory, and wanted especially to capture on paper the fast disappearing relics of early settlement and rural life. Her sketches, instead of portraying the new Commonwealth buildings, showed a quiet, largely unpeopled landscape with ruined barns and derelict cottages. The Commission, with its eye on the future, thought the collection 'unsuitable', and it was shown instead at a Sydney exhibition.

There had been hopes that many visitors from interstate might plan to visit Canberra for the opening of Parliament (and for a view of royalty) but only the most hardy and determined travellers made the trip. A Canberra winter was on its way – and the only option for travellers was a camp by the river, all hostel accommodation being fully booked for important visitors. The motorists' association, NRMA, felt that motorists had been actively discouraged from visiting, as the Commission had restricted visitors to 'five in a party', and the campsite was a good mile or two's walk from Parliament House. A few days before the opening, the campsite was shifted to within easy reach of the proceedings, but the authorities still could give no guarantees till the last moment – if interstate visitors failed to show – that a seat in the stands would be available. Neither could they make any provision for meals – or for tent poles. However, thousands of meat pies from Sargents Pie Company were ordered for consumption on the day. The Canberra and Queanbeyan folk who came must have been a thrifty lot who brought their own picnic baskets, and thousands of the pies ended up being buried as landfill. Thirty thousand commemorative florins were also printed with 'plenty left over' for later purchase.

The following day, the royal couple attended a public reception which took the form of a slow procession of people filing past the steps of Parliament House to doff their hats or wave at the Duke and his wife. Among the people in that procession were a group of Canberra pioneers who were invited to attend because of their special associations with the early years of white settlement on the Limestone Plains. The story of their lives reached back to a time when ticket-of-leave men still worked in the region and bushrangers accosted coaches and travellers on country roads. At least fifteen elderly gentlemen and womenfolk were among this group, most of them in their eighties or nineties. Mr John Gale, ninety-seven years of age, and his wife, Elizabeth, were driven to Parliament House in a Commonwealth car. Gale wrote to John Butters from his Queanbeyan home, 'But for my extreme age, I would walk out and back rather than miss the Culmination of my efforts for the past many years to see Canberra [as the national capital].'[21]

The one group who were not invited to this celebratory event were the Aboriginal people of the region, though two Wiradjuri men, Jimmy Clements and John Noble, walked over the mountains from Brungle Mission near Tumut to be present at the ceremony with their dogs. It seems that at least Clements was present at the opening on 9 May, when police tried to remove him as he was 'inappropriately dressed'. Clements refused to leave. His presence there gave novelty value to the scene for many white onlookers and perhaps aroused a half-acknowledged sense of fellow-feeling. 'He had a better right than any man to a place,' declared one onlooker, a clergyman.[22] The crowd, moved to a display of support, threw a shower of coins at Jimmy's feet. Clements was also among the crowd who walked in procession past the royal couple the following day.

Jimmy Clements, also known as King Billy, died three months later in Queanbeyan and was buried in unconsecrated ground. No Aboriginals received burial in consecrated ground in cemeteries.

*

The completion of Parliament House and its opening could be said to be the high point of the Federal Capital Commission's work for Canberra. Its chief officer and senior bureaucrats were all honoured with imperial awards that week. Butters received a knighthood; Daley, Rolland and Thomas Hill each received an OBE. Thomas Weston, in retirement in Sydney by then, came down for some months to supervise plantings around the new building and received the award of MBE.

From 1925 to 1929, Butters had oversight of a workforce of up to 3,000 tradesmen and labourers as well as men working on contract. There were plenty of obstacles on the way. In plastering the walls of Parliament House, the Commission had to bear the expense of moving the plasterers and their families to Canberra and returning them on completion of the work. Every aspect of building the city came under the management of the Commission and its decisive chief officer, and the range of its control was the widest ever entrusted to a single authority in Australia. Daley summed up the prime purpose behind the Commission's work: 'the building of a national capital on virgin soil [sic], adhering to a previously accepted plan, designed to serve not the present generation but the distant future'.[23]

In fact, the Commission represented a unique type of governance for Australia. Its files document the creation of great national institutions: Parliament House; the Solar Observatory at Mount Stromlo; the Australian War Memorial; the national School of Forestry; the Institute of Anatomy. At the same time, it functioned like a town council in a small rural township. It collected money from its ratepayers and it enforced the local ordinances that had been created for the territory: garbage collection; control of stray dogs; movement of stock through the territory; local bus services; road maintenance... It was at this parochial level that a good deal of friction occurred between the Commission and the territory's residents, whose complaints were all the stronger as they had no role in electing this form of local government. The Minister for Home and Territories summed up the problem succinctly in a statement in Parliament:

> ...although under the Commission system, much valuable work was done under conditions of extraordinary difficulty...eventually, it completely failed to obtain the approval of the citizens who were compelled to live under it...[24]

John Butters resigned from his position as Chief Commissioner in October 1929 to be replaced briefly by A.J. Christie, former Deputy Director of Queensland's Postal Institute. John Murdoch was appointed Second Commissioner. But by that stage, the Commission's role was coming to an end. The creation of a national capital, even on the modest terms outlined by the FCAC and the Commission, seemed extravagant and unnecessary to a country facing an uncertain economic and political future. As well, there was increasing dissatisfaction in Canberra with the lack of voting rights. In response to local agitation, the Nationalist government in late 1928 passed an amendment to the 1924 Seat of Government Act which provided for one of the three commissioners to be elected by Canberrans. The elected Commissioner, Dr J.F. Watson, took up duty on 7 February 1929 but refused to cooperate with the Commission, holding strong views in favour of a locally elected municipal form of government for Canberra.

When Labor assumed office in 1929, the incoming Prime Minister, Jim Scullin, made clear his opposition to Canberra. He condemned the city as a white elephant, 'miles on miles of roads, footpaths and kerbing... with barely a house in sight!'[25] Under Labor, the Commission was to be abolished and Canberra would once again find itself under the divided control of a number of government departments.

Charles Daley saw this as a backward step. He thought it of interest that the United States, democratic as it was, had for the past fifty years governed its federal territory by a commission of three men nominated by the President. For himself, he had found the years of hard work and single-minded focus on a national goal to have been worthwhile and productive: he called the Commission era 'the Golden Years' of Canberra, and he remained a strong defender of Butters and his work.

A farewell social was held for Butters and his wife at the Albert Hall on 11 October 1929. There were about 200 people present, with speeches from staff members including Daley. 'I have never worked among a better body of men than the officers of the Commission,' he told an attentive audience. Mr Rowe, President of the Returned Servicemen's League, expressed his appreciation of Butters with a cryptic message but one that the audience clearly understood: he was 'a big-minded man and his shoulders have carried many burdens which others should be carrying...'[26]

At this gathering, Butters himself reflected on the sense of high purpose that had prompted their work. 'In the first year, every scrap of work I asked from the staff was done willingly.' Later he was to respond to Scullin's disparaging remarks, defending the Commission's work with pride and some degree of bitterness:

This Commission not only achieved the almost impossible task of building a city from the ground upward – and a good bit under the ground too – but has managed an enormous business in which nearly £12 million was invested; administered a territory of approximately 1,000sq miles; operated and managed a huge land estate and home rental business; constructed ten hotels, 1,500 homes and public buildings; managed a hospital, a dozen schools, a bus system – in fact everything from the maternity homes to the cemetery. The Commission has built and now operates a water supply system, a sewerage system, a fire brigade, electricity supply, brickworks, pipeworks – recreation halls and grounds for the people.

It has been between the Scylla of the public servants and MPs wanting cheap accommodation and the Charybdis of Parliaments and Governments complaining of the cost. It is nonsense to suggest a task as has been accomplished in Canberra by the Commission during the last five years could have been carried out by officers of existing departments who are reasonably fully occupied in their existing duties.[27]

7 Town and Country

The concerns of rural landholders formed a regular part of Commission business.'

Eddison family at 'Yamba'.
Reproduced with permission of Canberra & District Historical Society

The Federal Capital Commission's work reached into every aspect of life in the territory and affected suburban householders, private businesses and rural landholders to various degrees. Many criticisms were levelled at it over the years. It was labelled 'a quasi-feudal domain'; it was condemned for living in the Victorian age in its attempts to regulate citizens' behaviour.[1] Above all, it was considered undemocratic in its governance.

One area of territory life that needed the Commission's early attention was the liquor question. In 1911, King O'Malley's rhetoric had won enough support in Parliament to allow him to introduce a liquor ordinance. A clause in the 1911 Act stated that no new liquor licences were to be issued in the FCT; the one hotel in operation, the Cricketers' Arms, was closed in 1918 after its licence expired. This clause did not establish a prohibition state; it was still quite legal for people to purchase liquor outside the territory and bring it back for their own consumption.

As the building of the provisional Parliament House progressed and members began seriously to consider the prospect of moving to Canberra, anxiety was expressed about the supply of alcohol. Would a bar – a parliamentary fixture in Spring Street – be installed in the new House? After questions were asked in the House of Representatives in March 1926, the press announced that a bar would be installed in Parliament House in contravention of the 1911 law.

The government received a deluge of letters, mainly from national church bodies and women's organisations, opposing changes to the law.

The officers of the Commission knew quite well that the law as it stood was not working. In July 1926, Butters submitted a report to Parliament. He pointed out the law's absurdity: '1,000 square miles of the country was dry and the rest of Australia as wet as can be'.[2] This posed a special problem in Canberra. Up to 50% of the territory's workforce would be in Queanbeyan on Friday or Saturday afternoons, drinking in long sessions that brought a roaring trade to the local pubs and left a trail of mayhem in their wake: fights in the street; men vomiting in the gutters; the police lock-up crowded at weekends. Men also brought liquor back to their mates at the camps or purchased it from illicit stills down by the river. Alcohol left its potent mark on lives which in many cases were already damaged by the war, by loneliness and hardship and by the alienation that came from a life of drifting.

Butters found that there was a noticeable drop in work output in the territory on Mondays and that the road to Queanbeyan was becoming dangerous to drive on at weekends. He reported that about 7,000 dozen empty bottles were consigned by rail to Sydney or Goulburn in the first three months of 1926: there were 3,000 men in the camps at that time. Butters stated that it was only the vigilance of the local police, Sergeant Cook and his constables, that had kept the situation in check. He felt that the law was inequitable: the rich could afford to order cases of liquor for delivery from a Goulburn merchant and could drink their whisky or beer in the comfort of their own home. The poor had to make the trip to Queanbeyan at the weekend or consume their purchases in the chilly solitude of their camp barracks.

Over the years, a number of police reports were made relating to alcohol-fuelled violence in the camps leading to injury or death – sometimes a lonely suicide. Harry Crawford, returned soldier, 'a quiet, inoffensive man', cut his throat with a razor after drinking heavily for two weeks. Percy Winburn, a returned soldier who had lost a leg during the war, died at Eastlake Camp 'after excessive drinking of methylated spirits'.[3]

Prime Minister Stanley Bruce took a public stance to support the current liquor law. As guest of honour at the Returned Servicemen's Banquet on Remembrance Day in 1926, he directed that the luncheon was to be a 'dry' event or he would decline to attend it. Consequently, the luncheon was held without alcohol.

However, the banquet after the opening of Parliament House on 9 May 1927 had an extensive drinks list including champagne, whisky and beer – probably purchased from one of the Queanbeyan hotels.

The double standards operating in the community could not be ignored.

Throughout 1928, a number of lobby groups petitioned the government about a proposed plebiscite. The No-Licence League wanted the law to remain unchanged. A group of Canberra businessmen led by a Commonwealth Bank officer hoped for a reasonable adjustment to the law as they were losing a lot of business to Queanbeyan.

The plebiscite was held in Canberra on 1 September 1928. It was to be the first ballot ever to be conducted in the Federal Capital Territory, though residents had voted in the two conscription referenda during the war. Four options were given to the voters: complete prohibition; continuation of the present ordinance; sale of liquor under public control; sale of liquor at licensed premises. A majority of citizens voted for the last option, with licensed hotels obtaining the right to sell alcohol.

'It will mean a lot more work for me,' a policeman declared morosely, 'but there will be some compensations.'

'It'll be all right to get a drink after work,' one man asserted, 'and it won't be my fault if I can't get it.'[4]

William Mildenhall, the Commission photographer, captured on film the moment when workers from the Ainslie Hotel met the first truck load of cartons of Cascade Ale brought in from Tasmania.

For the time being, NSW liquor laws would apply in the territory, with one or two alterations. No barmaids were to be employed: the Commission considered it to be a morally compromising and degrading job for women; and there were to be no bars in hotels, drinking to be done at seated tables in saloons. The Commission controlled the licensing of the hotels, and to cater for the workmen in the camps, it leased shop premises in three centres, Civic, Kingston and Manuka. These premises, to be known as 'cafés' and modelled somewhat optimistically on a European model of social drinking, brought in a steady stream of customers when they first opened on 23 December 1928.

The territory's own Liquor Ordinance came into force in July 1929. It allowed licensed hotels in Canberra (there were three of them) to serve liquor between 9 a.m. and 6 p.m., and also at evening meals to bona fide travellers. Booth licences were created so liquor could be served at places like sports carnivals or horse races. The Commission still maintained control of two liquor cafés, at Kingston and Civic; the one at Manuka had closed for lack of business. The cafés were a lucrative source of income for the Commission, but to most of the populace they were seen as offensive, dirty and disorderly, with roughly constructed counters and sawdust-strewn floors. A departmental memo likened them to the saloons of a mining township. *The Canberra Times* compared them to 'the worst type of drinking booth at some outback race meeting'.[5] In effect, the newspaper accused the Commission of being 'Australia's worst publican'. Temperance groups considered the cafés a disgrace that had brought great discredit to the city. Many people also felt that the Commission was not respecting the results of the plebiscite, which had clearly indicated people's wish for all drinking establishments to be run by independent licensed hoteliers.

The liquor cafés were finally closed after 1935, when all establishments came under the ownership of licensed hotels. The Commission's failure in what it had seen as a 'civilising' step, is surely an ironic footnote to its story, for these were men guided by high moral principles who believed they were acting in the public's best interests.

*

John Butters had years of experience of the large construction camps built in the Tasmanian highlands for the Hydro Electric Commission. It was a bleak environment and a harsh workplace and not conducive to a settled community life. Butters was determined to create something different as the new city took shape, with the first public servants arriving from Melbourne and hundreds of workers moving into temporary cottages with their families. He had in mind an ideal community in which workers from all levels of society pooled their talents, energy and interests to create amenities that were valued and well used and that promoted social harmony. The Commission booklet set the tone for what he hoped to achieve and the Social Service Association was created as an expression of his hopes. He was calling for an act of goodwill from all, backed up by close supervision by the Commission of programs he regarded as in the public interest.

The modern reader is bemused by the minutiae that took up the Commission's attention as they organised the life of the citizens. In January 1925, Butters initiated the idea of a regular Saturday dance at the Hotel Canberra (Hostel 1 became known as the Hotel Canberra under the Commission). In memos circulated to staff and to Surveyor General Goodwin, he pondered on the planning of the event: should dinner jackets be compulsory? (Butters thought not – due to 'the local difficulties of laundering boiled shirts'). What was to be provided for supper? Was an electric piano player available? After all, Butters conceded, the main thing to ensure an enjoyable evening for all was 'a satisfactory tone; this can be achieved by rigid supervision'.[6] There were to be no dances or playing of music in Commission hostels on a Sunday. Butters also instigated a ruling prohibiting organised sport on Sundays, an unpopular ruling which was still in force in the 1930s.

School welfare issues also occupied the time of the Chief Commissioner, though many of the details were delegated to the child welfare branch of the Social Services Association. In July 1925, Butters agreed to the erection of a shelter shed at Westlake next to the school bus stop; and a crossing was provided at Yarralumla Creek so that children living at the Cotter could reach home safely. In August that year, Butters wrote to Broken Hill Smelters at Port Pirie asking for plans and advice on children's playgrounds.

The first half of the century saw a fashion for house names engraved on brass at the front door. This was an appealing idea in Canberra, where in the early days houses had no street numbers. In 1925, Butters asked for a schedule of proposed names to be submitted to the Commission for approval. George O'Neill wrote to Butters with a proposal:

W. Willmott and I, returned diggers, decided to try our luck at Canberra City. Being sign writers and decorators we thought it would be nice if every house had a nice Aboriginal name. We have a number done (in Black and Gold) and orders for a lot more... Major Butters, I am trusting and hoping you will give this stint of ours a hoist. We are living in the small railway cabin opposite the Canberra Railway Station. Please Major, see us through this deal...[7]

George O'Neill's offer was not taken up by the Commission. However, a committee to investigate street names for the new capital had been set up in 1923 with Charles Daley as one of its members.

The Commission was often accused of promoting class distinctions in Canberra through its housing policy. This meant that the more expensive range of government-designed homes, affordable only by senior public servants, were being built in Blandfordia and Red Hill and more modest dwellings including weatherboard cottages, with a cap on the price that would put them in reach of lower-income officials, were being built in Reid, Kingston and Ainslie. Social differences did develop between suburbs, as they do in any Australian city, but conditions in early Canberra favoured a certain amount of democratic mingling. Everyone shopped at Kingston, where J.B. Youngs had opened the first general emporium, went to the moving pictures at the Manuka cinema and attended outdoor sports events at the newly built ovals. Telopea School catered for the children of senior officials, businessmen and workmen alike, as well as the children of local pioneering families, though the opening of the Church of England Boys Grammar School and St Gabriels School for Girls introduced the privileges of private schooling to middle-class families; and in 1927 St Christophers school for Roman Catholic families was opened at Manuka.

The concerns of rural landholders formed a regular part of Commission business. In 1923, the Minister for Home and Territories had approved the establishment of a three-member Land Board to recommend details in the administration and control of FCT lands. The board comprised John Goodwin, Percy Sheaffe and an accountant Charles Horsburg – all government men. The Commission reconstituted the board with Commissioner Clarence Gorman as chairman, Lands Officer James Brackenreg, and a territory lessee, Edward Crace of Gungahlin. Charles Daley was to act as secretary to the board, which was to interview applicants for new leases and to oversee the conditions of the leases.

Rural leaseholders had many concerns they wanted to bring to the attention of the Commission. They felt their lease conditions were onerous: they considered they were burdened with unfair rents and with the heavy cost of improvements yet they had only limited tenure on their land and often their holdings were too small to be profitable or give economies of scale. In April 1926, they formed a lobby group, the Federal Capital Lessees Association, which represented 'the Primary producers who supply Canberra'.

At their second annual dinner, held on 19 July 1927, Daley, as a spokesman for the Commission, appealed for 'the development of a civic spirit' in Canberra. John Goodwin, another guest speaker, spoke of the importance of primary production in the territory: about £40,000 was received as revenue from primary producers in the territory in one year compared to £12,000 in the city area. There were 244 lessees in the territory outside the city area, and these included dairy farms, market gardeners and poultry farms. One man had a rooster valued at sixty-five guineas.[8]

After Clarence Gorman's death in 1929, Daley was appointed as new chairman of the board. It was a position that attracted a great deal of animosity from lessees, as the board was seen to be administering territory lands without proper consultation with the leaseholders. The coming Depression was to cause great hardship for many small leaseholders.

James Brackenreg, Chief Lands Officer for the Commission, knew the land and knew the men who often struggled to make a living on it. Before coming to Canberra, he had been rabbit inspector for the Narrabri Pastures Protection Board, with seventy miles of rabbit-proof fence under his control. Arriving in Canberra, he set about vigorously attacking the rabbit plague which was destroying the capital lands. Knowing that their property was eventually to be acquired, many landowners had not destroyed rabbit warrens for years. Along the southern banks of the Molonglo River, near where the Hotel Canberra was to be built, was a rabbit warren two acres in extent.

Brackenreg began a process of eradication that involved netting, trapping, poisoning and ripping of burrows. The dogmen with their packs of twenty dogs rounded up the last few rabbits in what was to become the city area. As well, Brackenreg was advising landholders on weed and pest control on their rural blocks. His skills on the land saw him assisting with the valuation of properties during the acquisition of freehold land by the Commonwealth.

Brackenreg brought his family to Canberra in 1913 and in 1915 moved into the groom's residence at Yarralumla House. He was away frequently, driving off alone into the mountains with food and gear for five days as he inspected lonely properties in the south and west of the territory. By 1925, his duties included valuation of city blocks, management of city as well as rural leases, management of travelling stock, bushfire control, abattoir supervision, administration of Jervis Bay land, promotion of pastoral and agricultural education, forestry and management of Commission cottages.

This array of responsibilities meant that Brackenreg was well known to most Canberra residents in one capacity or another. He was a strong defender of the leasehold system – he knew how hard it was to acquire land without capital – and he often served as a spokesman for men struggling on their properties. In defence of a man who needed help to prevent theft from his market garden, he wrote, 'Murray's war service and actions as a lessee stamp him as one deserving of more than ordinary consideration.'[9] At the same time, he was assiduous in guarding government interests and expected that lessees would not try to exploit the system. He wrote to Daley in March 1932, pointing out that there were 'occasions when the government is being imposed upon'. He quoted two examples, one a city block, one a rural block, which had long outstanding rent payments but whose lessees were 'frequent visitors and competitors at the golf links. While this is purely their own business, I think it is also ours, in that some of that money might be diverted to the Treasury.'[10]

The roads through the territory formed part of the travelling stock route system of NSW. To reach the abattoir or the trucking yards at Queanbeyan, men had to travel their stock across the Molonglo River, which was known to flood. Brackenreg took up their cause in requesting the urgent construction of a bridge over the river at Coppins Crossing. At the same time, he was vigilant in supervising and encouraging better land management, with fines imposed on leaseholders who were careless about weed control, carried out unnecessary ringbarking or let their stock stray.

In 1926, he recommended that dogs not be allowed in work camps, till some officials expressed the opinion that men in the camps were as much entitled to a dog as a person in a residence. Brackenreg was prepared to give it a trial; he thought the Dog Ordinance would be able to handle any problems. He paid many visits to grazing properties which were troubled by large losses of sheep by marauding packs of dogs which had escaped from their owners and were running wild or had come across the border from NSW.

Brackenreg's wife, Helen, clearly shared his energy and initiative. When the family first arrived in Canberra, they had use of a few rooms at the old Springbank farm at Acton, where Helen cooked on an open fire in the garden. In later years, she was taken aback by the negative attitudes of families coming from Melbourne to a Commission-built house. She had known the surveyors' wives in the early days who often lived in tents: newly-wedded Percy Sheaffe and his wife Katie lived under canvas with the surveying teams in 1913. Even David Miller's wife lived for a time in a tent while the Residency was being built.

Helen Brackenreg had left school at twelve to look after younger siblings. The death of a sister as a child and her acquaintance with the health problems of isolated women gave her a strong interest in maternal and child welfare and she later trained as a nurse. She was a foundation member of the Canberra Mothercraft Society and served it continuously for the next twenty-one years. Helen was active in many community organisations in Canberra and also proved to be an astute businesswoman. At the first sale of private residential blocks in December 1924, Brackenreg had purchased six blocks. Helen arranged for houses to be built on the blocks and subsequently sold them and purchased three commercial blocks in the Sydney Building, one of the colonnaded business and shopping blocks designed by John Sulman for the Civic Centre.

The family built their own house in 1928 on a spacious block of land at Red Hill. The garden was designed by friend and former colleague, Thomas Weston, who came down from his retirement in Sydney to inspect the block and advise on garden design. The Brackenregs' daughter, Ruth, remembered that Weston was always a kind and gentle person and a very close friend of her parents. After Thomas Weston died in December 1935, James Brackenreg and Weston's successor, Alexander Bruce, were chosen by the family to scatter his ashes among the trees and parkland he had designed in front of Parliament House.

*

The Commission's final year was marked by Percy Owen's departure from Canberra to take up a new life in Wollongong. After divorcing his first wife in June 1928, he had married Sylvia Hoad in April 1929 and retired from Commonwealth service the next month. The *Canberra Times* wrote an editorial on 10 May, referring to 'the monumental service to the Commonwealth and to Canberra of a gentleman [who had] done more for the establishment and development of the Federal Capital than any other single man'. Even the eccentric King O'Malley considered Owen to be 'one of the ablest men south of the equator'.[11] The *Canberra Times* urged that some commemoration of his work should be made; they suggested that the site of the first Commonwealth structure in Canberra – the bunker housing the survey plans near Capital Hill – could be renamed Owen Place. This suggestion was never taken up and Owen remains without due recognition in Canberra. *The Australian Dictionary of Biography* considers that Lake Burley Griffin remains in part his legacy, as much of his work involved investigation of the Queanbeyan and Molonglo Rivers, essential research for the building of the lake; and its design conforms more to his ideas – and to Scrivener's – than to Griffin's. But Owen himself felt that his work had never been properly acknowledged. In September 1930, he wrote to Daley, 'Sir John, as far as I know, never sent on to the Commission my report on the Molonglo River and ornamental waters – the outcome of years of experience and a long period of investigation.'

For all his new-found domestic happiness, Owen still felt an exile, cast adrift from those vital professional concerns that had been such an important part of his life.

> I often think of Canberra and wish I could still have some hand in advising upon its development. I wonder at times whether many Canberrans think of me nowadays! And I wish I could meet again some of my old friends, you included. I seldom go to Sydney or Canberra – money so scarce now that I cannot well afford to.[12]

Charles Daley had worked under Owen's direction and then in close collaboration with him for over twenty years. After Owen's death in July 1936, Sylvia Owen wrote to Daley expressing her sense of loss, 'I am without ballast, a plant pulled up by the roots…' She sent Daley some reminders of their years of service together: '…he was always very fond of you'.[13] There were all the survey maps; a sketch of Parliament House; and a framed sample of the woods used in the building, which Owen had taken great pains to procure from every state in the Commonwealth.

8

The long slump

'Men from Parkes Barracks
appealed for a week's work, after
months of stultifying, enforced
idleness and semi-starvation.'

Workmen mixing concrete for roadworks, Duntroon Road (now Fairbairn Avenue).
From the collection of the National Archives of Australia

The financial crisis that engulfed the developed world in 1929 did not spare Canberra. By that stage, Owen had left the city, putting his years of involvement with the federal capital behind him. Charles Daley, a senior public servant by now but unsure what awaited him under the new dispensation, remained with his family in Canberra. He looked for other options, applying for a number of positions including Commissioner of Patents with the Registrar of Trade Marks and Design in March 1930.

John Butters would reach the end of his five-year term of appointment in October 1929. He had decided by then not to seek a second term, even though the government was planning to extend the life of the Commission for a further twelve months. It was clear to Butters that the financial constraints upon the Commission would only become more severe as time went by and the recession deepened. In June 1929, the government had required the Commission to reduce its estimates by 10%. In August there were to be further reductions of £450,000 in loan estimates. Charles Abbott, Minister for Home and Territories, wrote to Butters that 'the allotment of moneys will remain at a low figure for the next few years, and all idea of completing the transfer of the rest of the Public Service must be abandoned for the present...'[1]

Knowing that the Commission's days were numbered, Butters decided to resign. In accepting the job in 1924, he had anticipated there would be at least ten years of solid, challenging work ahead of him in Canberra. He was a man who liked meeting challenges: a combination of scientific and commercial knowledge in his management of the Tasmanian hydroelectric scheme saw it become the most profitable arm of the state government. It was a position which gave him a great deal of autonomy and allowed him to take bold initiatives. To stay on in Canberra meant he would be at the mercy of an unstable political climate and subject to the vagaries of departmental rule. 'I do not care to continue with Canberra as my principal work if it is reduced to an administrative job,' he wrote to Abbott in October 1929.[2] He requested annual leave for 1929 from 12 October, plus four weeks additional holiday, as he had taken very little leave in the previous four years. After his resignation, A.J. Christie was appointed as Chief Commissioner as an interim measure until the Commission was formally disbanded on 30 April 1930.

Butters was quite aware of the growing animosity directed at him and his officers. He knew that as long as the Commission carried out government policy, there was bound to be agitation against it. Public servants had been moved unwillingly from Melbourne and were a ready source of discontent about their houses, shopping facilities, transport and the cost of living. Landholders complained of high rentals, the leasehold system and interference by the Land Board. Manual workers and tradesmen complained about the condition of their temporary quarters and pressed for permanent housing. The local newspaper, the *Canberra Times*, ran a vigorous campaign for local representation in government. Its owner, Thomas Shakespeare, became a powerful spokesman for the community, firing off editorials which attacked the Commission as an autocratic system and gave voice to many community grievances. Increasing opposition to the Commission, and its claim to know best what citizens needed, saw the end of the Social Services Association which was disbanded in 1929.

In response to growing popular feeling, the government had restructured the Commission in late 1928 to allow the ratepayers of Canberra to elect the third commissioner. Dr Frederick Watson took his seat as Commissioner on 7 February 1929, and from the start made clear his hostility to the Commission and its work: he saw his role as agitating on popular issues, criticising Commission policy and attacking its chief officer. After a few weeks 'of most unseemly squabbling', he resigned as he felt he could not carry on his function 'as trustee for the Australian nation'.[3]

The next elected candidate, Dr John Alcorn, joined the Commission on 29 April 1929 and held this position till the Commission was disbanded on 30 April 1930 with the passage of a new Seat of Government (Administration) Act. Alcorn was another combative personality, complaining to Butters of his, Alcorn's, lack of power in the Commission. He accused Butters personally of excluding him from any meetings with departmental heads, and insisted that Butters seek £50,000 from Treasury to fund a full building program for tradesmen, even though Butters explained that 'there was no earthly chance of getting it'.[4]

With the passing of the 1930 Act and its accompanying Ordinance, a new administrative order for Canberra was established – the fifth since 1913. A Federal Capital Territory branch of the Department of Home Affairs was established, with C.S. Daley as its head as Civic Administrator. The branch was to carry out the activities of the former Commission except those transferred to three other departments: the Department of Works, the Attorney-General's Department, and the Department of Health. It was Daley's most senior position yet, but the job which had fired his imagination as a young man – to be involved in the creation of the federal capital – now seemed further out of reach. He wrote to Butters in the first week at Home Affairs, 'The situation has been very depressing, as you can well imagine. There has also been considerable confusion about practical matters that have not been worked out.'[5] Daley sent a memorandum to all his staff, many of whom had been specially selected for their position by the late Commission: '...the work upon which you have been engaged will in future be a responsibility of the Department of Home Affairs'.[6] This transfer of responsibilities could not have happened at a less favourable time. Daley was to find himself managing the impact of severe spending cuts and dismissal of staff over the next several years.

On 21 August 1930, an agreement had been signed in Melbourne between the Commonwealth and the states, based on the advice of a British financial mission led by Sir Otto Niemeyer. Niemeyer, concerned that Australia would not meet its obligations to repay debts to London bankers, insisted that the country's state and federal governments must reduce their deficits by cutting government spending, which meant, in effect, cutting the wages of their employees, sacking government workers and suspending development projects. This was acceptable economic rationale at the time but it was to worsen the effects of the Depression; as incomes were cut, spending fell and government deficits increased.

Canberra, still at an early stage of its development, desperately needed stimulation of its economy to encourage growth and employment opportunities; but instead it was faced, like the rest of Australia, with severe cuts to wages and a cessation of all new development works. Under the Financial Emergency Act of July 1931, there was a 22.5% cut in all public service salaries between £82 and £4,000. There were corresponding cuts in land rents, rates and electricity charges. Some rentals on rural properties were reduced by as much as one-third in view of the drastic decline in wool prices. All pensions, including age and repatriation pensions were reduced by 20% and there were cuts as well to maternity allowances and Commonwealth superannuation.

On 30 September 1930, rationing of employment, to which the Australian Workers Union (AWU) had agreed, was to begin in some Commonwealth departments. Daley had the task of rationing jobs in his branch. It would affect firstly the work of men in the Parks and Gardens section, though not those in a supervisory role. The ratio Daley suggested was one week's work in every three weeks for married men, three days' work in every four weeks for single men. The allocation of this work would depend upon the continuance of the Unemployment Relief Fund, to which the Commonwealth contributed 50%, with the rest coming from community fund-raising. At that time, September 1930, there were 154 unemployed married men in Canberra and 150 single men. By June 1931, the figures had jumped to 277 married men and 200 single men unemployed. Daley pointed out in his memo to the department that if single men were excluded from the rationing of jobs, the only alternative left would be supplying them with food rations, as the department could not expect that these men could be forcibly removed from Canberra. Rations had in fact already been issued to numerous deserving cases since May 1930. As well, sixty-seven youths from the territory were placed in various NSW government experimental farms as part of the Australian Youths' Settlement Scheme.

Daley spoke strongly against cutting jobs and expenditure in certain vital areas in the territory. Matters to do with public health and safety had first priority. There was to be an upgrading of sewerage works at Western Creek; additional pumping equipment at the Cotter; and repair of rotting timber on bridges. A 'one-armed, married returned soldier' attended to sanitation in the city area and must be kept on so that these services were not affected. In the Lands section, Daley insisted that the field staff of eleven rangers and seven labourers in rural districts be kept on; they had special knowledge of the territory and their work in catchment protection, rabbit control and fire control could not be compromised.

The east-west plantation area that Thomas Weston had advised planting as a windbreak in northern Canberra was another project that could not easily be abandoned. Lack of maintenance there would pose a grave fire risk to the area as well as destruction of the trees, a vital part of early urban planning for the city. Daley also advised against any reduction in forestry work, both to protect existing forests and to provide nursery stock for future plantings. Many gangs worked out in the Stromlo and Cotter catchment forests and in tree planting in the city area, work which was labour intensive and required little capital. Other relief work included chopping thistles on government land and clearing firebreaks around the city area.

Projects under the control of the Department of Works – the building of new houses, for example – were to be cut and no new loans were to be advanced for housing. The minister suggested to Daley that to offset this, money could be advanced for improving main road surfaces 'to lessen the dust nuisance' and for gravelling the Federal Highway to Goulburn. For the next few years, gangs of unemployed men working on roadsides and culverts would be a common sight in Canberra, many travelling to work in winter in their old AIF coats dyed navy blue.

There was to be no new acquisition of territory land for the foreseeable future. The education budget was cut by £15,000, which meant the new Canberra High School could not be built, even though Telopea public school was sorely overcrowded.

One of Canberra's first Commonwealth institutions, the Royal Military College, felt the impact of the Depression. Scullin's Labor government suspended compulsory military training from 1 November 1929 and there were cuts of 40% in defence expenditure. There were retrenchments in the permanent military forces and a drop in the number of graduates needed. The staff and students of the diminished college were to be transferred to Victoria Barracks in Sydney for the foreseeable future. From 1 January 1931, the Department of Works took over the college and houses at Duntroon, and in April transferred responsibility for the site and all its fixtures to Daley's Federal Capital branch. This branch was also to take over care and maintenance of General Bridges' grave. The Defence Department, 'owing to a shortage of funds', could not help with maintenance of the property, though the rifle range was to be retained by the department, and the cricket oval used for local matches. The laundry and boilers were dismantled and used at Canberra Hospital and the abattoirs. The college was not to return to Canberra until 1937.

The building projects that went ahead were the Institute of Anatomy, the Solar Observatory at Mount Stromlo and the swimming pool at Manuka, the latter project seen as an essential aid to public health and fitness. For many years, locals had swum in a weir below the Power House on the Molonglo River until tests conducted by Dr Robin Tillyard showed it to be the source of toxic bacteria.

Daley prepared a speech to be delivered at the opening of the pool on 26 January 1931, though in the end he was unable to be present. His notes referred to Walter Burley Griffin and his vision of the importance of water to a dry inland city: 'Some day Australia will realise the pleasant waters of Mr Griffin's dream. That day seems in these times so far ahead that none of us care to think much about it.'[7]

If that speech did not sound the note of bright and bland optimism expected of a public official, it did reflect Daley's own sense of the difficult times they were living through, from which there seemed no easy way out. Perhaps it also reflected his growing pessimism about the capacity of the present government to do anything constructive for Canberra.

As more and more men swelled the ranks of the unemployed, the prospect of people dying of want became for the first time a spectre to haunt Canberra and the rest of Australia. The issue of food rations – the last resort of a desperate government – came into force, with the Commonwealth Department of Health providing guidelines as to what would 'provide ample nourishment to sustain life in health during enforced idleness or very light work'.[8] The ration scales adopted from NSW contained bread, meat, flour, tea, sugar, oatmeal, jam, condensed milk (with fresh milk for children), butter, golden syrup, sago and rice, soap, cheese, potatoes, onions and prunes. Residents were encouraged to grow green vegetables for their vitamin content. In fact, vegetable gardens were found in most residents' backyards including many of the temporary workmen's settlements. In February 1933, Medical Superintendent Dr Nott found 'little or no evidence of deficiency diseases due to limited diet', though many older vagrant men were poorly nourished and had appalling teeth through unemployment and hard living. He saw a major problem as 'the profound ignorance among housewives in the provision of family meals'.[9] He suggested simple publicity and education at the ration depots might help.

Two camps were set up in Canberra for 'itinerants' coming to Canberra looking for work. In 1930, an old sewerage camp was renamed Parkes Barracks and housed single men, and Mount Ainslie camp served for married men with families who built humpies out of hessian and corrugated iron. With winter coming on, the men from Parkes Barracks scrounged for dead wood for their fires, pulling up wooden pegs to burn and collecting flood debris along the river, until firewood was supplied. Other small, unofficial camps cropped up, to which the administration turned a blind eye. Itinerant men received rations when they arrived in the territory and when they left, but they could not apply for work unless they were residents. Canberra Hospital treated many itinerant men who had heard of the fair and kindly treatment they received there.

In November 1931, men from Parkes Barracks appealed for a week's work. All were staunch Labor supporters; 50% were returned soldiers. They'd suffered 'months of stultifying, enforced idleness and semi-starvation'.[10] Many were in poor health as a result of their war service, so the cruelty of the Depression hit these returned men perhaps harder than any other class. They were given a week's work before Christmas. At the same time, eleven men turned up from Yass, penniless and hungry. They were given a day's work clearing grass around government stores.

During those difficult years, Oaks Estate, an historic settlement of between 300 and 400 people, stood out as a community whose needs the Commission did not properly address. Just across the Molonglo River from Queanbeyan, the estate had originally been part of Robert Campbell's property, Duntroon. With the establishment of wool scouring works, a tannery and warehouses and placed right next to the railway, the area became a busy industrial estate serving Queanbeyan and the region by the 1890s. However, the border survey defined the railway line as the eastern border of the territory and so Oaks Estate, being just north of the railway, became part of the Federal Capital Territory in 1911. No subsequent administration made any attempt to acquire the estate and so it remained freehold land. This status brought no advantages for the residents. The area was not part of Griffin's City Plan and territory officials hoped that the estate could be ceded back to NSW, thus absolving them of the problems it posed. Daley, as spokesman for the Commission, made clear its policy in a letter to the NSW Premier in October 1927.

The Commission wanted to transfer Oaks Estate back to NSW 'owing to the embarrassment to the Federal Capital Commission in providing services and assisting development contrary to the intentions of the city plan'.[11] That argument might have made good bureaucratic sense but to the residents of the estate it just seemed callous. In September 1926, J. Braithwaite of the Oaks Estate Progress Association had this to say: 'The Chair of the Commission will not do anything for us. If it is true they are going to hand us back to the State, the sooner the better.'[12] By December that year, Daley reported to the minister that survey information was being prepared so as to enable the incorporation of the estate into Queanbeyan. A legal problem arose that was to defeat the move: a majority of NSW electors had to agree to the transfer and no steps had been taken to hold a ballot on the issue.

So Oaks Estate remained a sort of no man's land. Until 1930, the residents had no garbage collection. Rubbish was tipped into a nearby allotment and spilled out through a gateway. James Brackenreg recommended that a Queanbeyan contractor be employed to remove garbage, and when none could be found, the Commission invited tenders for the service. Henceforth, garbage was disposed of at the city tip at Red Hill. The estate had no school; but the children were not allowed to cross the railway line to Queanbeyan and had to walk to the distant railway crossing.

As the estate was not connected to town water, tanks were used, and the Commission had installed a standpipe in 1929. It was removed after a few months as the residents refused to pay for what they regarded as an inadequate supply. They wanted water pumped direct from Queanbeyan, which enjoyed the same Cotter River water as Canberra. Without the standpipe and with tanks running low in the drought of 1931, some people had to buy water from Queanbeyan residents or draw water from the stagnant Molonglo River. There was a similar standoff regarding electricity connection: only fourteen residents when surveyed were willing to pay for electricity in their house at Queanbyean rates – so the connection did not proceed. This spirited but stubborn stand by Oaks Estate was seen by some people as bloody minded; others saw it as a move to obtain citizens' rights that they were owed as FCT residents. Dr Cumpston, Commonwealth Director of Health, argued that reticulated water should be available to every household in the territory, as should electricity, whether households agreed to it or not.

By 1930, when Daley had taken on the job as Civic Administrator, it seemed clear that NSW had no intention of assuming responsibility for Oaks Estate. In July 1930, Daley wrote to the Minister for Home Affairs urging him to extend water and electricity supply services to the estate. Some estate residents suggested that unemployed men could carry out this work, but time went by and nothing was done. As the drought of 1931 continued, Daley asked that the standpipe be restored for the residents.

Water mains were not extended to Oaks Estate until 1938, and electricity was not connected until 1940. The Commonwealth acquired Oaks Estate in 1974 and brought it under the leasehold system.

*

As Civic Administrator, Daley represented the territory in civil and ceremonial duties and he played host to many visiting dignitaries. This meant there was a regular call on his time and private resources; he and his wife hosted many gatherings, semi-official functions and meetings at their own home. His request for a modest entertainment allowance of £150 was knocked back, in view of the tightening of all budgets at this time.

One of the tasks of the Civic Administrator was to chair a newly formed Advisory Council, established in 1930 to strengthen the community's voice in territory affairs. The Council consisted of three men elected by the residents and three government nominees, plus C.S. Daley as chairman. Proceedings were open to the press, which reported in detail on the meetings. Councillor Thomas Shakespeare proved to be a formidable spokesman for the community and made clear from the beginning that he would fight for an introduction of some form of local government and for parliamentary representation for Canberra. Other councillors echoed his words and felt that, since the Council only had advisory powers and had no say even in the framing of local ordinances, it was easily ignored: the only purpose it served was as a channel for expressing grievances.

Daley was placed in an invidious position on the Council. As government spokesman, he defended its role though this made him the butt of public criticism and often led to fiery debate in Council meetings.

On 30 May 1931, a leading article in the *Canberra Times* expressed hostility towards the administration and pointed to Daley as a lackey to the minister and accused him of blocking any of Shakespeare's proposals from getting a fair hearing. The paper called for the Civic Administrator to be removed from the Council or for his status to be altered to that of an ordinary member.

Daley vented his own sense of frustration in a letter to Sir John Sulman a few weeks later.

...the public, fearful of autocracy, favours any scheme by which a large number of doubtfully qualified persons can dabble in the most difficult operations of government. The elected representatives [on the new Council] strain at the leash to obtain executive functions and become very critical of the Government and administration.

Daley pointed out that the financial crisis prevented the government from conceding any serious measure of self-determination; 'the revenue of the Federal Capital Territory represents a very small portion of its upkeep...'[13] This was a broad view of the federal capital as a national responsibility, with the government being accountable to all Australian taxpayers for its administration and development. A local municipal council could not take on this role, though Daley was happy to concede that local taxpayers should be able to have a voice in the framing of local ordinances.

As well as dealing with the inflammable politics of the Council, Daley was faced in April 1931 with another attack on his credentials by the Returned Servicemen's League (RSSLA), who questioned the minister as to why a returned soldier had not been appointed as Civic Administrator (government policy being to always give preference where possible to returned men when recruiting staff). The minister strongly defended Daley against the claims and said he was chosen because 'his association with the problems of Canberra had been longer and more intimate than that of any other available candidate'.[14]

There were other attacks on Daley's integrity. Thomas Shakespeare often wrote hostile editorials that criticised Daley's handling of land and leasing issues. Then, at a Council meeting in May 1932, Daley expressed regret at the retrenchment of some highly qualified officers who had served with him in the Federal Capital Commission. A stiff reprimand from the Departmental Secretary followed; '…it is contrary to Regulation 34 for officers to comment publicly upon the actions of the Government. Please explain why you disregarded the regulation.'[15] Daley successfully defended his actions, making clear that his words were solely to express appreciation of long-serving officers. He also questioned whether the regulation would apply to Council meetings, as it would effectively bar all public servants from taking part in most Council debates. Daley won that round, but was left bruised by the encounter: it only served to strengthen his disillusionment with the new order of affairs in the capital.

In March 1932, as a cost-cutting measure, the Prime Minister announced that the Departments of Works and Home Affairs would be amalgamated into a single Department of the Interior. The new department would have three branches: Civic Affairs; Works and Services; and Lands and Surveys. The role of Civic Administrator was abolished and Daley, while retaining a seat on the Advisory Council, would no longer be its chairman. He took on a new role as Assistant Secretary, Civic Affairs. This was the sixth change to the Territory's administration and to Daley it heralded further difficult times. Files and historical records would now be split among three separate branches and many of the officials who would take charge would have little or no experience of Canberra matters. Daley lobbied unsuccessfully to have all Canberra matters to do with lands, works and surveys allocated to his branch. He was only too aware from past experience of the many headaches caused by a division of authority, and also the wastage brought about by duplication of resources.

The Depression lingered on in Canberra, as it did elsewhere in Australia, till a new war brought changes. In the winter of 1935, the Advisory Council urged distribution of blankets to men who had been without regular employment for three years. In March 1937, the Council was still urging the government to find work for youths and unmarried men whose search for work so far had been unsuccessful.

*

The most significant national institution to be affected by the Depression was the Australian War Memorial, with its construction and official opening being delayed many years. While Charles Bean was based at

Tuggeranong Homestead working on the early volumes of the official history, he was also investigating possible sites for his planned museum. His history would tell the story of the part Australians played in the war but the museum was to be the repository of all the records, relics and artefacts that had been collected and the works of art that were being commissioned. They would bring the story alive for ordinary Australians. The museum would embody the collective 'spirit' of the AIF, 'that famous army of generous men' whose story Bean would devote a lifetime to recording. While still with the AIF overseas, Bean had obtained official permission to begin collecting material for the future museum. All the material was being held in Melbourne awaiting decisions about its permanent home. Temporary displays set up in the Exhibition Centre attracted huge crowds. In January 1925, the display was closed and transferred to the Exhibition Building in Prince Alfred Park in Sydney.

In August 1923, Sir George Pearce announced to the Senate that the Australian War Memorial would be built in Canberra ('Museum' becoming 'Memorial' in the authorising act of Parliament in 1925). Bean had already inspected possible sites for the museum in the company of the Surveyor General, John Goodwin. The favoured site was the area below Mount Ainslie looking south along Griffin's main axis to the future Parliament House and to the mountains that formed such a dramatic backdrop to the future city. Charles Daley had suggested this as the ideal site; it would provide a layout like that in New Delhi, where the war memorial lay at the end of a long avenue with the viceroy's palace its terminating point two miles away. With that site decided upon, Daley accompanied Bean on a walk around the grassy slopes below Mount Ainslie as Bean explained his plans for the buildings and grounds. At that stage, he envisaged a design inspired by classical Greece, whose associations with Gallipoli were so striking. Bean himself had been a classics scholar: the Memorial would be a shrine to those who fell at 'our Thermopylae'.[16]

Of all Commonwealth officials to be connected to the story of the War Memorial, Daley had the longest and closest association with its founding members. John Treloar, first Director of the Memorial, wrote to Daley in April 1936, thanking him for 'the interest you have shown in the Australian War Memorial since it first came before you officially nearly fifteen years ago. You have given the War Memorial the most beautiful site in Canberra.'[17]

The first stage of the project was an architectural competition for the design of the memorial. This was delayed by the changeover of government from departmental to Commission rule in January 1925. But the chief reason for the delay was that the Commission was also holding a competition for the design of the permanent administrative building. Daley, given the job of organising the memorial competition, was advised to delay it further by the various state Institutes of Architects, most of whose members were engaged upon designs for enlarging St Pauls Cathedral in Melbourne.

The competition was finally ready to be launched in August 1925, with press releases throughout Australia and in New York and London for the benefit of Australian architects working there. Only Australian architects at home or living abroad, or British subjects living in Australia, would be eligible to enter. The three adjudicators were to be J.S. Murdoch, Sir Charles Rosenthal and Professor Leslie Wilkinson, all respected architects with an international reputation. An early decision, later withdrawn, was to invite a British architect to be final arbiter of the designs.

There were sixty-seven competitors. Daley arranged for their designs were to be displayed in a large room at Sydney General Post Office for adjudication in August 1926. The twelve shortlisted designs all earned an award of one hundred guineas, but the judges faced a dilemma with the final choice. John Crust and Emil Sodersteen had both produced excellent designs but only Crust's fell within the required (but unrealistic) costing limit of £250,000. In January 1927, both architects were invited to collaborate on a new design, which they agreed to do and which was accepted. In March 1928, the plans were submitted to the Parliamentary Joint Committee on Public Works, which investigated the feasibility of the plans and after hearing evidence from experts, reported favourably on the plans. Walter Burley Griffin, having been called before the Committee, reported that 'If...the architectural standards of the whole city are up to the standard of the proposed structure, it would be a very handsome city.'[18] The contract between the Federal Capital Commission, John Crust and Emil Sodersteen was signed on 9 August 1929. Parliament voted £50,000 for the financial year 1928–29 but little progress was made in the Depression years that followed.

Charles Bean was most anxious that this great national project not fade from public view because of lack of funds. For him it was something in the nature of a sacred task to ensure that the memorial was built and that it include on a roll of honour the names of those who had died. That the project was kept alive and did not disappear from public view was due in large part to the work of the first Director, John Treloar. Treloar tried to keep the claims of the permanent building before the public, even arranging for the Governor General to unveil an 'inauguration stone' in a bare paddock on Anzac Day 1929, and commissioned Louis McCubbin to paint the event. After the ceremony, the stone was taken away and stored until building operations were finished.

In May 1917, Lieutenant Treloar had been appointed to manage the newly created Australian War Records section in London, tasked with the enormous job of collecting and preserving all material connected to Australia's part in the war. After the war, and with the memorial project foundering in the depressed economy, Treloar designed innovative and profitable ways to advance the Memorial's cause. The Memorial Trust Fund was made up of soldiers' money built up in cooperation with RSSLA branches. Treloar found ways to augment the trust fund through public lectures, film shows and sale of guidebooks and souvenirs. There was also a national tour of Will Longstaff's *Menin Gate* painting. Longstaff's painting of ghostly soldiers marching past the Menin Gate memorial in Belgium attracted large crowds wherever it was shown. Admission charges added handsomely to Treloar's Memorial Trust Fund, and reproductions of the painting were sold in their thousands by door-to-door salesmen, all ex-servicemen. Many Australians were still grieving for the sons or husbands they had lost on the Western Front and whose bodies would never be brought home. With a treasured copy hanging on their wall, the painting gave families some sense of connection with those faraway events and the men who died there.

In March 1931, Treloar arranged for the Memorial's salesmen to begin selling copies of Bean's first histories – *Volume I and II, The Anzac Story* – and the first volumes on the Western Front. Ex-soldiers in the Public Service could have payment deducted from their salary and secure more books as they became available. The venture proved a great success. In the inter-war years, it was considered that many Australian households would have held copies of Bean's official history. By 1942, 150,000 copies had been sold and the funds would be instrumental in allowing the completion of the Memorial.

In June 1933, the Memorial Board and the Returned Servicemen's League had urged the government to proceed with the project, giving pressing reasons for doing so: relief of unemployment; development of the national capital; and suitable housing for the collection. By December 1933, revised drawings were ready and tenders for the first stage were being called. This would involve the erection of the lower and ground floors of the building to display the collection. The building would have a temporary facing of cement, to be later replaced by stone. The heart of the Memorial, its Hall of Memory, Cloisters and Honour Roll, would be erected later when economic conditions improved.

Simmie and Co., a Melbourne building firm, won the contract. In August 1934, John Crust agreed to come to Canberra as resident architect for the project. By September that year, he could report that excavations were finished, drainage and concrete foundations were nearing completion and the brickwork for the walls was underway.

There were further delays. 1935 was a record wet year. Quarried building materials were proving hard to come by and the architects asked for at least a six-month extension. Extensions were granted from June 1935, to July, then October, January, March 1936... The project seemed mired in problems.

Not all Australians supported the idea of the Memorial. Ms O.W. Calvert of the Women's Non-Party League wrote to the Prime Minister in March 1934, protesting against thousands of pounds being spent on a soldiers' memorial which could go for the alleviation of national calamities like fire and flood. Others questioned why the funds could not be spent on the welfare of injured and maimed soldiers.

In July 1935, the Quarrymen's Union NSW wrote to the departmental minister,

> In July 1933 we were informed by the Prime Minister that the financial problems precluded authorizing stone work [on the exterior walls]. We realize that stone is a luxury but it is one of the oldest industries...and has character and dignity. The majority of our members are unemployed or on relief work, and if you can see your way to get the stone work started you

would do much to rehabilitate the stone industry and give many men regular employment...[19]

The response was as expected. 'Authorized funds would not allow for stonework.'

The transfer of the collection began before the building was complete, partly to save rents in Sydney and Melbourne and also because the security of the collection could not be guaranteed. It was therefore a sad irony when the lower ground floor of the Memorial was flooded in a cloudburst on 12 January 1936. Major damage was averted as all important records had been duplicated, with copies stored elsewhere.

In 1936, preliminary work began on the design of the Hall of Memory and the Cloisters. There was ongoing controversy about how the names of the dead should be commemorated in this, the heart of the Memorial. But another war was to intervene before these questions were resolved.

Charles Bean's dedication to the project did not falter, nor did his clear grasp of the function of these memorial spaces. In October 1936, he wrote to Emil Sodersteen,

> I hope the Hall of Memory goes on well. I meant to tell you why I was so anxious about drawing that band of names around the heart of the shrine – it gives a sense of the presence of the individual men. The men of the AIF consisted of the same tramloads and trainloads of individual citizens that are poured out of Wynyard station and that go about their daily business. The presence of these names will add a tense human interest to the feelings with which the visitor will enter your inner hall. *This hall belongs to these men. This is their place.*[20]

9
A People's City

'Single people moved into hostels: they found a sense of adventure in moving away from home...'

Office workers leaving front entrance Of West Block.
Reproduced with permission of Canberra & District Historical Society

The new city was a place of exile to many. It was still a raw construction site, the westerly winds stirring up clouds of dust on the unsurfaced roads and cleared paddocks. In 1925, Canberra had a population of about 4,000 people of whom one-third were workmen. There were no shops, no street lights and very few roads. The meeting hall at Acton was a tin shed. The main centres of activity were the work camps and the construction site at Parliament House. The Molonglo River and its flood plain separated the small administrative enclave at Acton from the planned new suburbs of Kingston, Blandfordia and Westridge, where mobs of sheep still grazed the intervening grasslands. The concrete bulk of the Power House dominated the southern bank of the river and its lights – burning twenty-four hours a day – would become a beacon to guide residents home at night. Journalists, sent to Canberra in the 1930s and used to more cosmopolitan excitements, made the glum observation that it was 'the only illuminated cemetery in the world'.[1] One 1930s resident recalled, '…the biggest parties were given by those who were transferred back to civilisation, meaning Melbourne. Their colleagues came to drink to their good luck and envy them.'[2]

Charles Daley believed that this new environment – offering so few of the familiar comforts of life in Melbourne – nevertheless acted as a tonic and stimulus to many of the men and women who came to Canberra in the 1920s. He observed that many who were previously little interested in affairs outside their own home began to take an active part in the work of the local sporting and cultural societies. Their children, whose own youth matched that of the growing city, accepted Canberra as their home. 'Eventually we came to love the upland stillness of Canberra, where in winter any sound seemed as sharp as the frosty stars.'[3] They were the feelings of Patience (Pat) Tillyard, who came to Canberra as a young girl when her father, Robin Tillyard, was appointed Chief Entomologist with the new Commonwealth body, the Council for Scientific and Industrial Research (CSIR). Pat was to become one among many active supporters of cultural and community life in the young city.

John Butters, familiar with the bleakness of life in the Tasmanian camps, was anxious to establish a better social environment in the territory, and he was particularly concerned that the public servants arriving from Melbourne take a positive approach to their new home. *General Notes for the Information of Public Servants* was published in April 1926 and distributed through a Commission branch office in Melbourne, where people could also inspect maps of subdivisions and cottage plans, and could fill out a form stating their requirements for housing. People were urged not to grumble 'more than is humanly possible, make up your mind to make the best of everything for a little while, and then when you are settled come and tell us what we can do to eliminate any troubles you may still have'.[4] Commission officers were expected to present a helpful face to the public, and would soon be approached by residents to fix broken gutters, knock down garage walls and remedy electrical problems. Front hedges were trimmed free of charge, and water, courtesy of the abundant supply from the Cotter, was freely available for gardens and young trees, with no water rates charged until 1928. That year, the Commission supplied electric stoves for public service families and gave public cooking demonstrations for women more used to gas or wood stoves.

The Commission was doing its best to settle people into their new environment, though more cynical observers saw them as officious and interfering, instructing people as to the design of their letter box, the colour of their eaves and window frames and the fittings in their laundry. Wider questions about social behaviour, including the ban on Sunday football and the design of men's swimming trunks, were other issues on which the Commission exercised an opinion and enforced their view.

In May 1925, Butters convened a meeting in Acton Hall to formulate a 'social service' scheme that would have the support of local residents. Committees were formed to deal with indoor and outdoor recreation, education, libraries, children and women's welfare. The Commission offered to supply material for the erection of children's playgrounds, recreation halls and tennis courts, with the community providing the necessary labour. More divisive issues – many at the meeting wanted a better housing scheme for workers – were banned from discussion that night. If many at the meeting held grievances against the Commission for this stand, nevertheless they were ready to cooperate and join the committees, which they appreciated would benefit their families and the community generally. The story has already been told of the building of the Causeway Hall and its opening in February 1926. This was probably the most ambitious of the social service projects and the one that most successfully embodied Butters' community service ideal. Mr J.H. Honeysett was appointed by the Commission to take charge of the Social Service Association and under his management, there was much constructive activity. Cricket and football grounds and tennis courts were laid down by voluntary labour in the scattered settlements; children's playgrounds were constructed at Acton and Ainslie, with more to be built at Eastlake, Westlake and the Causeway. A central library was established in the Social Service building at Acton where, for a small subscription, Canberra residents could borrow from among 2,000 volumes, and a library truck did the rounds of the settlements. A Canberra gymnasium was established and the first boxing contest held in Canberra, 'heavily patronized, and conducted in a manner reflecting credit on the promoters'.[5]

The Canberra Community News was issued monthly by the Social Service Association. There were reports for tennis, various football codes, cricket, golf, boxing and bowls, and community representatives sent in reports from each of the settlements. It was necessarily a voice for the Commission and its hearty tone and rather erratic typesetting were reminiscent of a school or scouting magazine.

Another magazine appeared in November 1925. Two workmen at the sewer camp at Westridge, D. Bernard O'Connor and Robert Jones, brought out what was to be a quarterly magazine, *Canberra Illustrated*, but only one issue appeared. Described on the front page as 'The Federal Capital in Picture, Verse and Story', the magazine was – unexpectedly – supportive of the three commissioners and their work: the building of Canberra was described as 'the most gigantic scheme now operating in the whole world'. There was an article on education in the territory, contributed by the principal of Telopea School, Mr Cecil Henry, and other entries about the Cotter Dam and forestry projects. The main hint of work camp irreverence in this workers' magazine came in the illustrations, which were clever caricatures of the territory's public servants, drawn in the droll style of the *Bulletin*. As well, the magazine directed some barbs at the *Community News*, its rival, which the editors rightly saw as a taxpayer-funded public relations exercise. An article on working conditions, 'Toilers of the Territory', extolled the benefits of the trade union movement and was generally positive about life for the working man in Canberra. Judging by the number of sponsors paying to advertise in the magazine, the business community were quite happy to support this publishing enterprise.

By 1923, a central portion of the Telopea Park School had been developed and there were small schools at Duntroon and the Molonglo settlement. Parents and citizens' committees served an important function in bringing parents together with common interests in the education of their children. A pioneer in the Telopea Park P & C was its secretary, A.K. Murray, a journalist who gave Canberra its first newspaper, the *Federal Capital Pioneer*, which appeared monthly until 1926 and then quarterly for another year. Murray was a devoted Canberra person and a keen local historian. He wrote regularly to a Sydney friend, J.A. Ferguson, with news of the steady growth and success of the *Pioneer*. 'What pleases me most is the type of person subscribing – with an interest historically in Australia and Canberra in particular.'[6]

Murray was a supporter of the Presbyterian Church: he and Henry Rolland, the Commission's chief architect, were both elders at the church and dreamed of building a cathedral for the faithful in Canberra. Murray was a great admirer of John Gale, both as a journalist and a lifelong supporter of the Canberra region, and he organised Gale's ninety-fifth birthday celebrations at the Hotel Canberra in April 1925.

In December 1924, when the first business and residential auctions were held, Thomas Shakespeare obtained a lease at Ainslie near the Civic Centre, to erect headquarters for a modern newspaper, the *Canberra Times*, whose first edition was to appear on 3 September 1926. The liberal ideals of the Shakespeare family, three generations of whom managed the paper, were expressed in the verse which for many years stood at the masthead of the editorial column:

> For the cause that needs assistance
> 'Gainst the wrong that needs resistance
> For the future in the distance
> And the good that we can do.

The new paper adopted the American standard, with a smaller sheet and a front page devoted to the principal news of the day (unlike the *Times* with its unwieldy format and front page of classifieds). From the start, the paper saw itself as having a national not just a local focus, and it fervently supported the movement for self-government in the territory. Thomas Shakespeare, one of the early members of the Advisory Council, battled for an extension of its power until his death. He was scornful of what he saw as the Commission's attempts to stifle democracy in the territory, and there were many heated clashes with the Commission's chief spokesman on the Council, Charles Daley. However, Thomas Shakespeare's son, Arthur, was to express warm respect for Daley when the latter retired from the Council and from the Commonwealth Service in 1952.

Canberra's 1924 land auction proved a stimulus for the building of private residences and the first shops and businesses in Canberra. The first residential lease was purchased by a Sydney developer, Henry Halloran, for £400. This flamboyant businessman launched land development schemes on at least fifty-nine different areas in NSW, including some in Queanbeyan. In April 1924, Halloran launched his ambitious Canberra Freeholds Estate, which included a subdivision that ran along next to the railway line, the NSW/FCT border. His promotional tactics included placing advertisements in English publications (including on the back of Inland Revenue forms), extolling the attractions of his subdivision 'Environa', promising buyers 'a plot of the nearest freehold land to Canberra – the new capital city!' Environa, whose long thoroughfares bore names like Parliament Boulevard and Speakers Avenue, capitalised on its proximity to the new federal city. Stone pillars, archways and walls were erected to provide dramatic vistas on the estate and a bust of Sir Henry Parkes, atop a forty-foot-high column, stood at the end of an imposing avenue of stone pillars.

The Depression put an end to Halloran's grand scheme for a dress-circle freehold estate with easy access to the new capital. A few of the blocks were sold to overseas visitors but never built on: this remained a source of embarrassment to the Queanbeyan Council for years. The estate was well known to many Canberrans during the inter-war years. When Sunday competition football was frowned upon by the Commission, 'Environa' became the unofficial football oval for the capital, and a race track down on the flats attracted keen punters. The Tuggeranong Picnic Sports was held there on Easter Sunday 1929, when Mr Jeremiah Dillon of the Westridge sewer camp and president of the Federal Football Club, challenged the Tuggeranong team to a strenuous game of tug of war.

'Environa' is now in private ownership but the structures Halloran built are still standing, scattered about the property like the melancholy ruins of an abandoned city.

*

In the story of the city, a number of entrepreneurial individuals stand out. One of these was Jack Ryan. Previously a signaller in the AIF, he ran a small radio and electrical business in Canberra. After obtaining a radio licence, he decided to build his own transmitter, purchasing a second-hand transformer from the Department of Interior, two radio masts from the Royal Military College when they closed down, and other second-hand equipment from disposal stores. Working back at night in the store, he kept warm with a small stove obtained from the Molonglo camp.

Opening night for the radio station was Saturday 14 November 1931. There was an address by Thomas Shakespeare, a poem by Robert Broinowski and a recital by Charles Daley's ensemble the Canberra Trio. The evening finished with a playing of the national anthem. A.J. Ryan Broadcasters Ltd was launched as a public company to manage Station 2CA in February 1932. Shakespeare was opposed to Ryan's venture at first, fearing competition for his paper, but he came to see that the city would benefit from a variety of news and entertainment sources. Daley was a keen supporter from the start, seeing the obvious advantages that would flow to the wider community from this venture. There were daily radio sessions: early breakfast session, lunchtime and 7 p.m. evening session. Jack had many novel ideas to attract listeners. He paid £10 to Lance Sharkey, union leader and professed Communist, for a ten-minute interview – the first broadcast of a Communist speaker in Australia. Ryan offered all the religious denominations equal air time, but none were interested except Father Patrick Haydon, the popular priest of the local Catholic community, so Ryan abandoned the idea. However, the station was on hand to record significant events in the church calendar, such as the sanctification of a new saint at St Christophers (in the presence of the Catholic archbishop) and a thanksgiving service at St Johns on its ninety-third anniversary.

As a member of Rotary, Jack recruited visiting celebrities, including Charles Kingsford Smith. He broadcast events from the Albert Hall, Hotel Canberra and the aerodrome, and in a noteworthy broadcast from Wirth's Circus, he set up a microphone inside the lion's cage and fed him ginger nut biscuits (giving a free plug for Arnott's biscuits). When Holyman's Airways started flights between Sydney, Canberra and Melbourne, Jack was given the job of guiding the early morning flight in from Sydney: fog on the low-lying river flats made plane landings a hazardous business in winter.

The radio station gave a voice to Canberra's emerging community, which in truth had a lot in common with much of rural and urban Australia between the wars. It became a significant social asset during the Depression, providing popular music on gramophone recordings, supporting bushfire and flood appeals and even running an adventure serial, a session of gentle mayhem, on air five nights a week for four or five years. Sporting events were important, both the performance, keenly followed, of local teams, and as well those glamorous imports from abroad, like the visiting Indian hockey team in 1935 and the English cricketers, who played in Canberra in 1937. There was even a broadcast of the Melbourne Cup, with the radio team heading out into the bush and picking up an appropriate station to relay on their own equipment. Aviators, both men and women, and visiting swimming and cycling champions, were always a source of fascination to the public, as were any events to do with royalty. The station broadcast accounts of the visit of the Duke of Gloucester in 1935 and the church service after the death of King George V in 1936.

George Barlin, a friend and colleague of Jack Ryan, called him 'the most remarkable man I have ever known'.[7]

*

A young woman played a creative role in Canberra's story between the wars. Verity Hewitt, one of the Tillyard daughters, came to Canberra as a teacher in 1930 and taught English and history at Telopea High School; the young Gough Whitlam was one of her pupils. In 1936, she married Laurie Fitzhardinge, a classical scholar appointed as Research Officer to the new Commonwealth National Library. The traditional role of a middle-class married woman, pursuing either domesticity or voluntary charity work, did not appeal to Verity and she decided to set up a small bookshop, using as stock the many antiquarian volumes her husband had collected in England. Her shop began in a small upstairs room in the Sydney Building in Civic and soon became known for its individual character and personal service. People were encouraged to browse and often came in just to chat. Patrons of the early days included Dr J.H. Cumpston, first Director-General of Health, who came regularly for detective novels. The Governor-General, Lord Gowrie, brought some friends along one day, telling them, 'This is the nicest little bookshop in Australia.' During the war, 'we became a centre for all sorts of drifting soldiery,' Verity recalled.[8] Just as the war began, she had a visit from the Japanese ambassador, accompanied by two policemen. He'd come for some reading material for his detainment in Melbourne before being repatriated.

Verity recalled the great demand for Everyman Classics. Books on art, travel, politics, geography, history and music all did well. The bookshop moved to a number of different locations but remained a well-loved part of Canberra's life until the 1970s.

*

Another individual who stands out in the story of those interwar years is Willliam Mildenhall. He came to Canberra in 1920, employed as paymaster to the Department of Works and Railways. There were not many amenities in Canberra but the place could satisfy two of his abiding interests, fishing and photography. In January 1921, he wrote to the secretary of the department offering his expertise in an official capacity as a photographer. If the department allowed him the cost of materials, he was willing to do any official photography in his own time. The value of his work was recognised by senior officials and in 1926 he was appointed information officer for the Commission. After its demise in 1930, he resumed his former pattern of taking photographs for government departments alongside his full-time clerical position. He also took on assignments for Fox Movietone, sending their Sydney office moving pictures of newsworthy material from Canberra.

In 1929, a local professional photographer complained that Mildenhall's work constituted an unfair business monopoly, and Mildenhall was forced to give up his work as an official photographer. He continued to work for many years in the Department of the Interior and raised his family in Canberra. His black and white photographs are now a precious archive recording the building of the city; they captured in arresting detail the everyday and human aspects of life in the young capital.

A public service job was waiting for William Mildenhall when he came to Canberra and as well he found satisfying outlets for his creative interests outside work. His wife was less fortunate. 'Where are we? Where are the shops?' she asked when they arrived in 1921.[9] Adele Mildenhall remembered that her mother 'cried for a week' after arriving, such was the wrench at leaving Melbourne. Without the stimulus of an outside job and interaction with new work colleagues, Canberra's womenfolk had to discover their own ways of settling into the new city. Very few women found themselves in satisfying professional jobs after marriage. One who did was Ruth Lane Poole, the wife of Charles Lane Poole, head of the Forestry School. Ruth had a privileged and artistic background as part of the extended family of the Irish poet W.B. Yeats, and as a young woman she became part of the Arts and Crafts movement in Dublin. For much of her married life, her husband was stationed abroad on forestry business, but in 1925, Ruth and her three daughters joined him in Melbourne, where Lane Poole had been appointed Commonwealth Forestry Advisor, soon to be transferred to Canberra. In Melbourne, Ruth Lane Poole soon made a name for herself as a talented designer. She was formally engaged by the Federal Capital Commission in March 1926 as Furniture Specialist to design the furnishings of both Government House and the Lodge, in consultation with their future inhabitants, Lady Stonehaven and Ethel Bruce. She then submitted her design report and costings, which were greater than the Cabinet estimates. When she offered to resign the commission, which she considered impossible without sufficient funds, Cabinet ordered a review of the costings and increased the allocation.

Lane Poole's interior design, using exclusively Australian timbers and high quality fabrics and fittings, was distinctive at the time, and was as much a part of the federal capital design aesthetic as were J.S. Murdoch's buildings. In Canberra, the Lane Pooles lived in Westridge House, Yarralumla, a house built for them and renowned for its beautiful Australian timbers.

For most Canberra women, their status was defined in the term 'home duties'. This in itself, in the raw young suburbs, brought plenty of frustration. Many of the early houses were built hastily to cater for an imminent influx of workers. The houses in Ainslie were built of timber that was not properly cured, and cracks often appeared. One woman recalled a rose bush forcing its way through the bedroom floor. Even in the more select suburbs of Forrest and Red Hill, houses were built with little consideration for the climate and aspect, with living areas often facing south and kitchens facing into the hot western sun (this at a time when the only source of refrigeration was an ice chest whose contents rapidly deteriorated in heatwaves once the ice had melted). Sheep paddocks brought blowflies in their thousands: one of Robin Tillyard's first research projects concerned the 'blowfly menace'. Kept out of the houses by wire screens, they came down the chimney to add to the housewife's woes. The open fire in the living room was the source of heating, but if it did not draw properly, the south-westerly winds of winter would push the smoke back down the chimney.

Food was more expensive than in Sydney or Melbourne but, in compensation, orders were taken and deliveries made door to door, a service that Canberra residents enjoyed until petrol rationing in the coming war put an end to the practice.

Church gatherings (still taking place in community halls for the most part) were important sources of friendship and support, with ladies' guilds formed to carry out women's work in the church – anything to do with children, social events or catering. Above all, women needed help through the difficult, lonely years of child-rearing. There were no parents or in-laws close by to turn to for advice, reassurance or a helping hand, and it was not an age when men took any part in the rearing of young children. So the Mothercraft Society was a great friend to many young Canberra women. The society was founded in October 1926; Helen Brackenreg (who had been a nurse) was a founding member. A Baby Health Centre was established in a cottage at Eastlake and was opened by Lady Butters in February 1927, just in time for the first influx of public service families. Women could bring their babies there for check-ups and discuss with the resident nurse any problems they had. To get there, they had to push their pram along some of the numerous dirt tracks that connected suburb to suburb.

Charles Daley's wife, Jessie, joined the council of the Mothercraft Society and from the early days was involved in efforts to furnish and equip the small cottage. Jessie must have been a woman of remarkable energy and resource and was to contribute much voluntary time to a wide range of Canberra community groups. In 1927 she had four young children: Margaret and Geoffrey were in primary school but of her two youngest, Arthur was about three years old and Nancy was still an infant. Her fifth child, Joan, was born in the family home at Acton in July 1928. Like most comfortably placed Public Service wives, Jessie Daley would have had home help: in fact, we know that she employed a young Irish girl, Mary, to act as children's nurse. Mary found herself disagreeing with Jessie about medication for childhood illnesses and she left the Daleys' employ after a few months. Jessie Daley was a Christian Scientist, with pronounced views on the rightness or otherwise of human intervention in serious illnesses. This religious community, which had a huge following in America, sought to return to early Christianity with its elements of 'healing through prayer'. It is not clear exactly what role her religion played in Jessie's life. Her daughters remember going to Sunday services with their mother at the Christian Science rooms next to the Kurrajong Hotel, but her husband spent Sunday worship at St John's, and then from 1934 played the organ at St Andrews Presbyterian Church. Charles Daley subscribed at one stage to the *Christian Science Monitor*, an American journal of news and commentary. (Its international standing was recognised with the award of seven Pulitzer prizes between 1950 and 2002.)

Jessie Daley had a long record of service to the Canberra community. In August 1928, she was elected vice-president of the Mothercraft Society and continued in this role until 1935, when internal disagreements about the role of the resident nursing sister led to Jessie's resignation. Many other groups benefited from Jessie's engagement with them: the Canberra Ladies Choir, Women's Hockey Club, the Girl Guides Association, school P&C associations, the Society of Art and Literature, and the Young

Women's Christian Association (YWCA). Their club room was opened in Civic in April 1931 by Lady Isaacs, and the centre became a favourite meeting place especially for young unmarried women, hosting a drama group, a discussion group, Women in Government, and a library of 500 novels. In 1937, Jessie Daley became vice-president of the local branch and a member of the national board of the YWCA. She put her skills as an organiser and her experience in sporting and cultural activities to good use, holding frequent welcoming parties and card afternoons at her home on behalf of the association to raise funds for charity and to welcome newcomers to the city. One of the YWCA's meeting rooms is named in her honour. Jessie Daley used her influence in the YWCA to form an FCT branch of the National Council of Women and was its founding president. Under her leadership, the branch brought representatives of community organisations together to coordinate their activities and give them a stronger public voice; their objectives were the advancement of women and the welfare of society through women's participation in politics, religion and all facets of community life. In July 1943, Jessie Daley was unanimously asked to remain as president, but that was to be her last meeting before ill health forced her to quit.

Patricia Tillyard (mother of Pat Tillyard) was another among the small band of resourceful, outward-looking women who helped to shape a better life for other women in the early years of the capital. Patricia became president of the Canberra branch of the YWCA and was to become the first (and only) woman on the council of the newly formed University College.

It is of interest to note that both Jessie Daley and Patricia Tillyard enrolled some of their girls at the newly founded St Gabriel's School but transferred them to Telopea High School because the latter offered a wider (and in their view, better) education. Patricia had studied botany at Cambridge; Jessie had studied dentistry at the University of Melbourne but had left before gaining her degree in order to marry.

*

In the interwar years and beyond, Charles Daley was given credit for 'nurturing the feeble flame of Canberra's early musical life'.[10]

He was a gifted musician, a pianist since boyhood. His mother, while musical herself, disapproved of her son's passion, fearing that a musical career would offer little security. In an ill-considered move, she burnt some of her son's sheet music – light popular melodies – that he'd saved his pocket money to buy. This did not deter the young Daley, who told her defiantly that 'he had all the music in his head'. He was devoted to the keyboard for the rest of his life. On the day before he died, he kept a regular engagement to play for elderly people at a community club in Canberra.

In June 1927, soon after the official opening of Parliament House, a group of about fifty men and women inaugurated a society for the promotion of literature and fine arts in the capital. There were four sections: fine art, music, drama and literature, and Daley was convener of the music section. If the Social Services Association was broadly democratic and inclusive in its reach, this new society was inevitably more elitist, attracting those confident, well-educated individuals who already held positions of authority in the city. The inaugural president was Sir Robert Garran, legal mind behind the framing of the Constitution and now head of the Attorney-General's Department. He and his wife had, from the start, been enthusiastic about what Canberra had to offer, and both were to play a prominent role in the city over the coming years. Other members of the society, besides Daley, were Colonel Percy Owen; Robert Broinowski the Clerk of the Senate; John Butters and his wife; Dr Tillyard and his daughter, Pat; Dr Allen (at that time Professor of Languages at the Royal Military College); and Kenneth Binns, head of the new National Library. Jessie Daley and a few other women joined a few months later; she took up the role of wardrobe mistress for the drama group. A number of plays were produced in the next few years but the group ran into trouble managing its fiery director, Dr Nott, and plays were discontinued. Dr Nott formed a breakaway group which became the Canberra Repertory Society.

The Arts and Literature Society's program, while worthy in spirit, was hardly likely to attract a large following. The monthly meetings generally took the form of a lecture, say, on Scottish poetry or the short story in literature. In November 1934, the Poet Laureate, John Masefield, visiting Canberra as a guest of the government, gave a lecture to the society members at the Albert Hall.

The society faded away in 1938, as people in Canberra gained access to a wider range of cultural programs through the ABC and 2CA and could attend concerts, plays and other public events at the Albert Hall.

The Canberra Musical Society was to play a large role in Canberra's public life in the 1930s and 40s. Daley was a founding member and for many years its president and guiding force. The society's first concert – extracts from *La Bohème* and *Madame Butterfly* performed by a group from Sydney Conservatorium – was held at the Albert Hall at its opening by Prime Minister Bruce on 10 March 1928, fifteen years almost to the day since Lady Denman announced the naming of Canberra. Its initial name, 'Assembly Hall', was deliberately chosen: it suggested the Regency equivalent in England where men and women could for the first time gather together in public to socialise and enjoy music and other entertainment. Its subsequent name, the Albert Hall, had further British connotations, evoking London's premier venue for classical music performances. Canberra's Albert Hall became the centre of cultural and community life for the next forty years.

Daley was keen to persuade visiting singers and musicians to include Canberra in their circuit tour. Having secured an August date for a visiting English opera singer, John Brownlee, the society had to warn Brownlee's agent not to expect a big financial success.

> The Albert Hall has good acoustic properties but it is situated nearly two miles from the residential areas. Transport facilities are not very good…if the weather is cold or wet, the folk here are more inclined than in larger cities to stay at home.[11]

There was no mention of the hall's notorious chilliness: only a few small electric heaters protected the audience and cast from the worst of Canberra's winter nights. At one event, a visiting singer refused to go on stage without her fur coat.

Many artists toured Australia from Great Britain, Russia and Central Europe before the war put a stop to such visits. From June 1928, Canberra citizens could subscribe to four concerts a year with an ambitious program that brought visiting chamber groups, instrumentalists and singers to the Albert Hall as well as local artists: a December performance of extracts from *The Messiah* with local performers was guaranteed to fill the hall and bring in a profit. The society had an orchestra under the baton of Jeffrey Haydon, senior lecturer in modern languages at the Royal Military College, and a small chamber group, the Canberra Trio, with Daley as pianist. The society's choir took part in the inauguration of the War Memorial on 4 April 1929.

Visiting artists were given a reception after the performance at the Daleys' home, 20 Balmain Crescent, and often stayed overnight. Afterwards, letters appeared with thanks to the family for their 'wonderful hospitality'. Jessie Daley often met visiting artists at the railway station and showed them around the growing city.

The early years of the Depression brought a drop in membership and the society had to cut expenditure, with no more visiting artists. The Christmas concert of 1931 was in aid of the Canberra Unemployment Relief Fund. From 1934, Daley arranged with the ABC to bring some of the station's touring celebrities to Canberra: these included such notables as Artur Rubenstein, Lotte Lehman, Gladys Moncrieff and the Budapest String Quartet.

Alfred Cunningham, a Sydney baritone who had performed at the Albert Hall in September 1934, wrote to Daley,

> You must be a happy man to be there – at the heart of things – with all your scope for constructive thinking – and the more so that you are contributing so literally to the 'harmony' of the city.[12]

Not all visitors to Canberra spoke of it with such warmth. Ernest Crutchley, appointed as Acting British High Commissioner, arrived to take up residence in Canberra House in January 1931. For the three years of his residence, he kept a diary which records the gloomy observations of a career diplomat missing the pleasures of London and Court society. Everything came in for acid commentary, from the shiny blue suit Prime Minister Lyons wore to a Parliament House levée, 'the Australian's regard for his clothes is negligible…' to the beery, noisy conviviality of RSL 'smoke socials', which he loathed. He was furious at the discourtesy of shop assistants and dismayed at Australians' uninhibited and vulgar exuberance: 'toilet rolls as streamers at a wedding!' An official guest at the Roman Catholic Debutante Ball in September 1933, he found it to be 'like a musical comedy. How different from the court life of our own dear

Queen. I had to sit with Her Excellency [Lady Isaacs] and inwardly support her the whole evening.' There were harsh words for the Canberra Musical Society at the Albert Hall: 'A terrible nursery duet and a comic song by a woman! And then eternal highbrow gramophone and endless speeches by Daley. Hard chairs.' [13]He did, however, find congenial company and conversation at Rotary dinners and luncheons, often organised by Daley as Rotary president.

Canberra, in fact, stood out from other capital cities in that it had a high proportion of educated middle-class people, brought from Melbourne to join the Public Service or to work in one of the new national institutions: the Forestry School, the CSIR, Mount Stromlo Observatory or the Institute of Anatomy. (Women of course had to be content with minor roles as secretaries, typists or stenographers.) Single people moved into hostels: women to Gorman House and men to the Bachelors' Quarters at Acton. Young and high-spirited, and without the responsibilities of marriage and family, many of these young people found a sense of adventure in moving away from home, with the freedom to be able to enjoy the unchaperoned company of their peers. Cycling, tennis, picnics at the Cotter, swimming in summer, and dances at the Forestry School were all popular recreations. A new drama group, the Repertory Society, was formed by Dr Lewis Windamere Nott in September 1932 as a breakaway from the Arts and Literature Society. It attracted many of Canberra's lively and intelligent young people, who enjoyed the chance to take part in informal play-readings or in productions staged at 2CA's new broadcasting hall.

Cla Allen, a scientist at Mount Stromlo, was part of an active group of mainly young men and women who began venturing out into the mountains to the west of the territory on their weekends or longer breaks. They explored the rugged country in some epic bushwalks, including a trip up through deep snow to the territory's highest mountain, Bimberi, in August 1931. In January 1931, Dr J.H. Cumpston, a keen bushwalker who was also interested in the source of Canberra's water supply, arranged to take his two sons on a four-day walk that traced the Cotter River from its source to the dam. Charles Lane Poole, Director of the School of Forestry, was also keen to explore the forested country to the west of Canberra. He was an accomplished skier and he encouraged his young friends by helping them make their own skies in workshops at the Forestry School. In 1934, Lane Poole was voted in as president of the newly formed Canberra Alpine Club. After a lodge was built for the club at Mount Franklin on the Brindabella Range, keen groups of skiers made the rough journey by hired truck or borrowed car along a narrow, winding and often muddy road up the range to the hut for an exhilarating weekend of skiing.

Robin Tillyard, the new Chief Entomologist with CSIR, and his wife, Patricia, were both English, Cambridge-educated and liberal-minded. They became enthusiastic supporters of the new city and found great interest and solace in some of the small organisations being formed in Canberra by like-minded individuals: the University Association; the local branch of the Royal Society; and, on a more domestic level, the Horticultural Society. This society was founded in 1929 and attracted Canberrans of all backgrounds. They were keen to transform their surroundings, coaxing the harsh soils into productive life with vegetable plots, hardy flowers like dahlias, and fruit trees in abundance, many of which seemed to flourish in this climate. Gardeners were given every official encouragement; they were, after all, to be partners with the government in creating this new Garden City. Thomas Weston and his successor as Manager of Parks and Gardens, Alexander Bruce, were always ready with practical advice for gardeners about pruning, soil improvement and seed varieties. Bruce was elected first president of the society, which held its first spring show in November 1929 in the Albert Hall and attracted 263 entries. These shows were to be held thereafter every year except for two years during the war, which suggests that the society's work made an invaluable contribution to community life.

Roses found a special place in the landscape of this Garden City. They flourished in the harsh environment, and had done so since colonial times, indifferent to the assaults of drought, neglect or disease. Dr Arthur Butler, visiting C.E.W. Bean at Tuggeranong Homestead in connection with the war history, came across a climbing rose on the property that so entranced him that years later, in 1932, he wrote a description of it in the *Canberra Rose Journal*.

> As I neared the homestead, I crossed a little rippling creek and saw what appeared to be a massive pillar of yellow…a vision of roses [with] the flowers

so thickly placed and so large as to make all else invisible besides the glory of their red-splashed gold. The bush, I ascertained, had been there for many years. It still flowers, though not, perhaps, as I saw it then.[14]

Charles Daley was so taken with this article that he suggested to the departmental secretary that 3,000 copies should be printed to provide favourable publicity for Canberra. The response was negative: it was not thought that the expense could be justified.

Robert Broinowski, parliamentary officer and later Clerk to the Senate, created rose gardens to enhance and humanise the new grounds of Parliament House. He persuaded the President of the Senate, Sir Walter Kingsmill, to allow him to start a rose garden on the Senate side, with each state having its own section, prominently labelled. His rose donors included city councils and businesses, and many House employees – cleaners, cooks, attendants and gardeners – donated a rose bush. After the success of this venture, Broinowski planned a ladies' rose garden on the House of Representatives (eastern) side of the building. With the support of Dame Mary Hughes, wife of former Prime Minister Billy Hughes, he had the wives of many parliamentarians contributing roses. Later, under Broinowski's direction, many trees of different deciduous species were planted there. Over the years, the rose gardens became favourite meeting places for visitors and Canberrans alike. One Senator, an amateur apiarist, kept his bees in the Senate garden.

The last year of the decade opened with heatwaves and fire. The Black Friday bushfires of January 1939 burnt for the whole of that summer in Victoria, killing seventy-one people and consuming whole townships. Bushfires menaced the federal capital as well, burning great swaths of forest and farmland to the west of Canberra. The city endured its longest ever heatwave, with seven consecutive days above 100 degrees. That extreme weather coincided with Canberra's hosting of the 24th ANZAAS Conference, which was to be held for the first time in the federal capital and attracted distinguished writers, academics and scientist from interstate and overseas. Charles Daley senior travelled up from Melbourne for the conference; he was a founding member of the organisation and had given a talk on Aboriginal art at the 1911 conference in Melbourne.

His son was heavily involved in planning the details of the 1939 conference and was a member of the executive committee that prepared a detailed handbook on Canberra's origins and development. The program of excursions included an afternoon visit to Lambrigg and excursions to Mount Franklin, Lake George and Burrinjuck Dam. Daley was required to prepare the conference's opening speech for the minister, as well as speeches to open the Forestry section of the conference and the speech at the dedication of the Farrer memorial. William Farrer's widow, Henrietta, had died since the Commonwealth acquisition of her property and she was buried in a grave next to her husband on a knoll above the homestead at Lambrigg. In 1938, the government decided to go ahead with the erection of a memorial there 'as an enduring token of the gratitude of a nation to a great man of science'.[15]

A number of international scientists were among the group that gathered at Lambrigg for the ceremony. Charles Daley senior was also there, identified as the man who had arranged to build cairns along the routes of the early colonial explorers in Victoria. The minister gave his speech and unveiled the obelisk in honour of William Farrer. Thomas Shakespeare, on behalf of the Country Press Association, unveiled the new headstone and slabs for the graves. Surveyor General Arthur Percival was there with his wife. He said the scene 'brought back a flood of memories' of the years 1911 to 1916, when as a young surveyor he camped on Mount Ainslie, on the Gudgenby and Molonglo Rivers and many other corners of the territory whose hills 'had been stripped of grass, denuded and eroded by the rabbit plague'.[16]

After the ceremony, everyone drove back to the Hotel Canberra for afternoon tea. It must have been a welcome relief after the stifling heat of the day.

Of the speakers at the conference, none attracted more attention than the English science fiction writer, H.G. Wells, who spoke in other capital cities as well as in Canberra. Wells, with an acute awareness of impending war, wanted to encourage Australians to talk about peace and to work towards intelligent resolution of conflict in world affairs. The Albert Hall was packed for his address, with 400 more people listening on the lawns outside on the public address system. Wells's speech was uncompromising, foretelling a bleak world where a brutal master race has enslaved all other races; salvation would only come with an intellectual 'reawakening' of the English-speaking world and its defence of liberal and civilised values. Australian audiences shrugged off his message, which they found disagreeable and fantastic. Charles Daley had ordered a copy of the author's *An Outline of History* only a couple of years before, so he may have had a deeper appreciation of Wells and his broad vision of human history.

'Curtin had been Prime Minister for a brief era in Australia's history, but people recognized how much his leadership had meant to the country.'

John Curtin and Ben Chifley outside Parliament House, Canberra.
From the collection of the National Archives of Australia

The last decade before the war was a troubled time for Charles Daley. His role in the civic administration of the territory was a demanding one that brought plenty of controversy and ill-feeling his way, but offered little scope for progressive action. Once again, Canberra had been put under the divided control of several departments, with all its potential for delay, confusion and poor management. And this change coincided with the worst years of the Depression. Daley's old friend and mentor, J.S. Murdoch, counselled a spirit of resignation.

> I am sincerely sorry that matters at Canberra are not so pleasant for you – one of those situations to be accepted as unavoidable in a spirit of patience until the political wheel makes another revolution…[1]

But Daley, finding such an attitude hard to adopt, looked for work outside the Commonwealth service, applying in July 1931 for the position of secretary of the Commercial Travellers Association of Victoria. In July 1932, he applied for the position of manager of the newly formed Australian Broadcasting Commission. Then in June 1934, there was an application for another government position, as Chief Electoral Officer.

These years found Daley's life at a low point. In the winter of 1930, his youngest son, Arthur, died of meningitis. Perhaps it was no accident that each attempt to leave Canberra for a new position took place in the winter months, recalling for him that earlier season of anguish and loss.

The young family had been struck down with sickness in May 1930, when the *Canberra Times* reported an outbreak of scarlet fever in Canberra, mainly in the areas to the north of the river. The two boys, Geoffrey and Arthur, were taken to the isolation block of the small Canberra hospital at Acton. Their sister, Margaret, was kept home from school as a precaution, but in June she developed symptoms and was hospitalised as well. The two older children recovered, but six-year-old Arthur grew worse and he was taken to Melbourne to see a specialist. Margaret and Nancy stayed with family friends in Canberra.

Despite a number of comments by Daley's contemporaries, suggesting that Arthur's death might have been caused by his mother's reluctance to seek medical help, there is no evidence that that was the case. Medical advice to isolate the children in hospital was acted upon and, as Arthur's condition worsened, Jessie Daley took the difficult decision to travel with the sick child to Melbourne, taking Geoffrey and two-year-old Joan with her. Daley, confiding in a Sydney friend, spoke of their hopes being raised as Arthur seemed to get better in hospital, 'playing with toys, and taking an intelligent interest in everything'.[2] Developing meningitis from an abscess on the brain, Arthur died in hospital on 22 July.

Daley drove down to Melbourne and brought his wife and two children home in the car. He was back at his desk by 31 July dealing with government business and responding with courtesy to the condolence letters that arrived. One of the letters was from the principal of Ainslie Primary School, where the young Arthur Daley had begun school. Many of his pupils had known the little boy.

The sadness of their loss was aggravated by the rumours that both parents would have heard: hints of culpability on the mother's part... an implication that her religious beliefs had influenced her actions. If they were aware of this, both parents chose to ignore the rumours. Jessie Daley's engagement with Canberra women and her support with many community programs, continued as before. The strain that the family was under led to a doctor warning Daley that he must take an extended rest from work. His deputy, H.R. Waterman, took over Daley's administrative work and the family went to Sydney for an extended summer holiday at Balmoral. Daley was back at work at the end of January 1931.

In the long term, consolation came for Daley through family, music, friendship and even the difficult demands and distractions of the workplace. For all his rather grave and upright public persona, it is clear that Charles Daley had a gift for friendship which many people valued. To Percy Owen, he was always a very dear young friend. John Sulman, in a written reference, spoke of his considerable ability 'combined with a most agreeable personality'.[3] Among Daley's wide circle of friends there were architects, musicians and artists. In an undated letter, his Sydney friend, architect Henry Budden, wrote, 'The next time I visit Canberra it will be purely for pleasure. You always did me good Daley.'[4] Ross Thomas, a retired teacher, wrote of 'looking back with pleasure on the association I had with you, which ripened into a firm friendship'.[5] Musical collaboration brought its own pleasures. Violinist Alfred Ackland, coming to Canberra for the ABC, looked forward to some informal music making, accompanying Daley in a piano and violin sonata. Daley himself remembered his friendship with Thomas Hill, Chief Engineer in the early construction days: 'Some of my happiest recollections of early visits to Canberra are centred on evenings spent with him round the piano.'[6]

Harold Herbert, exuberant and free-spirited artist, was on the selection panel to choose the winning design for a statue of King George V. A series of letters to Daley indicates a warm and sympathetic relationship between the bureaucrat and the artist, with an easy exchange of light-hearted banter. In January 1936, Herbert wrote from Melbourne, asking Daley, 'for old times sake to do what you can for a dear friend of mine, Louis McCubbin', who was to be stationed in Canberra engaged in art work for the War Memorial. 'I'll do the same for you some day,' Herbert promised Daley.[7]

Even within the dour confines of the Public Service workplace, the office, there was affection, loyalty and good humour, especially between Daley and his long-standing deputy, H.R. Waterman. While Daley and his family were on holiday in January 1933, Waterman wrote, 'Miss Smiles and I pine for your return. The office has been singularly free of discord, not because of your absence but probably owing to the heat.'[8]

As the decade wore on, Daley's correspondents had darker stories to tell. His younger brother, Frank, was in Germany studying automotive engineering processes. In July 1936, Frank wrote that Germany was now

a masterpiece of efficiency; the most wonderful roads...the country self-supporting in foodstuffs and other ways. But one senses the undercurrent of something sinister. Nobody will tell you their real feelings. They worship Hitler, but they also fear him. While we were there, 300 men 'struck' at our works at Opel; they were simply packed off to a concentration camp.[9]

Fritz Kramer was pianist for a popular middle-European group of men who sang traditional and classical songs in close harmony and delighted audiences world-wide. The Comedy Harmonists first toured Australia in 1937 under the auspices of the ABC and Charles Daley arranged for them to sing in the Albert Hall for the Musical Society. In May 1938 they were touring South America when they heard that Austria had been invaded. Kramer wrote to Daley,

> We have lost our wonderful Vienna… Many Austrians are homeless. A friend of mine has asked for a permit to Canberra. He is a bachelor, twenty-four-years old, with a medical degree of the University of Vienna – has too a musical degree of the Vienna Conservatorium. Dear Mr Daley, wouldn't you help him, with your great influence? I would be very grateful.[10]

There is no record of what Daley advised, but it is unlikely that many Jewish artists were able to seek residency in Australia at this time. After the *anschluss* (annexation of Austria) in March 1938, Australia House was inundated with 120 enquiries a day about coming to Australia. There were strict quotas on non-British migrants, and those who did come needed to provide a cash payment and guarantee from friends and family already in Australia.

Artur (Arthur) Schnabel was one of the many great European artists who, seeking refuge from Nazism, found a new life in America. Austrian by birth, Schnabel left his homeland in 1933 and became an American citizen. He was said to be the greatest living exponent of Beethoven's piano music. He toured Australia in July 1939 and his performance at the Albert Hall on 20 July was keenly anticipated. On 15 July the *Canberra Times* advertised the coming visit of 'Australian pianist Arthur Schnabel'. Daley, in a gentle correction to the editor two days later, wrote,

> Much as we would like the honour, Australia cannot claim the birthplace of Arthur Schnabel, who was a native of Austria, if one can still use that word. In these times when we see evidences of so many spurious forms of nationalism… it is satisfying to find that in music we have one of the greatest forces making for world unity. Arthur Schnabel and other famous artists who are making their contributions to these times and generations, belong to no particular country; they have a wider family than mere territorial boundaries.[11]

Earlier that month, the Vienna Boys Choir had performed at the Albert Hall. The young boys were billeted locally, two of them staying with the Daleys at 20 Balmain Crescent. The daughters remember them lining up for plates of hot porridge in the morning. Their tour finished in Perth on 3 September, as war was declared. This left them stranded and classed officially as 'enemy aliens'. Archbishop Mannix offered them foster homes with his parishioners in Melbourne and a place in a new cathedral choir. The boys stayed in Melbourne for the duration of the war; by 1945 they were young men. All but one decided to stay on in Australia, their families back home pleading with them to take the offer of a better life away from the chaos of post-war Europe.

With the onset of war, Daley's civic responsibilities grew heavier. In September 1939, an air force squadron was stationed at the small aerodrome to the east of Canberra. The Canberra Technical College, a small establishment based at Eastlake near the Power House, was directed to begin sixteen-week courses for mechanical fitters and aircraft riggers, with new batches to be trained for the duration of the war. Daley was given responsibility for coordinating the scheme. The first 100 recruits began their course on 1 December 1939 and were accommodated in huts at the aerodrome. They would be attached to the local squadron and after the course would proceed elsewhere for further training. The Department of Defence would meet all costs, including the extra teaching staff. It was an intensive regime, similar to that being organised at training centres and army bases throughout the country to deal with the vastly different defence requirements of this new war with its advanced weaponry and technology. Hours of instruction were 9 to 5 on weekdays, 9 to 12 on Saturdays and two evenings a week, plus a half day on Wednesday to allow for sporting activities. There was to be a two-day break over Christmas that was extended to six days so that trainees had a chance to travel home.

In 1940, the Air Board requested that Daley arrange a wider program of training to include courses for welders, electrical fitters and cooks.

The aerodrome at Canberra, up till then, was a sheep paddock, originally part of the Campbells' Duntroon holdings. The land was leased to a local grazier whose sheep kept the grass under control. In the 1930s, Holyman Company's aircraft made use of the airstrip but sometimes the pilot had to circle the field for fifteen minutes or so until the sheep wandered off the airstrip or the shepherd arrived with his dogs.

The RAAF tolerated this practice until December 1940, but as flight activity increased, with the possibility of aircraft having to land without warning or at night, they arranged with Daley for the sheep to be removed and the grazing lease withdrawn.

On 15 February 1942, Singapore had fallen to the Japanese and nearly 15,000 surviving troops of the Australian 8th Division were sent to prisoner of war camps. By March, Japanese planes had bombed Darwin. Australians saw that they were no longer fighting the Empire's battles but their very own. The Air Board needed urgent expansion of training programs for ground staff to service the RAAF. Could Canberra train an extra 200 fitters? When Daley explained the problem of serious accommodation shortage, the board sought out alternatives: Canberra Grammar School; the Causeway Hall; the Albert Hall...? Pressured to make something available, Daley arranged, reluctantly, for the Causeway Hall to be occupied for two months by the trainees; it meant disrupting valuable outreach work that the YMCA was doing there with young people. Church services and a baby clinic were temporarily moved to another small hall in Kingston. In August, more huts were erected at the aerodrome and even a large marquee, to accommodate the trainees on their shortened, twelve-week courses that now included training for electricians, instrument makers and repairers and wireless assistants. All courses included refresher instruction in very elementary science and chemistry and calculation, presented in a way that all trainees could master.

In June 1942, Daley and the principal of the technical college visited Melbourne to discuss the future training needs of the RAAF. They conferred with Daley's younger brother, Frank, who by this stage in the war was Acting Director of Ordnance Production. They also visited the Commonwealth Aircraft Corporation's works to see the mass production of equipment.

As the Pacific war expanded, the pace of training increased. By mid-1943, there were 350 trainees per course, each course now shortened to eight weeks. The courses ran from December 1939 to August 1945, with a 95% pass rate – the highest of any unit in the Commonwealth. This was something of which Daley and the teaching staff he employed were very proud.

In December 1943, the RAAF base also became a training centre for three Dutch squadrons displaced from the Dutch East Indies by the Japanese. The presence of these tall European men introduced a note of novelty and excitement to the predominantly Anglo-Saxon community.

Some of the men were to marry local women and to settle in Canberra after the war. Then American troops were stationed at the new Canberra hospital before being sent north. The Daley girls remember seeing them strolling round, flirting with the locals. Encountering Mr Daley on his walk home for lunch at Acton, they asked if he had any girls 'of marriageable age'.

Another important defence establishment came to Canberra in May 1939, when wireless stations were established at two bases near Canberra, Belconnen and Harman. Harman was set up to receive ships' messages, which were then transmitted to Belconnen for transfer elsewhere. These were some of the earliest such wireless stations to be set up anywhere in the world. There were about thirty families at each base, with the children going to school at the Molonglo camp school.

With the coming of war came the need for the country to produce its own military equipment, including the optical instruments needed for anti-tank guns. The Optical Munitions Panel was created in June 1940 to investigate how this could be best achieved. Daley's brother, Frank Daley, was on the panel, as well as Richard Woolley, Director of the Commonwealth Solar Observatory at Mount Stromlo. Woolley, setting aside his own astronomical research, offered the staff and technical expertise of the Observatory to the war effort, and for the duration of the war Mount Stromlo became one of the Commonwealth's main sources of optical munitions. All optical design was under Woolley's supervision and the director worked seventeen-hour days in the first year of the program. By 1942, the Observatory had been converted into an optical munitions factory, employing at its peak up to seventy people. Most of these workers were brought out to the isolated mountain site by bus and returned to Canberra at the end of the day. They were expected to observe security rules and not talk to anyone about the work they were doing. Women were among those employed at the site, including Unity Cunningham, a trained nurse, who carried out meticulous work inserting lenses into the metal frames of binoculars in a special dust-free room. Unity became a friend and companion to the artist Rosalie Gascoigne, whose husband, Ben Gascoigne, was an expert in astronomical optics. Rosalie, raising three young children in a staff house at the observatory during the war, felt an oppressive loneliness in the cold and isolated atmosphere of Mount

Stromlo, with its ranks of dark pine trees and its exposure to the biting winds of the Brindabellas in winter. In later years, Rosalie Gascoigne was to become a noted artist with an international reputation, but most of the raw material for her work came from the landscape and abandoned artefacts of rural life around Canberra.

Other strangers came to Mount Stromlo during the war, refugees from Europe. Woolley, in urgent need of trained staff, learnt that a number of refugees and wartime internees had first-class optical experience. Most had fled Nazi Germany and had skills in optics and mechanics. The War Cabinet agreed to release a number of internees into Woolley's personal custody, and they became an invaluable part of the team at the Obsevatory. A number of them married Australian women and set up businesses after the war.

Many public servants were working very long hours and up till 10 p.m. on Wednesdays to cope with the extra workload which war brought to the administration. The Works branch of the Department of the Interior worked overtime to cope with the designing and construction of defence and civil works. While the Prime Minister's Department and Department of External Affairs were both based in Canberra, it was clear that the real focus of the war effort still lay in Melbourne. Paul Hasluck, seconded to External Affairs in 1941, was bemused at the muddle and informality that seemed to prevail in the office at West Block. The departmental secretary brought his dog to work and it kept him company in his office, occasionally being given water from the tea lady's saucers. As well, the records clerk had a blue heeler dog who slept under his table. Sensitive files were slipped under the desk blotting paper for future reference, and the filing of documents was in the care of a 'cheerful and imperfectly educated band of youths' or some helpful housewives who worked part time. The department was certainly not the nerve centre of foreign operations. The Department of Defence was based in Melbourne, as were the departments of the Navy, Army and Air, Munitions, Aircraft Production and Defence Coordination. This meant that there was a constant shuttling of ministers, senior administrators and service chiefs between Melbourne and Canberra, with consequent massive waste of time and resources. Most commuting was done on the overnight train to Melbourne unless officers were lucky enough to get a lift in a ministerial car. When war broke out, the *Canberra Times* urged the relocation of senior defence officers to Canberra in the interests of national security and efficiency, and there were many who supported this. Opposition leader John Curtin was very critical of the government's indifference to Canberra as the centre of government. William Woodger, the president of the Canberra Chamber of Commerce, and Dr Nott, elected member of the Advisory Council, both felt that Menzies' government had broken faith with the purchasers of leases and businesses in Canberra, by transferring new war departments to Melbourne. The city, in their eyes, had been abandoned. The reality was that Canberra, chronically short of office space and accommodation, would not have been able to host a massive influx of the Public Service at that stage.

The Melbourne press remained unremittingly hostile to Canberra. An article in the *Argus* on 14 November 1939 headed, 'Aloofness of Canberra: politicians hate it', deemed that 'even now it would not be too late to scrap it and bring back the National Capital to its proper sphere in one of the great Australian capitals'.

The problems caused by trying to conduct a war from widely separated bases were tragically illustrated in the disastrous plane crash on 13 August 1940. It took the lives of ten people, including three Cabinet ministers and the Chief of General Staff, who were flying to Canberra from Melbourne. The plane, coming in to land at Canberra, was seen to circle the aerodrome and then disappeared behind a nearby hill and soon afterwards there was an explosion and a cloud of smoke. Vehicles rushing to the scene found the plane had disintegrated on impact and burst into flame. All on board were killed instantly. There were four crew and six passengers, who included James Fairbairn, Minister for Air and Civil Aviation; Brigadier Austin Street, Minister for the Army and Repatriation; Sir Henry Gullett, Vice-President of the Executive Council; and Sir Cyril Brudenell White, Chief of General Staff. For Prime Minister Menzies, this 'dreadful day' took from him not only his senior advisors and colleagues, but 'some of his greatest friends'.[12] The death of Gullett and Brudenell White saw the passing of two men closely associated with C.E.W. Bean and the story of the 1st AIF. Gullett had written the story of the men of the Light Horse for Volume VII of the Official War History, *The War in Palestine* and Brudenell White had been in command of the

1st AIF after General Bridges' death. Bean wrote later, 'It was unbelievable that four of the noblest of Australia's leaders – two of them among my dearest friends – had perished in that dreadful moment.'[13]

With troops heading for the Middle East and later to the Pacific theatre, and with the RAAF training in Canada and England, Australian families waited hungrily for overseas news. A concert by the ABC Symphony Orchestra at the Albert Hall on 28 November 1942 was to commence at 8 p.m. sharp so people could be home for the 10 p.m. news bulletin on the radio.

Charles Daley, in his annual report for the Music Society in 1942, urged the Canberra community to keep up their association with the society. Not only did the regular program of concerts, with both local artists and some ABC celebrities, provide a useful way to raise money for the war effort; music offered something 'fundamental' to the human spirit, giving consolation and also recreation in times of stress, anxiety and grief. He pointed out that music could also provide a practical way to entertain members of the fighting forces who were coming to Canberra in increasing numbers: the 7th Light Horse, the RAAF and Dutch squadrons, and American troops stationed in Canberra before being deployed north with General Macarthur.

As elsewhere in Australia, fund-raising and volunteer efforts became part of everyday life in Canberra. The Musical Society held many benefit concerts in the war years, with proceeds going to the Red Cross, the Australian Comforts Fund, the POW Fund, the Canberra Volunteers Welfare Association and the Y.Y. Hospitality Centre, an initiative of the YWCA to provide a recreational centre for visiting servicemen and women. A concert held in aid of the Red Cross in April 1940 with the popular Peter Dawson as guest artist attracted a record crowd to the Albert Hall, with hundreds being unable to gain admission. Noel Coward, touring Australia for the Red Cross in 1940, also gave a concert at the hall.

In June 1944, the Sydney Symphony Orchestra performed with guest conductor Eugene Ormandy. He was the first official Lend Lease musician to tour Australia, a visit arranged jointly by the ABC and the US Office of Information. Pianist Isador Goodman performed in April 1945, having already given over 200 concerts for the army in Australia and New Guinea as well as nationwide recitals for war fund charities.

Organising these events was a large and time-consuming job, and Charles Daley as society president took much of the responsibility for them. Hotel bookings for the artists; publicity; invitations to VIPs; hall seating and stage arrangements; conveyance and care of instruments; meeting the artists at the railway station and often hosting a post-concert party at Balmain Crescent: all this had to be done outside office hours.

His daughters recall wonderful occasions at their home: a late-night dinner for a group of Italian opera singers (Hotel Canberra having refused to provide an after-show meal); a visit from the Borovansky ballet troupe; and Artur Rubinstein playing for them on the piano in the drawing room. Jessie Daley had been an active member of the society in the 1930s and a great help to her husband, but the early years of the war saw her succumbing to an illness which increasingly prevented her taking an active role. From May 1943, there were no more cheerful social gatherings at Balmain Crescent. Jessie Daley went to Sydney to the Christian Science Rest Home at Mosman, suffering from the advancing symptoms of cancer. Her eldest daughter, Margaret, went with her as carer; the two younger daughters, Nancy and Joan, were both preparing for end-of-year exams and were not told of their mother's illness. They stayed in the Hotel Kurrajong with their father, as no housekeeping help was available at that stage of the war. Their elder brother, Geoffrey, was in New Guinea serving in a commando unit.

Jessie Daley died in Sydney on 10 November 1943, in the presence of her friend and counsellor, a Christian Science healer. If there were alternative endings to her story or even the possibility of medical intervention that might have prolonged her life, they were not outcomes that Jessie Daley either sought or desired. She died peacefully early in the morning, her friend having read with her the Sermon on the Mount.

*

The Governor General, Lord Gowrie, and his wife Lady Gowrie, were in residence at Yarralumla from 1936 to 1944. Gowrie's term of office was to have ended in September 1939 but with the outbreak of war his appointment was extended. Then in 1942, the couple were persuaded to stay another two years, in spite of Gowrie's ill-health and their desire to see their grandchildren. Despite their patrician background, the Gowries were warmly regarded by Canberra residents. Lady Gowrie, especially, earned wide affection and respect for her engagement in many community projects and her assiduous fund-raising efforts during the war. The grounds of Government House were thrown open for fetes and other public occasions and she helped organise musical events in the ground and at the Albert Hall. She is remembered especially for her support of the Canberra Services Club; she was active in raising funds for this project and took a personal interest in its construction. Opening in March 1941, the club provided a comfortable retreat for service men and women on leave or on duty in Canberra, offering meals, billiards, concerts, twice-weekly dances and reading facilities. Her other abiding interest was in the provision of nursery schools in cities throughout Australia. Conscious of the problems the present generation was passing on to the next, she wanted to see young children given every chance to lead a stable, happy and productive life; nursery schools could play an important role here.

On 24 April 1944, the Music Society held an afternoon concert to honour Lord and Lady Gowrie and farewell them before they left for England. Their only surviving son, Patrick, a gifted poet, had been killed in action in 1942, and people recognised that returning home would bring them grief as well as consolation. Canberra people, many with sons serving overseas, understood the loss this couple had endured, and wanted to wish them well. Daley's speech to the couple was heartfelt.

> You have given your active personal support in every worthy movement in this city. You visited our institutions, including all our churches, attended club and society meetings, sporting functions and gatherings of every kind. Our schools, both public and private, have benefited from your consistent interest. You have truly shared our joys and sorrows and enriched our social experience...[14]

Lady Gowrie and her husband stayed in touch with Daley after the war, with regular Christmas greetings. The 1947 Christmas card had a query, 'How is the music in Canberra?' Zara Gowrie was herself a trained musician.

On 16 June 1940, Prime Minister Menzies had given a rousing address to the nation, announcing far-reaching changes to government powers to put Australia on a full war footing. 'The watchword is "All in" – everything that we have, our savings, our property, our skill, the service of our hands, if necessary the service of our lives ...'[15]

Community groups and schools undertook to make camouflage nets and grow Victory Gardens where decorative flower beds or stretches of lawn were dug up and replaced by radishes, carrots and potatoes. There were Sheepskins for Russia appeals and schools and clubs served as depots where country people could bring their donated fleeces. Following a national appeal for scrap rubber, schoolchildren began collecting old tyres as well as bottles, tins and newspapers. John Curtin, who had replaced Menzies as Prime Minister in September 1941, warned in May 1943, '...it is not an exaggeration to say we could lose the war through lack of rubber, the supply source of which is now almost entirely in enemy occupied countries'.[16] An urgent directive went out to all Commonwealth departments to do their utmost to conserve rubber supplies. Daley forwarded instructions to all public and departmental vehicle users to be rigorous about correct maintenance, wheel alignment and careful braking. With the rationing of petrol and the shortage of rubber and spare parts, private vehicles soon disappeared off the roads. Canberra's streets reminded one observer of India, with people going about their business everywhere on bicycles.

While in many ways Melbourne had become the focus of the government's war efforts, an event on Remembrance Day in 1941 symbolised the central role that Canberra could still play as the national capital. This was the official opening of the first stage of the Australian War Memorial, when the exhibition galleries would be opened to the public for the first time. The Hall of Memory and the Cloisters would not be developed until after the war.

The two men who addressed the nation that day – ABC broadcast the event Australia-wide – were a study in contrasts: the Governor-General, Lord Gowrie, a senior and distinguished soldier of the Empire, who had earned a VC while serving with the Egyptian army in 1898 and been badly wounded on Gallipoli; and the Prime Minister, John Curtin, a former trade unionist, opposed to conscription in 1916 and briefly gaoled for failing to register for the call-up. If Gowrie was initially distrustful of the new Prime Minister, over the course of the war they developed a close friendship when they were neighbours at the Lodge and Yarralumla. At the Memorial, both spoke words that fitted the sombre mood of the times. Lord Gowrie asked those who would visit the Memorial to reflect on the terrible cost of war. The Great War had 'settled nothing; it was a war in which all concerned came out losers'.[17] He asked Australians to be prepared for any sacrifice in the present war to put an end to this 'menace to mankind' and to declare 'never again, never again'. John Curtin's speech emphasised the appropriate symbolism of siting the War Memorial opposite the Federal Parliament, whose elected leaders might look up and see in the Memorial a reminder of a people's sacrifice and endeavour.

Canberra people, as in every other Australian community, had their share of anxiety and grief as their sons enlisted to serve overseas, in some cases not to return or to return as changed men. Many who had caught malaria while serving in the Pacific found that it recurred to plague them after the war. Daley's own son, Geoffrey Charles Daley, enlisted with the Commando Squadron 2/7 and served in New Guinea on the Owen Stanley Ranges. Falling seriously ill with scrub typhus and malaria, he was evacuated to Port Moresby, carried out by native bearers. After recovering in a Moresby hospital, Geoffrey was discharged from the army on 26 November 1944. Unwilling to return to a desk job after the war, Geoffrey decided to finish his law degree full time at his father's old college, Ormonde College at the University of Melbourne. He suffered recurrent bouts of malaria. His sisters recall that there were 'a lot of adjustments' these returned men had to make, including recovery from nightmares about being under attack, the snipers hiding in the foliage...

James and Helen Brackenreg's son, Lieutenant James Brackenreg, of 2nd Battalion, was declared missing in the retreat from Greece in 1941. He was later reported wounded and a prisoner. He was among those who were liberated from German POW camps in May 1945, to be given a welcome home at the Lady Gowrie Services Hut in December 1945. Sir Robert Garran's son, John, was there too. He had endured captivity in Changi and forced labour on the Burma Railway, where his tall, gaunt figure and strong spirit had made him a leader among his fellow captives.

*

From 1934, Charles Daley had an important weekly commitment which he kept faith with for seventeen years. After the dedication of the new Presbyterian Church of St Andrew, Daley was approached by the church elders to see if he would be willing to play their organ until they could find someone permanent. Daley was already known as an accomplished organist, as he often played the organ at the old church of St Johns. He was appointed honorary organist at St Andrews in August 1934 and from then on became an indispensable figure in the musical life of the church. He played at Sunday services, weddings, funerals and baptisms plus weekly rehearsals. His daughters also recall how much time he spent in maintenance of the organ, a stately Hill, Norman and Beard instrument that often needed attention. He would take the girls along during the week and while he clambered up into the loft to attend to the organ pipes, he would shout down instructions as to which note they were to play while he checked it. As a reward for their help, he would have some fun with the girls by playing 'Who's Afraid of the Big Bad Wolf' and other bouncy airs in the empty church.

Hector Harrison was the moderator (minister) at St Andrews. He seems to have provided friendship, moral support and spiritual comfort to a range of people during those difficult years. A number of letters to him attest to the regard in which he was held by his parishioners. Lord Gowrie wrote 'to my neighbour and my warm friend' to thank him for his support after the death of Patrick, Lord Gowrie's son.

Prime Minister John Curtin was another neighbour and close friend of Harrison. By the middle of 1945, Curtin knew that he was dying, having already suffered one major heart attack from which he never fully recovered. A letter of 23 June 1945 requested

that my friend, Reverend Hector Harrison, should conduct any service which is held in Canberra and also conduct the service in Western Australia should he find it convenient to go there. I am aware that there is a hereafter and that men are required to account for their misdeeds in this life.[18]

Curtin had abandoned his Catholic faith years before but here it seems he was groping toward some kind of religious consolation. He had lived long enough with the burden of alcoholism, and fought hard enough to overcome it, to recognise the claims that some kind of spiritual repentance might have on him.

Curtin died at the Lodge on 5 July. He had been Prime Minister for a brief era in Australia's history, but people recognised how much his leadership had meant to the country in the days after the fall of Singapore and for the years of war that followed. Thousands gathered at his funeral on 7 July at the Karrakatta cemetery near his home of Cottesloe, with Hector Harrison conducting the service. The day before, a simple memorial service had been held in Kings Hall, Parliament House, with Harrison reading the eulogy. After the service, the plane bearing Curtin's body left Canberra airport for Western Australia. A high school football team, training on the school oval, stood to attention at the request of their coach: a line of fifteen boys looking up as the plane circled low over the city before heading west into the evening.

11

A New Beginning

'Canberra became a richer and more interesting place because of these waves of migration.'

Citizenship Convention, Canberra 1950.
From the collection of the National Archives of Australia

On 15 January 1943, Treasurer Ben Chifley took charge of a new Ministry of Postwar Reconstruction to plan for Australia's transition from a wartime to a peacetime economy. The Depression had convinced many progressive thinkers of the strong need for government intervention and forward planning to prevent the recurrence of the social disruption and human suffering that Australia had gone through in those years. There was also a strong desire to maintain full employment and to avoid the mistakes made after World War I, when so many men returned to years of poverty and struggle. Chifley had bitter memories of 'hundreds of men queued up outside the Lithgow small arms factory gate, all after the one job...'[1]

Between 1942 and 1946, widows' pensions, maternity allowances for Aboriginal mothers, funeral benefits and unemployment and sickness benefits were introduced; old age and invalid pensions and other payments were adjusted to allow for increased price levels. These were all measures that bore the stamp of a Labor Party committed to social reform. The department also worked with the states to provide housing and hospitals and gave financial support to the state universities. Under John Curtin's leadership, the Labor Party supported the establishment of a national university in Canberra and more university scholarships to give working class students greater access to higher education. Charles Daley was to play a part in this era of reconstruction in his own city, especially in the field of education, in which he had a lifelong interest.

Daley played a very active role in the establishment of the early schools in Canberra. Telopea Public School was opened on 11 September 1923 to serve as a central school in the first stages of the city's growth. Arrangements were made with the NSW Department of Education to provide staff and curriculum resources while the Commonwealth would bear the costs of the buildings and their upkeep. Much of the liaison with the department was Daley's responsibility. From the outset, Telopea accepted secondary as well as primary students, and in 1925 the school had successful candidates in the Intermediate and Leaving Certificates. The Department of Home Affairs officials sent their children to the school, and children also came from the outlying districts of Gibralter, Tharwa, Royalla, Weetangera and Hall, where some of the old pioneering families still lived on leased properties. As well, there were the children of construction workers from the camps at Westlake, Westridge, Molonglo and Duntroon.

In June 1928, Prime Minister Bruce opened the Technical and Trades School attached to the Telopea school before being moved to the Power House complex. He referred to it as one of the most up-to-date in the Commonwealth. In 1930, the new Canberra University College began to make use of the school after hours, with Dr Allen conducting classes in English and Latin and Professor Haydon holding French and German classes.

Telopea and Ainslie Public Schools were some of the best equipped and furnished government schools in Australia. Their parent body had a much more professional and educated background than was the case in most regional communities at the time. Many parents took an active role in fund-raising and serving on parents & citizens committees. The opening of Ainslie Primary School in September 1927 was one of the first important civic functions to be performed by Prime Minister Bruce in the new city. Many of his cabinet ministers were also in attendance that day. Charles and Jessie Daley were there as young parents and signed the visitors' book. Their elder son, Geoffrey, was one of the foundation students at the school and became dux in his last year.

When the school was extended in 1938, the new building provided rich opportunities for arts and crafts and an activity-centred approach to learning. The school was the first primary school in Australia to be planned with a purpose-built library, lecture room and needlework room. The library contained a valuable collection of paintings by a Sydney artist, T.F.W.S. Alban: a mural depicting the story of Peter Pan. The school magazine, *The Beacon*, was a high-quality production with poetry, linocuts and a stylish cover design, and a school choir established in 1930 won local competitions and eisteddfods. Daley often accompanied the school choir and he wrote the school song, 'Altiora'.

As a showplace, the school was often visited by delegations to Canberra. Paul Harris, the American founder of Rotary International, visited it in April 1935. Noted feminist and political campaigner Jessie

Street had warm words of praise for what was being done in Canberra's schools. After a visit in June 1940, she wrote to Daley,

> Many thanks for taking me to see those beautiful schools. We really have something in Canberra to be proud of in them... I hope you will get a minister sufficiently sympathetic to make it possible to start on the university.[2]

They would have shared, these two, a common desire to see a national university in the young capital. It was a part of Burley Griffin's plan, and the area designated on the gazetted city plan – between Black Mountain and the Civic Centre – was the site Griffin had chosen. There had been support for a university from the 1920s. Two forceful advocates were Sir Robert Garran and Sir David Rivett, a scientist appointed in 1927 to head the new Council for Scientific and Industrial Research (CSIR). In 1929, they formed a committee with J.G. McClaren which submitted a plan to the government for a university offering undergraduate courses as well as undertaking research and postgraduate work. In 1930, the government, as an interim measure, agreed to establish a university college which would provide undergraduate courses in arts and economics to suit the needs of Canberra's public service population. The college was affiliated with the University of Melbourne. Sir Robert Garran was chair of the College Council and Charles Daley was a founding member, remaining on the council for twenty-eight years. The council and the University Association (an informal gathering of intellectuals in Canberra, including Daley) made a number of approaches to Prime Minister Lyons over the next decade, urging the creation of a national university with a focus on scientific research and advanced study, but the Depression years were not an auspicious time for such a project.

The war provided a new momentum. Many intellectuals who were deeply engaged in the war effort were also looking ahead to what a post-war Australia would be like and what it might be capable of achieving. Most of the employees in the new Department of Postwar Reconstruction were young economists with university degrees. This was a contrast to the pre-war policy of the Commonwealth Service, which had always given preference to ex-AIF men. This meant that in some departments the higher ranks were often staffed by men who had gained their position by virtue of long service rather than intellectual ability. Many of the young people recruited to work in Canberra towards the end of the war found it an exciting place. There was the experience of being in a community with people 'who were there because they had the brains and ability to pull the country through the war and prepare for the post-war period'.[3]

The economist H.C. Coombs was a valued advisor to the Treasurer, Ben Chifley, who appointed him head of the Department of Postwar Reconstruction in early 1943. The department established a reconstruction training scheme to offer full-time training to ex-servicemen and women as a prelude to their suitable re-employment. Part-time training was also available to groups to upgrade or improve their occupational status. Another of the department's initiatives was an interdepartmental committee, chaired by R.C. Mills, to investigate the future role of the Commonwealth in education, which up till then was mainly a state responsibility. Charles Daley was invited to attend committee meetings as a representative of the Department of the Interior. It was Daley who suggested that the idea of a national university be included in the committee's agenda. With Garran's help, he prepared a memorandum proposing a postgraduate university with research of special concern to the Commonwealth in the emerging post war world: government and international relations; Australian literature and history; and Pacific affairs. The final report of the Mills Committee, submitted in October 1944, endorsed these proposals and supported a strong Commonwealth involvement in education: a Commonwealth Office of Education was set up in early 1945. Daley had made a significant contribution to this historic document and was invited to sign the final report.

Another area of research which was clearly vital to Australia's future was medical research, and there were hopes that the distinguished Australian scientist Sir Howard Florey might lead a national medical research centre in Canberra. With John Curtin's illness and death, this opportunity was lost but Coombs took up the initiative, urging the Mills Committee to recommend the immediate establishment of a university in Canberra with research focused in five schools: Medical Research; Social Sciences; Pacific Affairs; Town and Country Planning (later dropped) and Physical Science.

On 1 August 1946, the university Bill passed into law and the Australian National University (ANU) was formally created. Coombs saw the new university as an agent of change, 'a kind of intellectual powerhouse for the rebuilding of society', whose members could seek answers to the problems of poverty, unemployment, social injustice and international and racial tensions.[4] Sir David Rivett wanted to see both CSIR and the ANU engage in fundamental scientific research and he deplored the 'conscription' of science by totalitarian societies as had occurred under Nazi and Soviet rule.

An interim council for the ANU was appointed which numbered Coombs, Rivett, Garran and Daley among its members. Daley was on the building and grounds committee, whose task was to liaise with the government and the academic community about the many specialised building needs of the research schools and the university as a whole, including the vexed question of accommodation – this at a time when there was an acute housing shortage in Canberra. The interim council held monthly meetings throughout 1947, setting up many administrative and financial arrangements, appointing a registrar and a librarian and finally, in 1948, choosing a man for the crucial position of vice-chancellor, a person who, according to academics, 'would relieve them of their chores but not of their authority'.[5] The council chose Professor Douglas Copeland, Minister to pre-Communist China and Australia's Prices Commissioner during the war.

The council was determined to enlist the brightest talents available to head the schools and in 1948 a number of expatriate Australians were invited to visit Canberra with their wives, to meet the interim council and to discuss in detail the requirements for the research schools. Howard Florey, Marcus Oliphant and Keith Hancock were three Australians who had achieved international recognition in their respective fields of medicine, nuclear physics and modern history. Raymond Firth, a New Zealander, was Professor of Anthropology at the University of London and was keen to play a part as head of a school of Asian/Pacific studies.

There was a particular cachet attached to the physical science program. Marcus Oliphant had worked at Cambridge University's Cavendish Laboratory, and during the war he was part of the British team working on the Manhattan Project to develop the atomic bomb. His own vision was of a post-war world that would benefit immeasurably from the harnessing of nuclear energy for peaceful purposes. The council were very keen to appoint him to head a research school which would include departments of nuclear physics, particle physics and theoretical physics, geophysics and astronomy. Oliphant explained to the council his concept of the new university, where the heads of the research schools would each bring out a team of first-class colleagues and establish that communality of endeavour that marked the centres of advanced learning in Europe and America. His employment would be expensive, requiring a large budget for experimental equipment, running expenses and salaries. Keith Hancock the historian also had large claims to make. He would not be prepared to do any undergraduate teaching and both he and Oliphant were reluctant to see the Canberra University College incorporated into the ANU, a move they felt might compromise the work of the research schools.

Both Hancock and Oliphant suspected that they – and their wives – might find it difficult to adjust to life in the small community that was Canberra, whose population was still under 50,000. The shops were primitive but expensive, there were no good restaurants – and where were the theatres, the good bookshops? They would need generous sabbaticals to return to Europe for intellectual refreshment. What about their wives, who were educated women? They would not want to come to Canberra to spend all their time in the kitchen, but would they be guaranteed access to paid domestic help? The interim council promised as best it could to meet these requests for 'freedom from routine duties which is essential to success in original investigations', which included a promise that the men would not be required to take part in speeches or debates on behalf of the government.[6]

An ample budget and an absence of too many strict rules and regulations meant that the interim council was able to offer generous salaries and conditions to these academic 'maestros'. Oliphant, anxious to please his wife, who was reluctant to leave her home in England, wanted a home with plenty of land and spectacular views. Daley took him out to virgin scrub at Weetangara (now part of the suburb of O'Connor), which was just outside the existing survey limits of the city, where they inspected a block that seemed suitable. Oliphant later blamed Daley for choosing the site, saying it was probably chosen so as to make out a case for surveying the area for new subdivisions. As building costs soared and projects were delayed by the shortage of labour and materials, Oliphant, back in England, was ready to throw in the Canberra position. The interim council, alarmed by the potential loss of this key figure, prevailed upon Prime Minister Menzies, newly returned to office, to offer 'carte blanche' to Oliphant, including capping at £10,000 the amount he had to pay for the house. In the end, the house was rented to Oliphant, not sold. The city plan was in fact modified to allow for the extension of services to this hillside but soon afterwards the new suburbs of Turner and O'Connor were developed.

When it was finished, the large home stood on a rise looking over the new development of O'Connor. In May 1953, Oliphant made himself locally unpopular when he wrote to the *Canberra Times*, complaining in a letter of extraordinary arrogance that his hillside view was becoming 'increasingly depressing' as he looked out on the wooden cottages below.[7] These were 'Tocumwal houses', formerly sleeping huts from Tocumwal air base in NSW. In 1947, they had been transported to Canberra and refitted as family homes to help ease the acute post-war housing shortage. Oliphant thought they were little better than slums and he deplored the bare appearance of the suburb, where old trees had been cut down to make way for roads and other facilities. Two loyal Canberrans, Jim Fraser (the FCT's second elected member to the House of Representatives) and William McLaren, Secretary to the Department of the Interior, both wrote letters in reply, with a stinging rebuff of Oliphant's comments. Fraser suggested that Oliphant, instead of complaining about the views, might like to empathise with those families who had waited two years or more to receive public housing.

Early in 1950, when the first academic staff took up residence, the ANU was still just a shed in a grassy paddock. The shed was a former RAAF mess hut moved in sections from Cootamundra to Acton, where it served as a board room, offices and kitchen. By 1953, the paddock had become a construction site. Construction had begun on the Medical Research and the Physical Sciences buildings with their associated laboratories; housing for ANU staff was another priority.

In 1954, University House was opened and became a showpiece of the ANU with its collection of contemporary Australian art and fine furniture by the noted Australian designer Fred Ward. University House was built on the model of an Oxbridge college, offering postgraduate scholars a place to stay where they could meet like-minded colleagues and take part in academic social life. University House became an important part of Charles Daley's life after his retirement from public service in 1952. He paid his annual membership and regularly had his midday meal there, enjoying the stimulating company of the many international scholars who came to the university for terms of study or research. His home in Balmain Crescent was only five minutes' walk away from University House. The cottages built by the Commission now came under the control of the ANU, some of them being taken over for staff residences or office accommodation.

The post-war years saw Charles Daley still leading a busy working life as Deputy Secretary of the Civic Branch of the Department of the Interior. It was not a job many people would have envied him. The department had little better standing in the eyes of many people than the Commission had had. 'It ruled our lives,' was a common feeling.[8] The Civic branch was the public face of the bureaucracy for most Canberra residents. They visited the Acton offices to pay their rates, register their motor vehicle, complain about housing or leases, enquire about lost dogs, request maintenance on a cricket oval or a toilet block for a community hall. In the minds of most people, the branch consisted of dull, decent people doing a dull but necessary job.

Daley's own position of course involved work that was both more complex and more challenging than this. As the man with oversight of building regulations and ordinances, Daley had to reconcile the pressing need for more worker settlements with his obligation to adhere to the official city plan. There was a chronic housing shortage after the war: returned servicemen and their families needed somewhere to live, and as well there was an influx of new workers as the government promised to complete the transfer of the public service from Melbourne. A number of new workmen's hostels, built on austere and temporary lines, were erected after the war to house single men including emigrant workers. In 1946, a 'temporary' settlement for families was built at Narrabundah, with prefabricated steel frames and plywood walls. As mentioned before, huts brought up from Tocumwal air base became the wooden cottages of the new suburbs of Turner and O'Connor. As well, the worker settlements of the 1920s were still in use twenty years later. Westlake, for example, originally planned as temporary quarters during the Commission years, was now a strong and cohesive community and people rightly regarded it as their home. These scatterings of temporary and low-cost settlements were a feature of post-war Canberra. As well, many temporary and poorly built administrative buildings were erected during the war and post-war years in Griffin's governmental area, in clear contravention of the city plan.

In 1939, at Daley's instigation, the National Capital Planning and Development Committee was set up as a body of review and advice, with Daley as executive officer, all members, highly qualified architects and town planners, giving voluntarily of their time. It aimed to safeguard the Griffin plan and to set high aesthetic and architectural standards for building in the capital. It did successfully advise the government on the need for three key changes to the Griffin plan: the removal of the industrial area from north Canberra to Fyshwick; the elimination of the expensive Eastern Lake (which would have drowned most of the territory's dairying and orchard land); and the removal of the railway line through Civic and north Canberra. But the committee could only offer advice, it had no executive power and its advice was often ignored: it was reminded that it should 'confine its report to the suitability of plans submitted'.[9] The erection of temporary buildings continued, a consequence of population pressures, public service needs, and often, the wishes of government ministers with no interest in long term planning for the capital. Daley was later to admit, 'I could write a book about the frustrations we have suffered in building a capital, as a result of sheer lack of interest on the part of political authorities'.[10]

Daley found more satisfaction in other aspects of his work. When the Snowy Mountains Scheme was inaugurated by Prime Minister Chifley in 1949, Daley was proud that he had played a role in the early stages. In January 1946, he wrote a report for the Department of the Interior, referring to the 1909 Seat of Government (Surrender) Act which provided that NSW would grant the Commonwealth free access to the water of the Snowy River for electricity generation.[11] Daley urged the department to consider the future use of the Snowy River for hydroelectricity needs as Australia's demand for more electric power grew after the war. The Snowy River Authority was later to consult Daley for historical background to the 1909 Act, as it sought to balance the power needs of Victoria, NSW and the ACT.

There was also great satisfaction in showing overseas visitors around the young city, explaining its history and sketching out its future. In November 1944, Lieutenant-Colonel S. Ballard of the Air Corps, US Army, visited Canberra.

> The morning I spent in Mr Daley's office was the most instructive, the most fascinating I've had in years. He showed me the original Griffin plans and drawings, also new plans developed by the present government.[12]

While the Griffin plans and drawings were in the custody of Daley's office, he also found himself defending those plans against commercial or political interests. R.J. Casey, Treasurer in the Lyons government in 1936, wished to settle in Canberra. He chose a site for his residence at Acton, overlooking the future lake. It was a site marked for the hospital on Griffin's plan. Daley wrote to the Secretary of the Treasury on 11 November 1936, explaining that it would be a serious breach of the zoning provisions in the Griffin plan to locate a ministerial residence on a site reserved for hospital use. He also pointed out that it would be a serious reflection on the government as there were no convincing reasons for allowing this to happen. He concluded, 'It is the statutory duty of the Department to preserve the accepted plan of Canberra.'[13] Daley stood firm against the Treasurer on that occasion. Casey got his residence, a grand brick mansion on the south side of the river in the new diplomatic enclave that developed after the war.

There were other confrontations. An influential builder had a fur coat ready to offer to Mrs Daley if her husband had been willing to listen to his proposition for some changes to the zoning laws.

One long-running exchange concerned Mrs Helen Barton, who ran a private bus company in Canberra. She was a formidable character whom people did not willingly cross. She had first visited Canberra in 1925 and approached Daley about bringing her fleet of heavy earth-moving vehicles to the capital from NSW, where they were employed on railway construction. They operated under her name; Mr Barton takes a back seat in this story, as he did no doubt in the marriage. Daley explained to Mrs Barton that heavy trucks were not needed but there was a good opening for a motor bus.

In July 1926, Mrs Barton established a private bus company which had good patronage on the city to Queanbeyan run. By January 1927, she had purchased a second bus, two ordinary touring cars and an up-to-date limousine so that she could enter the taxi and touring car business. She and her husband and their pet dogs took up residence at Hotel Canberra and she parked her fleet of vehicles behind the hotel in a temporary extension built onto an open shed which was where hotel guests parked their cars.

With the approach of the opening of Parliament House in May 1927, all accommodation at Hotel Canberra was required for officials and the temporary bus shelter was to be dismantled. Mrs Barton and her husband would have to give up their rooms and also move their vehicles. Daley suggested that she arrange with a local garage to take her vehicles. No, the buses wouldn't fit. Could she not arrange to build a garage on an industrial block she was leasing at Ainslie? No, she couldn't justify the expenditure when her future business was so uncertain. Mrs Barton refused to move from Hotel Canberra unless the Commission could provide accommodation for her and her fleet of vehicles. It was only when Daley threatened her with an eviction notice that she and her husband and the pet dogs moved to the Hotel Ainslie, where the Commission allowed her to park her vehicles as an interim measure.

The Commission introduced its own city bus service in April 1926, with four vehicles operating a basic service around the new suburbs. Helen Barton soon accused the Commission of undercutting her. In fact, she had been asked to offer a quote for this city service but her high price had been unacceptable, the Commission being able to run the buses at a much lower rate.

By 1930, Mrs Barton's coach service was based in the industrial area at Mort Street, Braddon, and she was still conveying passengers on the Ainslie to Queanbeyan run. By that stage, the Commission had granted her a number of concessions: she was allowed to undertake special services during peak periods (such as when the Manuka picture shows finished); to use her two cars as private hire cars with appropriate vehicle number plates; to take group hire within the FCT; and to pay her registration fees by monthly instalments.

In spite of these concessions, she felt embattled. Writing to Minister Neville Howse in June 1928, she announced that 'negotiations are at a deadlock; how tightly the noose is being drawn...'[14] Registration fees hadn't been paid; her hire cars were not properly registered; her drivers on the Queanbeyan run were picking up passengers within the city area and thus competing with the city omnibus. Daley admitted to a colleague that she was 'a most trying woman; she has a mistaken idea of the extent to which she should be assisted'. After Mrs Barton erected a house and garage on her leased block, she asked for permission to run a miniature golf course on the block to supplement her income. This request was refused. When her file was closed, in June 1931, she was still asking for concessions from the department.

*

A much happier relationship was forged with William Hoffmann, a young musician who came to Canberra in July 1947. He was the first professional musician to be employed full-time by the Commonwealth Public Service, with the aim of re-establishing the Canberra City Band and initiating music training in schools. Hoffmann and his wife lived with Charles Daley for two and a half years while they waited for a house of their own to become available. Daley in fact was the man behind the whole enterprise. With his long involvement with Canberra public schools, he was keen to introduce a program of musical education and he found Prime Minister Ben Chifley sympathetic to the idea.

The Canberra City Band had in its former life been a community brass band formed by men coming to Canberra in the 1920s to work on construction sites. Part of the tradition of English working-class life, brass bands had a popular following in Australia, with men often inheriting a cornet, euphonium or trombone from a father or uncle. Many of these men were self-taught, but under the leadership of a dynamic bandmaster who organised regular practice sessions, they could create lively, tuneful music that was a feature of public gatherings between the wars.

John Butters and his Social Service Association wanted to support a community band and discovered that there were a number of brass players in the work camps who were keen to form a band but needed instruments and sheet music. Butters and Daley were able to arrange for the donation of instruments and music and the Commission provided free transport for men to rehearsals and performances. With annual subsidies from the Commission, the Canberra City Band was able to perform at a number of public functions, including the arrival of the Duke of York in May 1927 and the welcome to Bert Hinkler in 1928. Butters was patron of the band, whose confident slogan was 'Australia's best band for Australia's Capital'.

The Depression was a blow to the brass band movement everywhere. Men who were out of work and struggling to feed their family had neither time nor energy for musical recreation. In 1929, the Commission provided a subsidy to the band and contributed to the cost of uniforms and new instruments, but the real problem was unresolved. Men were out of work, and there was no preference given to bandsmen in filling jobs. Daley, Civic Administrator at the time, did what he could to plead their cause. 'A local band is a feature of town life and in proportion to the practical support and direct interest taken must be its quality and the pride residents take in it.'[15]

In 1937, an act of working men's solidarity put an end to the band's career. The men refused to perform at an Armistice Day ceremony at Parliament House unless the government guaranteed full-time employment for its members. Prime Minister Lyons instructed that all assistance to the band was to cease. The instruments, music and uniforms were put into storage, to be retrieved from time to time when there was a request for a loan. In June 1941, the wing commander of the RAAF base in Canberra wanted to start a brass band and Daley recommended that the instruments be made available for his use. However, by March 1942, as the war moved closer, the station had to return the instruments as the frequent comings and goings of RAAF personnel made regular rehearsals impossible.

With the ending of the war, people wanted to revitalise community and cultural life. Men returning from active service and ex-band members expressed interest in re-forming the band. Daley took their appeal to the secretary of the department, adding that it was crucial to appoint a full-time, well-paid conductor as a government employee. It was 'unreasonable to expect the best results of a man given two jobs to do'.[16] He had the backing of Prime Minister Ben Chifley, who had visited the UK in 1946 and been impressed by the concert bands he had seen performing in regional communities. In 1947, national advertisements for the position of bandmaster were placed. Daley was in charge of the interview and selection process and considered the twenty-eight-year-old Hoffmann the best applicant in view of his experience and 'his enthusiasm for this somewhat unusual set of duties'. Hoffmann played a range of musical instruments and had wide experience of promoting musical activities in the community; he had also commanded an army band during the war.

A former band leader, Les Pogson, who had his own popular dance band in Canberra in the 1930s, had moved to Albury during the war to entertain troops passing through. He would have liked to apply for the position but decided against it due to the scarcity of housing in Canberra.

The newly formed Canberra City Band under Bill Hoffmann had its first practice session on 22 September 1947. Ben Chifley was made honorary member of the band and retained an interest in it until his death in 1951. In fact, the band was known to some as Chif's Band or Mr Chifley's Baby. The first public performance was on Anzac Day in 1948 at the Australian War Memorial. Chifley was there, and two visitors for the Food for Britain campaign, Laurence Olivier and Vivien Leigh. In October 1949, the band played at the opening of the Snowy Mountains Scheme in Adaminaby and a week later at the laying of the foundation stone at the ANU: both great national projects initiated under Chifley's leadership. That year, the band had been transformed from a brass band to a military or concert band by the introduction of woodwind instruments. The band made its first appearance as a full concert band on Remembrance Day at the Australian War Memorial in 1949.

The band's profile grew under Hoffmann's energetic leadership. In November 1948, a performance was broadcast on local station 2CA; the Queanbeyan Municipal Band interrupted its practice to listen with great interest. In 1950 and 1951, there were free concerts on Sunday afternoons – in the Albert Hall in winter, outdoors in summer – which included performance of popular requests. The Jubilee year of 1951 celebrated fifty years since the opening of the first Commonwealth parliament. On the Australia Day weekend, the Canberra City Band played a special program of Australian music on the lawns in front of Parliament House, including a composition, *Murrumbidgee Panorama*, by Hoffmann. This work was also played in March that year at the small village of Tharwa, 'the first occasion in the history of the district that there had been a band concert'.[17]

As well as giving his active support to the band, Prime Minister Chifley decided that the government should play a role in encouraging all the arts in Canberra, now that the war was over and there were plans for the city's growth in development and population. In April 1948, he met representatives of cultural societies in Canberra. Under the direction of Sir Robert Garran, a report was prepared outlining a long-term program to build theatres, concert halls, cultural centres, and an art gallery and a conservatorium of music. All these lay well into the future, but in January 1949, Chifley informed the Arts Council that he and the Minister for the Interior had agreed to an annual grant towards cultural activities in the city, to be decided with the help of an advisory committee. Government money for the arts is well established policy these days but the Chifley government's grant to the arts organisations in Canberra was the first Commonwealth arts grant in the country.

The Jubilee year, 1951, was a milestone for Canberra and a milestone in Charles Daley's professional life. As chair of the committee set up to organise the territory's year-long celebrations, he had oversight of a program of events that gave every community group a chance to be involved. Daley was sixty-four and nearing retirement when he took on a program that these days would be the work of a highly paid and full-time director. People had confidence that he would do the job well. When Lady Gowrie had expressed a wish to start a Red Cross branch in Canberra in 1939, she was told by its secretary-general that if Daley took up the development of the movement, 'it would be a guarantee of its success'.[18]

The Jubilee year was crammed with events. There were sheep dog trials; performances by Canberra Repertory and Canberra City Band; Artists' Society exhibitions; an ACT youth week; numerous sporting events, including a long-distance bike ride ending in Canberra, organised by Hubert Opperman; a Jubilee poultry show and the annual show at the village of Hall of the ACT Pastoral and Agricultural Society. The Countrywomen's Association (CWA) met their world president, visiting from the US: a 'simple country woman' who called for world peace. Teachers came from interstate for a Jubilee education conference, with Margaret Mead as one of the guest speakers. There was a large program of public tree planting and Daley wrote the introduction to a reprint of the Canberra Horticultural Society's book *The Canberra Gardener* (still in print and an indispensable reference fifty years later). A large-scale pageant took place on Capital Hill as part of the celebrations, with a re-enactment of the day Lady Denman gave Canberra its official name. Canberra Repertory's professional producer, Adrian Borzell, created an extravaganza involving several hundred people: there was a Cobb & Co. coach, bushrangers on horseback, the Duntroon band and cadets, and the entire population of Canberra's schools, who wound up the pageant by making a huge map of Australia on the hill. John Garran, back in civilian life as a farmer and an enthusiastic member of Repertory, played the role of King O'Malley. This open-air spectacle was a great success and a popular highlight of the year's celebrations.

While the program included Canberra groups, it was anything but parochial. With a fine sense of history, it embraced both past and future, themes local and international, as all part of the city's story. Sir Robert Garran gave an address on Fifty Years of Federation; Marcus Oliphant arranged a conference at the ANU on Science in Australia; Dr Joanne Eder, president of the International Council of Women, addressed a women's gathering. A pioneers' night was held at the Albert Hall, and many members of old pioneering families on the Limestone Plains came along to reminisce and join in the dancing. One of their number, an eighty-year-old gentleman, sang an old ballad from his youthful days in the district.

The State Ball on the evening of 13 June was interrupted and then ended by the news that former Prime Minister Ben Chifley had died of a heart attack. There was widespread and profound grief at his death. 'No Australian party leader, no prime minister, has been mourned more deeply.'[19] The next night the Sydney Symphony Orchestra, conducted by Eugene Goossens, performed at a Jubilee concert held at the Capitol Theatre. The evening opened with the Funeral March from Beethoven's *Eroica* Symphony, honouring the passing of a man who so genuinely symbolised the ideals of the Labour movement.

There were two other gatherings of national significance during the Jubilee year. One was the second Citizenship Convention, held at the Albert Hall between 22 and 26 January. Its purpose was to celebrate the success of the immigration program since the war and the assimilation into Australian life of 'New Australians'. Giving the immigration program a sense of urgency and national importance in that era of Cold War unease was the desire to populate Australia's empty spaces and provide a strong workforce for economic development. At a naturalisation ceremony, certificates were presented to four people, all refugees from wartime and post-war Europe, who were taking on Australian citizenship; they were required to renounce their former nationality and to take an oath of allegiance to the king. As part of the conference there was an exhibition of arts and crafts from some of the emigrés' homelands and an open-air pageant of dance and ceremony in front of Parliament House, with 6,000 people attending. The first convention, held in January 1949, had been arranged under the Labor government, which then lost office. Harold Holt, Minister for Immigration in the Menzies government, took over its organisation. It aimed to instil in Australians 'a deeper appreciation of the privileges and obligations of citizenship, and the responsibility of sharing these obligations and privileges with immigrants…' Newcomers were expected to renounce old and foreign loyalties yet keep a pride in their cultural heritage. Perhaps we see the program as sending contradictory messages. Yet there was no denying the impact these waves of migration had on Australian life in the '50s and '60s, and Canberra, like other cities, became a richer and more interesting place because of it. Hoffmann recalled that at one stage in the early 1950s there were eleven different nationalities represented in the city band.

The second major conference of the year was held over four days in August. The Jubilee Congress on Regional and Town Planning brought architects, town planners, politicians and bureaucrats together to consider what the next fifty years might mean for the development of Canberra. The conference offered Daley a chance to bring Griffin's plans and his legacy to the attention of a new generation. Arrangements were made for his prize-winning designs to be on display at the National Library – the first time many would have seen them – as well as aerial photos showing recent development and plans of principal official buildings.

Daley gave the opening address as Executive Officer of the National Capital Planning and Development Committee, explaining its role as an advisory body modelled on the Washington Fine Arts Commission. His address, geared as it was to an event celebrating Canberra's story, glossed over the many obstacles and frustrations the committee had faced in trying to persuade successive governments to adhere to the official city plan. Nevertheless, his address made its mark at the conference. Professor Brian Lewis of the University of Melbourne, who was to be chief architect for the building of the ANU, wrote afterwards to Daley to thank him for the paper which was 'the most interesting and valuable of those delivered'.[20] He suggested that Daley should write a book, 'with your knowledge and experience of Canberra, which is unique'.

A British authority on town planning, Professor Brian Holford, was guest speaker at the conference and was later invited back to Canberra to advise on its development under Prime Minister Menzies. In time, the lake would be developed, and buildings set in spacious gardens. It would also be a city of free-flowing traffic where the placement of main roads was central to planning. It would be a comfortable and attractive city; but it would not be the city Griffin had designed.

'The city project had brought him congenial tasks for a lifetime.'

C.S. Daley at the gates of a mansion, San Francisco.

Charles Daley left the Commonwealth Public Service in 1952, at the statutory retirement age of sixty-five. There were official farewells from his fellow workers in the department and from the members of the Advisory Committee, including a warm farewell from Thomas Shakespeare's son, Arthur Shakespeare, who had taken over as owner and manager of the *Canberra Times* after his father's death.

You, Sir, have been one of a number of people in the history of Canberra who have glimpsed some future greatness in it as the centre of government... I hope that your talents will continue to be exercised within this city, because your viewpoint has always been a very broad one and your recognition of public responsibility an example to everyone...[1]

Community groups, including Rotary, held farewell dinners at which Daley was guest of honour, and Canberra High School decided to award an annual C.S. Daley prize to their outstanding senior student. A cheerful telegram arrived in July 1952 from cycling hero Hubert Opperman, who had taken part in the 1951 celebrations: 'Enjoy your chance to freewheel...'[2]

Charles Daley was a widower; his daughters had grown up and left home, though his son, Geoffrey, was still living with him and working in the Crown Solicitor's Office. Daley's retirement from service to the Commonwealth might have seen him face a period of depression that came from feeling out of touch and forgotten. His old friend and mentor, Percy Owen, had confessed to that frame of mind, wishing he could still have had some hand in advising on the city's development. Even John Butters, who had left Canberra in 1930 to take up consulting engineering and a range of private business appointments in Sydney, had, by the time he retired, a sense of being on the sidelines, largely forgotten in the new post-war Canberra. Reading an article in the *Sydney Morning Herald* in February 1963, he was amazed to find no mention of the work of the Federal Capital Commission; and even more wounding, he was 'overlooked' by the Prime Minister's Department when invitations were issued to VIPs to attend the fiftieth anniversary celebrations of Canberra in May 1963. As far back as September 1940, it seemed he missed the challenges that his work in Canberra had provided: he wrote to Daley 'wondering whether the Works people have some work for me to carry out (without of course letting them know I have approached you)'.[3]

Daley was more fortunate than many senior public servants who found life after retirement rather hollow. For one thing, he received an invitation to travel and do some research that few would have been able to resist. As a foundation member of the Canberra University College, he was invited to be one of its four representatives at a Congress of Commonwealth Universities to be held in Cambridge in July 1953. While he was overseas, he was to investigate new directions being taken in building and accommodation in the post-war expansion of tertiary education in the UK.

Embarking on the *Orion* for the six-week trip to England, Daley was accompanied by his daughter, Joan, who had just completed her nursing training at the Royal Melbourne Hospital and the Women's Hospital. Daley carried a document, complete with the Prime Minister's red seal, in which Menzies asked for all facilities to be offered to Mr Daley while he was abroad.

They arrived in London on 19 May, to the welcome of an English spring. That year, 1953, was the Coronation year, and England was emerging from its post-war austerity to what was fondly believed would be a golden 'new Elizabethan age'. There was a celebratory mood abroad, a sense of glorious new possibilities for the kingdom and its people. This was confirmed by the announcement – on Coronation day – that the world's highest peak, Mount Everest, had been climbed, considerably adding to British prestige at the time. For Australians like Charles Daley, a loyal supporter of the Crown Imperial and Australian connections to Britain, there could not have been a finer time to visit England. Daley took Joan to visit the High Commissioner, Sir Thomas White, at Australia House. There they had the chance to view the splendid marble interior whose history Daley knew so well; he corrected some inaccuracies in White's official records. He called on the Gowries, who were living in Mayfair, Lady Gowrie the same energetic person he remembered but Lord Gowrie considerably aged. Zara Gowrie was especially pleased to hear of the progress of nursery and preschool education in Canberra, 'It's so splendid when the parents play an active role – especially the fathers!'[4]

Then came the Rotary International Conference in Paris. Joan remembered with nostalgia the splendour of the occasion, with 1,000 Rotarians and their wives attending the conference, which culminated with a banquet at Versailles and fireworks exploding over the ornamental lake. They returned to England for the coronation, which they had planned to view from Apsley House, a museum at Marble Arch. They were greeted with 'command invitations' to the Abbey itself for the occasion, but not having the formal evening wear (white gloves and tiaras, top hats for men) they had to be content with a view of the procession. After the coronation they left for a Cooks tour of Belgium, Switzerland and Italy.

In July, Daley was in Cambridge for the conference, the seventh such conference to be held since 1911. It aimed to promote 'the commerce of knowledge and ideas, the freemasonry of intellectual ideals…' throughout the emerging Commonwealth.[5] Its program included discussion of some of the challenges and opportunities posed by the post-war expansion of universities: academic mobility and exchange schemes; the role of government; the selection of students; the changing nature of the curriculum.

In Cambridge, the Daleys met two of Patricia Tillyard's daughters, Honor and Faith, who took Joan under their wing and were very kind to her. After the conference, Daley was invited to speak to the Rotary Club of Letchworth – one of England's first planned post-war cities – about Another Garden City. Then came his research tour, visiting six of the new regional universities in England, the major universities in Scotland (Edinburgh, Aberdeen and Glasgow), Ireland (Belfast, Dublin and Cork) and Cardiff in Wales.

His colleague on the National Capital Planning and Development Committee, the architect Bertrand Waterhouse, had given Daley a list of places he must visit in London: galleries, churches, buildings, parks (and 'as many of the London squares as possible'). There were also concerts, including the Scottish National Orchestra at the Edinburgh Festival. He took in the fifth test match at Kennington Oval in Surrey; and there was a seat to view proceedings in the House of Commons on November, before he returned to Australia. Joan set off with a friend for Canada, for more youthful adventures.

Daley came back to Canberra with a renewed sense of energy and purpose. There were hints that there would be official support for his intention to write a history of the city. 'I understand that it is under consideration officially – the National Library has approached me about it.'[6] He expected it would take two or three years to do justice to the subject. It would run from pre-federation days to the end of the Jubilee year. He'd already shared an outline of his plans to John Butters; if the government didn't come good with an offer for him, he would still plan to do some writing of his own, a human story rather than the technical details about the building of the city. He confessed to Butters that he would not relish any period of mental inactivity. He typed up a synopsis to get him thinking: a 'Suggested Basis for writing the history of the Federal Capital'.

There were still many other demands on Daley's time, though the voluntary position he most valued, that of organist at St Andrews, was sadly no longer available. The church had had to find another organist while he was overseas, though they made clear that he should feel free to come and play the organ in the empty church whenever it suited him. He chose not to do this and began attending services at St Johns instead, though when invited especially to play for weddings at St Andrews he was happy to do so. He missed the interactions with people, often strangers, who heard him play at St Andrews. A Melbourne visitor had asked 'how he could get a copy of a very lovely number I heard you play on the organ...' Another listener wrote, 'The organ sang and spoke with such expression as I had not heard in years...it recalled to me the greater joys of a lifetime'.[7]

Soon after his return from England, Daley began playing the piano for the Thursday Club, a social centre for the elderly residents of the Goodwin Homes in Turner. These were named after the Surveyor General John Goodwin, who after retirement ran a small grazing property near Canberra and was an active supporter of St Johns and many charitable causes. Daley, aware of the benefits that singing could bring to elderly people, collected piles of sheet music of popular melodies and small song books for the group. Daley made his regular visit to the club every week until he died in 1966.

Many other community organisations provided a source of interest and companionship: the Rotary Club, with its dinners and guest speakers; the Canberra Classical Association; the Canberra Chamber Music Society, which was formed to provide venues for visits from the Musica Viva Society in Sydney. Musica Viva brought the great chamber music ensembles of Europe to Australia in the 1950s and '60s and Canberra now was to be part of the touring circuit.

Correspondence from those years shows Daley to have been in touch with a wide range of people, especially from the world of music, which he continued to believe provided a common language to cross national barriers and creeds. Ivan Laher was a 'New Australian', one of the thousands of displaced people emerging from the prison camps of Europe to be offered a place in Australia. It was a new life, but first they had to serve their two years wherever the government sent them. Laher was sent to labour on constructions sites in Canberra, staying at the Capital Hill camp. He came to know Charles Daley through playing together at community and church concerts; Laher played the oboe. He moved to Victoria to work for the Water Board, but appealed for help in finding a job 'less hard on my hands'. Daley was able to help with his naturalisation papers, which were finally issued in May 1956. Laher's final letters express how much Daley's friendship and help had meant to him: 'I will never forget you. Today I'm swimming in the ocean and don't see the earth... your old pal – Aussi! Ivan.'[8]

There were echoes of other wartime friendships. Lili Kraus was a Hungarian pianist who had been interned by the Japanese while she was touring in the Dutch East Indies. She performed in Canberra in 1946 and returned thirteen years later as part of an ABC Commonwealth tour. Daley arranged a reception for her at University House and took her to view the growing city. Leaving Australia, she wrote to him from Teheran, thanking him 'for your cherished friendship'.[9]

In December 1958, Daley submitted a tribute to Sir Robert Garran to the Canberra University College Association magazine, *Prometheus*. It was considered 'among the best things in the magazine' – together with Barry Humphries' offering, 'Sandy Stone's Big Week', and an extract from Manning Clark's *History of Australian Settlement*.[10] As the years advanced, there were occasional health scares: a two-month period in hospital with 'heart strain' in 1958 left Daley feeling he had become 'a kind of log'.[11] He was impatient to get back to work, especially as Arthur Shakespeare had offered him a small commission to write a series of articles on some of the figures in Canberra's development. By that stage, his two younger brothers were both nearing retirement from demanding and interesting professional jobs: Air-Vice Marshall Ted Daley as Director General of Medical Services for the RAAF; Frank as head of the design team who had produced the first Holden cars for GMH. Like Charles, they were contemplating life after retirement, and searching for some meaningful commitment that was more than just a hobby. They would need this, Charles warned them, 'to keep brain and personality well alive'. He admitted to his brothers that, as for himself, he could 'easily have continued for years' in his job. Retirement did not come easily to such men. At that stage, the three brothers were helping advance the publication of their late father's book *The Story of Gippsland*, which finally appeared in 1960. In 1957, Frank Daley revisited the Gippsland forests of their youth and was 'appalled by the suicidal destruction of whole forests. Dad would have wept openly. Where we had walked among the towering giants there is not even a tree …the mountains have been stripped and gaunt, ring-barked skeletons stand up on the skyline'.[12]

Frank asked his brother whether he had found a boarder, hoping this would help him 'feel less lonely'. By that stage, Geoffrey had married and Daley welcomed the chance for regular visits to the new household at Campbell and the arrival of grandchildren.

By 1957, it was clear that the government were not prepared to offer him the official history project he had hoped for, and he was therefore anxious to prepare his own personal record of the history of the city while his health and mental capacity allowed for it. Meanwhile, in 1955, Daley was called once more onto the political stage to give evidence to the Senate Select Committee on the Development of Canberra, chaired by Senator John McCallum.

Prime Minister Menzies hoped the Senate enquiry would lead to a new commitment to build a city worthy of the young Commonwealth. After the war, with a new focus on the Commonwealth government and its powers, Australia's attention turned to the federal capital, whose progress had been halted by two wars and the Great Depression. Inviting the future Queen Elizabeth to visit the capital in February 1953 to unveil the Australian/American memorial, Menzies was mortified at what lay on public view: a memorial standing in farm paddocks, the city nothing but a random scattering of provisional and temporary buildings.

The Senate committee called eighty-two witnesses over the course of eight months and tabled its comprehensive report in September 1955. Along with many of the witnesses, Daley presented a story of neglect and disorganisation, with many betrayals of Griffin's official city plan. He argued strongly for a single authority to replace the present system of departmental rule. The committee's findings supported this. It recommended that the development of Canberra be transferred to a centralised authority with powers similar to that of the Snowy Mountains Authority, and it issued a bold call for decisive political action: 'The time has come to take the responsibility of building the National Capital and placing it firmly and squarely on the shoulders of people living today.'[13] The committee also recommended an artistic standards committee, similar to Washington's Fine Arts Commission; it observed that the National Capital Planning and Development Committee had been given an impressive list of functions, but no authority – a fact that had been a continual source of frustration for Daley during his chairmanship.

Other recommendations of the McCallum Committee were that no more temporary buildings were to be erected; all government buildings were to be designed by highly qualified architects; and temporary housing was to be removed at the earliest possible opportunity. It also recommended an elected legislative council be established which would carry out legislative functions at a state level, thus satisfying local agitation for the franchise.

In the Senate debates arising out of the committee's findings, Senator McCallum had this to say: 'Some public servants have watched over the city very carefully.' He referred to '...the unsleeping vigilance of a very fine public servant, Mr Daley. If there had always been as much diligence and faith as Mr Daley has shown, Canberra would be a much better city.'[14]

The National Capital Development Commission was established in September 1957 and its first commissioner appointed in March 1958. Charles Daley lived long enough to see the creation of the lake, Griffin's formal basins much modified and his East Lake removed, but still offering in time that serene, open expanse of water such as Daley had admired in the cities of Oslo, Stockholm and Geneva. But other parts of Griffin's vision – concentrations of urban activity along wide boulevards, Constitution Avenue as a centrepiece of civic and cultural life, a busy public transport network of trams and trains – these features were never to eventuate, being replaced by through traffic corridors for private cars.

In 1961, there was another overseas adventure. In June, Daley travelled to Bahrain to visit his oldest daughter, Margaret, and her family, and with them toured the Greek islands. He travelled via Delhi so that he could see 'the sister capital in whose founding and development I have always had an interest'. In September, he was in England, staying with a Rotary family at Letchworth; then there were five weeks in the US, where he had letters of introduction to YMCA groups and to the secretary of the Washington Fine Arts Commission, and where he visited many universities.

Back in Canberra, a number of honours awaited him. He was elected a life member of the Canberra Chamber Music Society and a life member of Rotary. In August 1963, he was made an honorary associate to the ACT Chapter of the Royal Australian Institute of Architects. He confessed that the city project had brought him 'congenial tasks for a lifetime'.[15] Though he never trained or practised as an architect, his work had been closely linked to this profession and he owed much to architecture and its allied arts. After his death, the Institute was to honour him with the inauguration of a C.S. Daley Architecture Award, given annually for an outstanding example in Canberra of domestic architecture.

The growing city began to acknowledge his contribution in small ways. In October 1963, one of the main thoroughfares in the expanding Australian National University (by then offering undergraduate degrees) was named Daley Road, and in later years, when the new town of Belconnen had been built, a Daley Crescent was named after him. After his death, a small native garden was planted outside the Griffin Centre in Civic, which housed the ACT Council of Cultural Societies. A plaque announced that the garden was built in memory of C.S. Daley. After the Griffin Centre was demolished in 2005, the plaque was transferred to a new site in Glebe Park. An honour walk in Civic now includes the names of C.S. Daley and of Jessie Daley, both active and generous contributors to community and cultural life in Canberra.

In 1964, the plan was revived to contribute a regular column to the *Canberra Times*. John Douglas Pringle, managing director of the paper, had been impressed by an authoritative letter which Daley had written about Charles Scrivener's role in the selection of the city site. He invited Daley to write a weekly article of about 400 words, to appear every Saturday. He suggested they'd find a younger man for regular music reviews, which up till that time Daley had considered his responsibility. Pringle was pleased with Daley's first article, which appeared in July; he especially liked the title, 'As I Recall'. These articles were to appear weekly for thirteen months, with a break while Daley attended a world alliance of YMCA groups in Japan. They were then resumed in October 1965 and ran until September 1966. The last one appeared the day after Daley died. They ranged over the whole history of the city from the early days of federation and the search for a capital, through the formative years of planning and construction, with numerous pen portraits of individuals involved – for good or ill – in the building of the city.

The last days in 1966 were taken up with writing and research – Charles Daley was always ready to provide a paper for those who needed background information about Canberra. Music was a consoling presence, both to share with others as he did at the Thursday Club, and in times of solitude. Evenings in the empty house on Balmain Crescent would see him playing Mozart sonatas, or Chopin, or reading new novels – he was even tackling D.H. Lawrence's *Sons and Lovers*.

He died with family nearby, on Friday 30 September 1966. He'd had dinner with Geoff and his wife Billie at their Campbell home, and they found him in his favourite chair in their sitting room later that evening.

A funeral held at St John's Church brought hundreds of people in an official or private capacity, to express their respect and gratitude for his life and work. A letter appeared a few days later in the *Canberra Times* from Dorothy Hurley. She had known Charles Daley and shared 'his interest and deep affection for Canberra. Now he is dead there is a great blank in the annals of Canberra history. One cannot think of Canberra without him.'[16]

References

Abbreviations

AJCP   Australian Joint Copying Project
AWM   Australian War Memorial
C&DHS   Canberra & District Historical Society
CT   *Canberra Times*
FCAC   Federal Capital Advisory Committee
FCC   Federal Capital Commission
FCT   Federal Capital Territory
NAA   National Archives Australia
NLA   National Library of Australia
SMH   *Sydney Morning Herald*

Prologue

1. *Victorian Naturalist*, July 1933, 'Rock Shelters at Gudgenby River, Federal Territory', by Charles Daley.
2. *New York Times*, 2 June 1912, 'American Designs Splendid New Capital for Australia'
3. Senate Select Committee on the Development of Canberra, p. 7
4. Keith Arscott in correspondence with Billie Daley
5. Letter to Geoff Daley from Chief Archivist, 4 October 1966

1: The Victorian Years

1. NLA, MS 1946, folder 115, 20 December 1947
2. Ibid., folder 96
3. *As I Recall*, pp. 83–4
4. NAA: SP394/1, NL18/2474, Lithgow – Small Arms Factory – Housing Scheme, 15 February 1918
5. SMH, 9 May 1922
6. SMH, 29 March 1924
7. Commonwealth Joint Committee Public Accounts, 1924, Housing in Lithgow
8. NLA MS 1946, Folder 93, Parliamentary Standing Works Committee Report on Arsenal
9. NAA: A192, FCL 1920/1082, Survey of Proposed Commonwealth Arsenal Town, Tuggeranong
10. NAA: A411, FCAC minutes, 9 May 1921
11. NAA: A1 1916/24760, Secret Establishment of Arsenal in FCT
12. NAA: A179, GL 1918/698, Arsenal Town Committee, 11 July 1918
13. *As I Recall*, p. 131

227

2: Towards Canberra

1. Gavin Souter, *Acts of Parliament*, p. 104
2. NAA: A100, A1906/3799, Proposed Federal Capital sites
3. Ibid.
4. Ibid.
5. Senate Select Committee on Canberra, 1955, p. 7
6. NAA: A100, A1909/3286, Members' Trip Yass–Canberra
7. NAA: A100, A1909/10275, Correspondence relating to Federal Capital Territory
8. Ibid.
9. *The Bulletin*, April 1908
10. Chris Coulthard-Clarke, *Duntroon, the Royal Military College of Australia*, 1911–1986, p. 19
11. *As I Recall*, p. 59
12. H.M.Rolland, 'From Country to City', an address to C&DHS, 1957, p. 4
13. SMH, 9 May 1927
14. T. Griffith Taylor, *Journeyman Taylor*, p. 122
15. NAA: A100, A1908/2841, Commonwealth Accommodation in Melbourne
16. C&DHS Journal, December 1909
17. *As I Recall*, p. 33
18. NAA: A357, 1, FCT, Yarralumla Homestead and buildings – valuations
19. C&DHS Journal, December 2009. Weston Creek was named after Captain Edward Weston, Superintendent of Hyde Park Convict Barracks.
20. NAA: CP 362/3, 7, PM Bruce – address to Institute of Engineers

3: The most beautiful city in history

1. Peter Harrison, *Walter Burley Griffin, Landscape architect*, p. 13
2. NAA: CP 487/6, 4, Correspondence relating to receipt of Federal Capital Design
3. Ibid.
4. Paul Reid, *Canberra Following Griffin*, p. 45
5. *As I Recall*, p. 22
6. Ibid.
7. Ibid.
8. Ibid., p. 24
9. Ibid.
10. Royal Victorian Institute of Architects, July 1911
11. *Building*, June 1912, p. 53
12. Ibid., p. 54
13. John Reps, *Canberra 1912: plans and planners of the Australian Capital Competition*, p. 252
14. *Building*. p. 53
15. Reps, op.cit., pp. 252–3
16. Harrison, op.cit., p. 33
17. *As I Recall*, p. 25
18. NAA: A 199, FC 1921/76, Correspondence with Walter Burley Griffin in regard to position on Federal Capital Advisory Committee, 31 October 1920
19. Ibid., 23 Dec 1920
20. NAA: A199 FC 1921/759, Visit of Prince of Wales to Canberra
21. Alasdair McGregor, *Grand Obsessions: the life and work of Walter Burley Griffin and Marion Mahony Griffin*, p. 344
22. NLA MS 460, Folder 104, January 1947

4: Greening the Capital

1. George Taylor, *Building*, June 1912, p. 47
2. NAA: CP 209/1, B1, Inwards Correspondence, Afforestation Branch, Federal Capital Territory
3. NAA: CP 209/1 B7, 27 September 1917
4. NAA: CP 209/1, B11, 15 February 1921
5. Geoff Page, *Gravel Corners*, pp. 38–40
6. NAA: CP 209/1 B 9 Part 1, August 1919
7. Ibid.
8. John Gray, T C G Weston (1866–1935) horticulturalist and arboriculturalist, PhD thesis, University of Canberra 1999, p. 71
9. NAA: CP 209/1 B 10, August 1920
10. NAA: A361, DSG 18/262, Petition from Pupils of Tuggeranong Public School re Ringbarking, 11 February 1918
11. NAA: A 192, FCL 1921/1517, Timber – Federal Territory
12. Page, op. cit.

5: Transition

1. NAA: A199, FC 1922/1411, Extract from Hansard re: opposition to building Federal Capital, 20 July 1922
2. NAA: A414/18, Water Supply
3. NAA: A411, Minutes of the Federal Capital Advisory Committee
4. Ibid.
5. Ibid.
6. Alan Foskett, *The Molonglo Mystery*, p. 45
7. NAA: A 192, FCL 1921/1803, Valuation FCT lands, 13 October 1921

8. NAA: A192, FCL 1922/1296, The Residency, Canberra – Take over from Administrator
9. NAA: A192, FCL 1922/1104, Holding 166 Federal Territory, Mrs Farrer
10. Ibid.
11. NAA: A466, 1921/7577, Extra allowance for Mr C S Daley
12. Ibid.
13. NLA MS 1946, folder 243, undated cutting
14. NAA: A 292, C 2737 A, Provisional Parliament House erection, Canberra
15. Parliamentary Standing Committee on Public Works, Erection of Provisional Parliament House, Minutes of Evidence, 1923

6: Commission Rule

1. NAA: A414, 78, Administration of Federal Territory
2. C.S. Daley's evidence, Senate Select Enquiry p. 6
3. *Daily Telegraph*, 3 July 1920
4. *The Age*, 5 July 1920
5. NLA MS 1946, Folder 97, 25 October 1924
6. NAA: CP 487/6 27, Confidential files, Correspondence FCC
7. NAA: A414 1 FCAC Appointment of Committee
8. NAA: A414 92, Final report of FCAC, 18 February 1926
9. NAA: CP 487/6, 52, Federal Capital Advisory Committee – final report
10. NLA MS 1946 Folder 97, 21 April 1925
11. NAA: A 659, 1939/1/11457,

Transfer of officers to Canberra –
Regulations
12. Ibid.
13. Gavin Souter, *Lion and Kangaroo:
the initiation of Australia*, p. 84
14. A copy of the booklet is in C.S.
Daley papers, C&DHS, Box D
15. NAA: A6266 G 1927/4505 FCC –
welfare of workmen and dependents
16. NAA: A6265, 1925/1445,
Correspondence – Request by
Workmen for Improved Conditions
17. Ibid.
18. NAA: A1, 1933/2763, Causeway
Hall, Erection and administration,
part 1
19. *Canberra Community News*, 11
Feruary 1926
20. SMH, 10 May 1927, *Argus*, 10
May 1927
21. Susan Mary Withycombe, *Gale
Force*, p. 119
22. *Argus*, 10 May 1927, p. 19
23. NLA, MS 1946, Folder 8
24. Hansard, H of R debates, 12
March 1930
25. CT, 23 September 1929
26. CT, 11 October 1929
27. NLA, MS 1946, Folder 7

7: Town and Country

1. Warren Denning, *Capital City:
Canberra today and tomorrow*, p. 33
2. NAA: A 458, G388/1, Prohibition.
FCT, Individual Representations.
3. NAA: A 6268, 0/30/157, Police
Reports – Federal Capital Commission
4. CT, 3 September 1928
5. CT, 27 March 1929
6. NAA: A6265, 1925/297, Dances at
Hotel Canberra

7. NAA: A6265, 1925/1000, Names
for Cottages
8. CT, 19 July 1927
9. NAA: A6273, L1927/874, Federal
Territory Lessees Association- issues
raised with FCC and stock routes
10. NLA MS 1946, Folder 20, 17
March 1932
11. NLA MS 460, Folder 88,
O'Malley to Kenneth Binns, 2 July
1937
12. NLA MS 1946, Folder 98, 29
September 1930
13. Ibid., Folder 102, 6 July 1936

8: The Long Slump

1. NLA MS 4990, FCC folder (not
numbered)
2. Ibid.
3. *Argus*, 25 March 1929
4. NLA MS 4990, op.cit
5. MS 1946, Folder 9, 6 May 1930
6. Ibid., 30 April 1930
7. Ibid., Folder 18
8. NAA: A1 1936/191, Ration relief
to unemployed
9. Ibid., 6 February 1933
10. NAA: A6272, E175, Special Relief
Measures for Unemployed persons
in the FCT prior to Christmas
11. NAA: A570, L&S 1927/815,
'Oaks Estate', Queanbeyan,
Proposal to Retransfer to State
12. NAA: A1, 1933/2094, part 3,
Collection and disposal of garbage,
Oaks Estate
13. NLA MS 1946, Folder 18, 12
June 1931
14. NAA: A1, 1932/1127. Civic
Administrator, Canberra –
Appointment of

15. NLA MS 1946, Folder 20, 25 May 1932
16. NAA: A414, 69, Accommodation for War Museum
17. NLA MS 1946, Folder 25, 1 August 1936
18. NAA: A292, C20068 Part 1, Australian War Memorial (Erection)
19. NAA: A 292, C20068, Part 2, Australian War Memorial (Erection)
20. AWM 38, 3DRL 6673/665, Official History 1914–1918. Records of C.E.W. Bean

9: A People's City

1. A. Fitzgerald, *Canberra's Engineering Heritage*, p. 129
2. Anne Edgeworth, *The Cost of Jazz Garters*, p. 36
3. Wardle papers, C&DHS, Box 14 Folder 3
4. C.S. Daley papers, C&DHS, Box D, op. cit.
5. *Canberra Community News*, 12 July 1926
6. NLA MS 3538, April 1925
7. Jack Ryan, *Jack Ryan Remembers 2CA*, introduction by George Barlin
8. CT, Saturday 17 February 1979, 'Bookselling in early Canberra'
9. W.J. Mildenhall, *Developing Images*, p. 42
10. CT, 25 November 1963
11. NLA MS1946, Folder 294, 1 August 1928
12. Ibid., Folder 307, 11 September 1934
13. NLA, M 1830 AJCP 11830
14. *Australian Rose Journal*, 1932, p. 12

15. C.S. Daley Papers, C&DHS, Box F
16. *Country Life Stock and Station Journal*, 13 Jaury 1939

10: Another War

1. NLA MS 1946, Folder 100, 5 Nov 1932
2. Ibid., Folder 98, July 1930
3. Ibid., Folder 97, 10 March 1924
4. Ibid., Folder 98, undated
5. Ibid., Folder 108, undated
6. Ibid., Folder 112, 15 May 1944
7. Ibid., Folder 102, 9 January 1936
8. Ibid., Folder 22, 17 January 1933
9. Ibid., Folder 102, 23 July 1936
10. Ibid., May 1936
11. CT, 17 July 1939
12. Souter, *Acts of Parliament*, p. 328
13. C.E.W. Bean, *Two Men I Knew*, p. 221
14. NLA, MS 1946, Folder 112
15. NLA, MS 4936/6/6
16. NAA: A 659, 1945/1/929, Rubber – Necessity for conserving supplies
17. Michael McKernan, *Here is their Spirit*, p. 5
18. NLA, MS 6277, 23 June 1945

11: A new beginning

1. L.F. Crisp, *Ben Chifley: a biography*, p. 191
2. NLA, MS 1946, Folder 108, 24 June 1940
3. Edgeworth, op. cit., p. 50
4. Foster & Varghese, *The Making of the Australian National University 1946–96*, p. 19
5. Ibid., p. 31
6. Tim Rowse, *Nugget Coombs: a reforming life*, p. 177

7. CT, 27 May 1953
8. Edgeworth, op. cit., p. 36
9. ArchivesACT, C19902, Minutes of National Capital Planning & Development Committee, 24 February 1941
10. NLA, MS 1946, Folder 95
11. Ibid., Folder 60
12. Ibid., Folder 58
13. Ibid., Folder 30
14. NAA: A1, 1930/7174, Mrs H Barton Motor Bus Service FCT
15. NAA: A 431, 1946/40, Canberra City Band – General file – Part 2
16. NAA: A 431, 1949/1799, Canberra City Band – General File – Part 4
17. NAA: A 431, 1962/969, Canberra City Band – General Correspondence- Part 1
18. NLA, MS 1946, Folder 38
19. Michelle Grattan, *Australian Prime Ministers*, p. 268
20. NLA, MS 1946, Folder 119

12: A Private Citizen

1. ArchivesACT, A2942, 238, C.S.Daley papers
2. NLA, MS 1946, Folder 120
3. Ibid., Folder 108, 10 Sept 1940
4. Ibid., Folder 141
5. http://onlinelibrary.wiley.com/doi/10.1111/j.1468-2273.1954.tb00817.x/abstract
6. NLA, MS 1946, Folder 120, July 1952
7. Ibid., Folder 116, 24 Aug 1948, and 23 June 1948
8. Ibid., Folder 124
9. Ibid., Folder 127
10. CT, 13 December 1958
11. NLA, MS 1946, Folder 125
12. Ibid., 24 Feb 1957
13. Senate Select Committee on Canberra, September 1955, p. 17
14. Hansard, Senate Debates, 20 Sept 1956
15. NLA, MS 1946, Folder 131
16. CT, 12 Oct 1966

Bibliography

Manuscripts and microforms held in the National Library of Australia

M1829–30 AJCP, Diaries of E.T. Crutchley
MS MS 460, King O'Malley papers
MS 1946, C.S. Daley papers
MS 3538, A.K. Murray papers
MS 4936, R.G. Menzies papers
MS 4990, John Butters papers
MS 6277, Hector Harrison papers

Books and journals

Andrews, W.C., *Canberra's engineering heritage, Institute of Surveyors*, Canberra, 1990
ANZAAS Report, Sydney, ANZAAS, 1935
Architecture in Australia, RAIA Publications Board, Sydney, 1968
Australasian Association for the Advancement of Science Report, Sydney, 1921
Australian Rose Annual, National Rose Society of Victoria, 1932
Barrows, G., *Prime Minister's Lodge: Canberra's unfinished business*, Dagraja Press, Canberra, 2008
Bean, C.E.W., *Two men I knew: William Bridges and Brudenell White, founders of the AIF*, A&R, Sydney, 1957
Birtles, T., *Charles Robert Scrivener: the surveyor who sited Australia's national capital twice*, Arcadia, Melbourne, 2013

Boyd, Robin, *The Australian ugliness*, Cheshire, Melbourne, 1960
Broinowski, R., *A witness to history: the life and times of Robert Arthur Broinowski*, MUP, 2001
Brown, Nicholas, *A history of Canberra*, Cambridge University Press, Melbourne, 2014
Building: the magazine for the architect, builder, property owner and merchant, Sydney, 1912
Burkhardt, G.A. & McPherson, A., *A Jubilee History of Ainslie School, 1927–2002*, Ainslie School, Canberra, 2002
C&DHS Journals, 1960–2015, C&DHS, Canberra
Calthorpe, Dawn, *Chortles, chores and chilblains: cameos of childhood in Calthorpe's House*, Canberra, ACT Historic Places, 2002
Canberra Community News 1925–27
Canberra Rotary Club, *History of Rotary Club of Canberra 1928–1978*, Canberra, 1978

Clarke, P., *Eileen Giblin: a feminist between the wars*, Monash University Publishing, Melbourne, 2013

Cockburn, S., & Ellyard, D., *Oliphant, the life and times of Sir Mark Oliphant*, Axiom Books, Adelaide, 1981

Coltheart, L., *Albert Hall: the heart of Canberra*, New South Publishing, Sydney, 2014

—, *Nursery tales for a garden city: the historical context for the records at Canberra's Yarralumla Nursery*, Australian Garden History Society, 2011. www.archives.act.gov.au

Commonwealth Jubilee Citizenship Convention: Report of Proceedings, Canberra, 1951

Coulthard-Clarke, C., *Duntroon, the Royal Military College of Australia, 1911–1986*, Allen & Unwin, Sydney, 1986

Country Life & Stock & Station Journal, William Brooks, Sydney,1939

Crisp, L.F., *Ben Chifley: a biography*, Longmans, Melbourne, 1961

Daley, C. & Williamson, H.B., *Where the Murray Rises*, Field Naturalists Club of Victoria, 1922

Daley, C., *The Story of Gippsland*, Whitcomb & Tombs, Melbourne, 1960

Daley, C.S., *As I Recall: reminiscences of early Canberra, compiled for C&DHS*, Mulini Press, Canberra, 1994

—, *Canberra nomenclature*, C&DHS, 1958

—, Director's report of Jubilee Celebrations, 1901–1951, Canberra, 1952

—, *Early cultural activities in Canberra*, C&DHS, 1956

—, *Much ado about nothing*, C&DHS, 1960

Denning, W., *Capital city: Canberra today and tomorrow*, Publicist, Sydney, 1938

Federal Congress on Regional and Town Planning: record of proceedings, Canberra, 1951

Foskett, A., *ACT education: the formative years 1912–1978*, Canberra, 2000

Foskett, A., *Canberra's hostels, hotels and guest houses: a part of our heritage*, Canberra, 2000

Foskett, A., *A capital change: some recollections of the National Capital Development Commission's early years, 1958–1967*, Canberra, 1996

Foster, S.G. & Varghese, M., *The Making of the Australian National University 1946–96*, Allen & Unwin, Sydney, 1996

Frame, T.& Faulkner, D., *Stromlo: an Australian observatory*, Allen & Unwin, Sydney, 2003

Freeman, P. (ed.), *The early Canberra house: living in Canberra 1911–1933*, Federal Capital Press, Canberra, 1996

Fullerton, S., *Brief encounters: literary travellers in Australia 1836–1939*, Picador, Sydney, 2009

Gibbney, H.J., *Canberra 1913–1953*, AGPS, Canberra, 1988

—, *Calthorpe's Canberra: the town and community in 1927*, AGPS, Canberra, 1986

Gillespie, L., *Canberra 1820–1913*, AGPS, Canberra, 1991

Grattan, M. (ed.), *Australian Prime*

Ministers, New Holland, Sydney, 2008

Gray, J., T.C.G. Weston (1866–1935): horticulturalist and arboriculturalist, PhD Thesis, University of Canberra, 1999. http://webpac.canberra.edu.au/record=b1207820-S4

Griffiths, T. & White, D., *Lithgow small arms factory: a history in photographs*, Lithgow, 2012

Griffiths, T., *Lithgow's small arms factory and its people*, Toptech Engineering, Sydney, 2006–8

Gugler, Ann, *A story of Capital Hill*, Canberra, 2009

—, *True tales from Canberra's vanished suburbs of Westlake, Westridge and Acton*, Canberra, 1999

Hall, M., & Coltheart, L., *Canberra*, C&DHS, 2001

Harrison, P., *Walter Burley Griffin, landscape architect*, NLA, Canberra, 1995

Hasluck, P., *Diplomatic witness: Australian foreign affairs 1941–7*, MUP, Melbourne, 1980

Hoffmann, W., & Sharpe, J., *Mr Chifley's baby: the Canberra City Band*, Canberra, 2013

Horsfield, J., *Mary Cunningham. An Australian Life*, Ginninderra Press, 2004

Hungerford, T.A.G., *Riverslake*, A&R, Sydney, 1953

Johnstone, F.M., *Knights and theodolites: a saga of surveyors*, Edwards & Shaw, Sydney, 1962

Jones, M., *Cotter: nature's gift to Canberra*, ACTEW, Canberra, 2010

Lyon, Louise, (ed.) *Voices of old Ainslie: a collection of life stories from early residents of Ainslie*, Canberra, 1995

Mahony, D.J., & Taylor, T.G., Report on a geological reconnaissance of the Federal Territory, Government Printer, Melbourne, 1913

McDonald, D.I., *Canberra & District Historical Society: a brief history 1953–1973*, C&DHS, Canberra, 1974

McGregor, Alasdair, *Grand obsessions: the life and work of Walter Burley Griffin and Marion Mahony Griffin*, Lantern, Victoria, 2009

McKernan, M., *All in: fighting the war at home*, Allen & Unwin, Sydney, 1995

—, *Here is their spirit: a history of the Australian War Memorial 1917–1990*, QUP, 1991

Menzies, R.G., *The measure of the years*, Coronet Books, London, 1972

Mildenhall, W.J., *Developing images: Mildenhall's photographs of early Canberra*, NAA, Canberra, 2000

Mort, Eirene, *Old Canberra: a sketchbook of the 1920s*, NLA, Canberra, 1987

Noye, L., *O'Malley, MHR*, Sid Harta Publishers, Victoria, 2007

Overall, J., *Canberra: yesterday, today and tomorrow: a personal memoir*, Federal Capital Press, Canberra, 1995

Page, Geoff, *Gravel Corners*, A&R, Sydney, 1992

Payne, Jan., *Australia House: 75 years of service*, Australian High Commission, London, 1993

Power, K., & Gillespie, L., *Pictorial History of Telopea Park School*,

Telopea Park P&C Association, Canberra, 1983

Reid, P., *Canberra following Griffin: a design history of Australia's national capital*, NAA, Canberra, 2002

Reps, J.W., *Canberra 1912: plans and planners of the Australian Capital Competition*, MUP, Melbourne, 1997

Rolland, H.M., 'From Country to City', an address to C&DHS, April 1957

Rolland, H.M., *Over the years: an autobiography*, H.M.Rolland, Hawthorne, 1971

Rowe, R.& Aitken, A., *Building and furnishing of the Presbyterian church of St Andrew, Canberra, ACT*, Canberra, 1992

Rowse, T., *Nugget Coombs: a reforming life*, Cambridge University Press, Melbourne, 2002

Royal Canberra Golf Club jubilee history, Canberra, 1977

Ryan, Jack, *Jack Ryan remembers the early days of 2CA*, Canberra, 1984

Selth, P.A. (ed.), *The Canberra Collection*, Lowden Publishing, Victoria, 1976

Sinnayah, S., *Audaciousville: the story of Dacey Garden Suburb, Australia's first public housing estate*, City of Botany Bay, 2012

Souter, G., *Acts of Parliament*, MUP, Melbourne, 1988

Souter, G., *The Lion and the Kangaroo: the initiation of Australia 1901–1919*, Collins, Sydney, 1976

Stephenson, Freda, *Capital women: a history of the work of the National Council of Women (ACT) 1939–1979*, NCW, Canberra, 1992

Taylor, T.G., *Journeyman Taylor: the education of a scientist*, Hale, London, 1958

Watson, F., *A brief history of Canberra, the capital city of Australia*, Canberra, 1927

White, H.L. (ed.), *Canberra, a nation's capital*, A&R, Sydney, 1954

Withycombe, S M., *Gale Force: John Gale and the siting of the National Capital*, Queanbeyan & District Centenary of Federation Committee, 2001

Index

A

Acton 40, 41, 42, 43, 46, 47, 60, 72, 73, 74, 75, 76, 81, 91, 95, 112, 115, 116, 118, 119, 121, 135, 158, 159, 160, 168, 173, 180, 186, 204, 205, 207
Ainslie Primary School 181, 199
Albert Hall 48, 78, 125, 164, 170, 171, 172, 173, 174, 176, 182, 183, 185, 189, 191, 211, 213
Arts and Literature Society 170, 173
Australia House 21, 22, 24, 183, 219
Australian Association for the Advancement of Science 19, 50
Australian National University 14, 115, 201, 202, 203, 204, 205, 211, 213, 215, 225
Australian War Memorial 32, 84, 124, 150, 151, 192, 211

B

Barton, Helen 207, 208, 209
Bean 32, 81, 82, 94, 99, 120, 150, 151, 152, 153, 155, 174, 188, 189
border survey 29, 60, 146
Brackenreg, Helen 135, 167, 193
Brackenreg, James 72, 81, 117, 133, 134, 135, 136, 147, 193
Brickworks 62, 76, 91, 95, 99, 120
Bridges, Major General William Throsby 40, 67, 91, 144, 189
Broinowski, Robert 163, 170, 175
Bruce, Alexander 136, 174

Bruce, Stanley 48, 108, 121, 129, 171, 199
Butters, John 10, 48, 110, 111, 112, 114, 116, 117, 118, 123, 124, 125, 128, 129, 131, 132, 140, 141, 142, 159, 160, 170, 209, 210, 218, 221

C

Canberra and District Historical Society 15
Canberra City Band 209, 210, 211, 212
Canberra Horticultural Society 83, 174, 212
Canberra Mothercraft Society 136
Canberra Musical Society 171, 173
Canberra Repertory Society 170
Canberra Times 15, 131, 136, 141, 149, 161, 180, 183, 188, 204, 218, 226
Canberra University College 199, 203, 219, 222
Capital Hill 37, 41, 56, 57, 67, 94, 104, 119, 136, 213, 222
Causeway Hall 119, 160, 185
Chifley, Ben 14, 198, 201, 206, 209, 210, 211, 212, 213
Citizenship Convention 213
Civic Administrator 142, 148, 149, 150, 210
Clements, Jimmy 123
Comedy Harmonists 182
Coombs, H.L. 201
Corin, William 38, 90

Cotter Dam 47, 62, 90, 91, 92, 160
Cotter River 38
Crutchley, Ernest 172
Curtin, John 188, 192, 193, 194, 195, 198, 201

D

Daley, Arthur 168, 180, 181
Daley, Charles senior 9, 10, 18, 19, 20
Daley, C.S.
– early training in Melbourne 20–25
– Lithgow 25
– Arsenal Town Committee 30
– Duntroon 40
– city design competition 51
– views of King O'Malley 53–54
– Griffin's 1918 plan 64
– friendship with Thomas Weston 80
– work with FCAC 89–94, 101–105
– Molonglo Internment Camp 97–99
– work with FCC 109–112, 114
– opening of Parliament House 121
– defender of John Butters 125
– Land Board 134
– friendship with Percy Owen 137
– Civic Administrator 142–150
– association with Australian War Memorial 151–152
– Canberra Musical Society 169–172, 189
– William Farrer memorial 176
– death of Arthur Daley
– wartime responsibilities 184–185
– death of Jessie Daley
– St Andrews Church
– support of schools 198–199
– Australian National University 201–202
– Department of the Interior and NCPDC 205–207
– Canberra City Band 209–210
– Jubilee celebrations 212–215
– travel overseas 219–220
– official history 221, 223
– Senate Select Inquiry 223–224
Daley, Edward (Ted) 18, 20
Daley, Frank 18, 19, 20, 182, 185, 186, 223
Daley, Geoffrey 168, 169, 170, 172, 180, 181, 190, 193, 199, 218, 223, 225
Daley, Jessie 181
Daley, Joan 168, 181, 190, 219, 220
Daley, Margaret 168, 180, 190, 225
Daley, Nancy 168, 180, 190
Dalgety 34, 35, 36
De Burgh, Ernest 30, 38, 88, 90, 112
Department of Home Affairs 12, 20, 22, 34, 42, 43, 51, 63, 64, 142, 198
Department of the Interior 150, 166, 187, 201, 204, 205, 206
Duntroon 38, 39, 40, 46, 47, 67, 78, 81, 91, 96, 97, 144, 146, 161, 184, 199, 213

F

Federal Capital Advisory Committee 10, 80, 88, 99, 102, 105
Federal Capital Commission 10, 13, 48, 109, 110, 111, 119, 123, 128, 147, 149, 152, 166, 218
Federal Capital Territory Advisory Council 148, 150, 162, 188

G

Gale, John 36, 82, 122, 123, 161
Garran, John 193, 213
Garran, Robert 19, 35, 66, 109, 170, 193, 200, 201, 202, 212, 213, 222
Goodwin, John 25, 26, 29, 30, 31, 32, 80, 81, 84, 88, 100, 101, 131, 133, 151, 221

Gowrie, Lady 190, 191, 212, 219
Gowrie, Lord 165, 190, 191, 192, 193, 194, 219
Griffin, Marion Mahony 12, 52, 56, 58, 68, 78
Griffin, Walter Burley 11, 12, 13, 14, 29, 30, 47, 56, 57, 58, 59, 60, 61, 62, 63, 64, 65, 66, 67, 68, 69, 78, 79, 80, 88, 89, 90, 91, 92, 93, 94, 103, 104, 119, 137, 145, 146, 151, 152, 200, 206, 207, 214, 215, 224, 225
Groom, Littleton 25, 35, 65, 66, 67, 89, 105

H

Halloran, Henry 162, 163
Harrison, Hector 194, 195
Harrison, John 110, 119
Hewitt, Verity 164
Hoffmann, William 209, 211, 214
Hotel Canberra 78, 96, 97, 112, 131, 134, 161, 164, 176, 190, 208
Hughes, Billy 62, 66, 175
Hughes, Mary 175

L

Lake Burley Griffin 75, 137
Lambrigg 101, 176
Lane Poole, Charles 166, 167, 173, 174
Lane Poole, Ruth 166
liquor laws 130
Lithgow small arms factory 24, 28, 198

M

Maiden, Joseph 73, 75, 77, 78, 80, 82
Menzies, Robert 14, 188, 191, 192, 215, 219, 223, 224
Mildenhall, William 118, 130, 165, 166

Miller, David 36, 43, 44, 48, 50, 51, 54, 55, 60, 61, 62, 63, 72, 74, 92, 114, 135
Molonglo Internment Camp 97, 98, 99, 115, 118
Molonglo River 13, 29, 36, 37, 38, 41, 46, 47, 64, 74, 75, 77, 89, 95, 98, 134, 135, 137, 145, 146, 147, 158, 176
Mort, Eirene 121
Mount Stromlo Observatory 62, 173
Murdoch, John Smith 12, 22, 23, 24, 39, 40, 43, 46, 55, 60, 65, 89, 97, 103, 104, 120, 124, 152, 167, 180

N

National Capital Development Commission 224
National Capital Planning and Development Committee 206, 214, 220, 224
Nott, Dr L.W. 145, 170, 173, 188

O

Oaks Estate 146, 147
Oliphant, Kenneth 114
Oliphant, Marcus 202, 203, 204, 213
O'Malley, King 25, 43, 45, 52, 53, 54, 55, 56, 59, 62, 63, 68, 69, 72, 90, 92, 128, 136, 213
Owen, Colonel Percy 12, 21, 24, 28, 30, 31, 35, 36, 39, 40, 41, 46, 47, 48, 50, 51, 55, 60, 61, 62, 63, 64, 65, 66, 84, 88, 89, 90, 91, 92, 93, 97, 101, 102, 103, 109, 110, 111, 115, 120, 136, 137, 140, 170, 181, 193, 218

P

Percival, Arthur 29, 43, 54, 176
Pittman, Edward 41, 47
plane crash 188

Power House 46, 47, 62, 81, 91, 92, 95, 115, 117, 120, 145, 158, 184, 199

Prime Minister's Lodge 121, 166, 193, 195

provisional Parliament House 11, 12, 13, 67, 84, 93, 94, 101, 103, 120, 128

Q

Queanbeyan 36, 37, 38, 42, 45, 46, 47, 77, 82, 88, 97, 98, 104, 119, 122, 123, 128, 129, 130, 135, 137, 146, 147, 162, 208, 209, 211

R

Returned Servicemen's League 125, 149, 154

Rolland, Henry 40, 97, 115, 119, 123, 161

Rotary 164, 173, 199, 218, 220, 222, 225

Royal Military College 40, 67, 144, 163, 170, 172

Ryan, Jack 163, 164

S

Schnabel, Artur 183

Scrivener, Charles 35, 36, 37, 38, 39, 41, 43, 44, 50, 51, 55, 60, 62, 64, 66, 72, 73, 74, 84, 137, 226

Senate Select Committee on the Development of Canberra 223

Shakespeare, Arthur 162, 218, 223

Shakespeare, Thomas 141, 148, 149, 161, 162, 163, 176, 218

Snowy River 34, 35, 206

Social Service Association 131, 160, 209

St Andrews Church 168, 194, 221

Stewart, P.G. 104, 105

St Johns Church 38, 43, 164, 168, 194, 221, 226

Sulman, John 26, 50, 55, 59, 73, 80, 88, 89, 92, 105, 108, 109, 110, 111, 112, 119, 136, 149, 181

T

Taylor, Thomas Griffith 41, 42, 51, 77, 81, 95

Telopea School 133, 160

Tillyard, Dr Robin 145, 158, 167, 170, 174

Tillyard, Patience 158, 169, 170

Tillyard, Patricia 169, 220

Treloar, John 151, 153

Tuggeranong arsenal 28, 29, 30, 31, 63

Tuggeranong Homestead 31, 32, 81, 120, 151, 174

V

Vienna Boys Choir 183

Vigilance Association 45

W

Wells, H.G. 176

Westbourne Woods 75, 77, 79

Weston, Thomas Charles 13, 26, 27, 67, 72, 73, 74, 75, 76, 77, 78, 79, 80, 81, 82, 83, 84, 92, 119, 123, 136, 143, 174

Westridge 95, 96, 99, 118, 158, 160, 163, 167, 199

Y

Yarralumla Homestead 38, 44, 48, 63, 74, 78, 83, 102, 114, 134

Printed in Australia
AUOC02n1209191015
271028AU00003B/3/P